About the author

After gaining a degree in Russian and a mas-
ters in sociology of literature, Charles Buxton
worked in east London for over fifteen years
as a community activist, then coordinator of a
voluntary sector training programme for the
unemployed. In 1995 he took up a position with
VSO as regional manager, preparing projects
and sending NGO, education and health sector
volunteers to eastern Europe and the former
Soviet Union. Since 2001 he has been based in
Bishkek, Kyrgyzstan, as programme manager
for INTRAC (International NGO Training and
Research Centre), working with civil society
organizations across Central Asia.

RUSSIA AND DEVELOPMENT

CAPITALISM, CIVIL SOCIETY AND THE STATE

Charles Buxton

Zed Books
LONDON

Russia and Development: Capitalism, civil society and the state was first published in 2014 by Zed Books Ltd, 7 Cynthia Street, London N1 9JF, UK

www.zedbooks.co.uk

Set in Monotype Plantin and FFKievit by Ewan Smith, London
Index: ed.emery@thefreeuniversity.net
Cover designed by www.roguefour.co.uk

A catalogue record for this book is available from the British Library
Library of Congress Cataloging in Publication Data available

ISBN 978-1-78032-109-7 hardback
ISBN 978-1-78032-108-0 paperback
ISBN 978-1-78032-517-0 pdf
ISBN 978-1-78032-110-3 epub
ISBN 978-1-78032-650-4 mobi

MIX
Paper from
responsible sources
FSC® C013604
www.fsc.org

CONTENTS

TABLES

ACKNOWLEDGEMENTS

Francis Stevenson, Tim Binyon and Stanley Mitchell, who nurtured my interest in all things Russian at school and university. Max Adereth, Terry Wilson, Dan Jones and David Kessell, who in different ways affected my political thinking and commitments.

My colleagues in VSO and INTRAC in so much fascinating and fruitful work over almost twenty years. Civil society partners and allies across Central Asia and Russia without whom we couldn't have done anything. Activists from the arena of Soviet-Russian–UK relations – the Society for Cooperation in Russian and Soviet Studies, the Bearr Trust and Oxford-Perm link.

Ludmila and Sasha, close Moscow friends from the 1970s. Sergei Aleshenok – head of the VSO Russia office from the late 1990s and a friend since then. All the members of my family (three generations!) who took part in our expedition to Moscow in 1978–80, and my colleagues in the translation department of Novosti Press Agency. Isabel Gorst, who both visited Central Asia and hosted me on many occasions in Moscow in the 1990s and 2000s. The writer Yulian Semyonov and the publisher John Calder, with whom I had an enjoyable collaboration on translating projects in the 1980s. My father Paul Buxton, who loyally supported my interest in the region. Russian civil society experts at the Higher School of Economics, Association for Social Information and Institute for Collective Action, who helped arrange my visits to Moscow, the Urals and Siberia for this book. My partner Anara, who accessed materials, made contacts, accompanied me on travels, interpreted situations, and encouraged me throughout.

The staff at Zed Books: Tamsine with whom I first developed the idea, Jakob, who got it past the board, and Kim, who brought it to fruition.

Several of my family and friends named above are sadly no longer with us, so this is first and foremost a posthumous tribute to them. To the others: thank you very much for all your support.

INTRODUCTION

Russia and Development: Capitalism, civil society and the state – this is a small book on a big topic. Written over a period of three years in between work in international development projects in the former Soviet Union, it flows out of a previous book, *The Struggle for Civil Society in Central Asia*, at the end of which I felt the need to examine Russia's role, past, present and future, in this region more closely. Why? Because Russia's relations with the post-Soviet countries are clearly important but little has been written in the development field about them. So I chose a geographical focus – Central Asia, the Urals region and Siberia – and began to collect material. The book became a kind of travel companion – the main stops where different sections were written are Bishkek, Dushanbe, Almaty, London, Moscow, Perm, Yekaterinburg, Novosibirsk, Irkutsk ... The result is also a kind of reflection, an attempt to review more than thirty years of study and interest in Russian language and culture, Russia, Soviet socialism and the post-Soviet period through the prism of development thinking and practice.

Because the topic is a big one, perhaps it is worth stating the main aims of this book. First, I wanted to review development policies in Russia some twenty-five years after *perestroika*. The break-up of the Soviet Union in 1989–91, in what I follow other analysts in calling a pro-capitalist 'revolution', led to the abandonment of the socialist, state-led model of development. But elements of state-led development have remained across the former Soviet Union (FSU) and they deserve some attention; it seems to me that it is a bit early to consign this strategy to history. Secondly, I wanted to continue my analysis of civil society development in the region, and in particular to examine the activities of NGOs and social movements in Russia today. This is my own specialist area of work, and the political, economic and social crisis of the last twenty-five years in FSU shows in a multitude of ways how closely processes in civil society are linked with development in the wider sense.

I also wanted to go back, albeit briefly, to the period when Russia colonized the region, starting roughly from the sixteenth century. In the transition period, new international actors in the region – at least in the 1990s – often spoke and behaved as if they were launching development (in particular, civil society) from scratch. The same tendency could be seen in Central Asia seventy-plus years previously, at the time of the socialist revolution in Russia. However, events in both the 1920s and the 1990s proved that the past strongly influences the present; failure to take the previous period fully into account leads to a faulty set of plans for the future. If we look carefully at, say, British or French international aid programmes, we will see many connections with our history of colonization and empire; so it seemed to me that it might be useful to consider the same in Russia.

The book moves quickly through a number of locations, stories and case studies, but it has a number of main arguments that surface regularly.

It takes as a starting point that Russia's progressive development tradition suffered a major setback with the triumph of privatization policies as the USSR broke up. I do not try to describe the heady days of *perestroika* and *glasnost* in the mid-1980s or the battles between Gorbachev and Yeltsin at the turn of the 1990s – a multitude of authors have covered this topic and with much better access to primary source material than me. Like civil society groups across FSU, as a development worker I am dealing with the consequences of pro-capitalist coups – that is, development gone into reverse for large sections of the population. Here we are talking about the destruction of a social safety net, the absence of redistributive economic policies and the rapid growth of inequality.

But people are beginning to adjust and some of them to fight back. Political change in Russia and the FSU is slow and difficult. The capture of political and economic power by insider groups led to mass disillusion with democracy. Nonetheless, many citizens see little option now other than to campaign for free elections, to challenge the results of unfair privatization, to oppose new monopolies controlling basic services like water, electricity and gas, and to demand firmer action from national governments in holding down prices and in creating jobs. Civil society and social movements are active on this agenda across the region wherever they are given the space to organize and the freedom to express views. But they are still relatively weak compared with the business and state sectors.

Another argument advanced by this book is that the forces of nationalism that became so rampant after the destruction of the multinational Soviet state are being driven slowly by the forces of global capitalism to enter into new regional associations. Yeltsin's Commonwealth of Independent States (CIS) and Putin's Eurasian Customs Union are examples of the attempts to band together for greater influence in the international arena; the entry of the Baltic states into the European Union was determined by similar motives. I regard the development of transnational associations in FSU as a progressive move, not a step backward – as long as they are entered into freely.

Many ethnic groups and peoples inhabiting the Russian Federation and its neighbours do not have a nation-state. The question about how the 100-plus smaller peoples located in the Eurasian geographical space have fared from development policies in the Tsarist, Soviet and transition period is a complex one, and in the early chapters of this book I have provided only some essential background and ideas. I argue that the Leninist approach to the national question was fundamentally progressive, while it has also spawned many problems since the USSR disappeared. Indeed, the rate at which the fifteen ex-Soviet Socialist Republics have moved apart from each other and the distance they have gone since 1989 varies enormously.

The book argues that it is time to look with more interest at Russian development policies towards its own eastern and southern regions and its south-eastern neighbours. I am not so much concerned with Russia's relations with the West or what score Russia gets in comparison with the USA and Europe on various indices (democracy, GDP, economic competitiveness, etc.). There are many books on this topic already. In the south-east, by contrast, a feeling of disillusion with Western solutions has spread widely since the end of the 1990s. For example, ten to fifteen years ago, people in the FSU would often say, 'Maybe the CIS can become a Union like Europe, maybe we'll eventually create a common currency like the euro.' But with all the problems facing the European Union, you don't find so many people saying that now. So while some citizens and NGOs still hold up the banner of European culture and values, others look east or south and inward at themselves.

What is my overall view of Russia's model of development as it emerged from Tsarist through Soviet to post-Soviet times? Probably it goes something like this. From the sixteenth century, Russian colonialism moved gradually out from its European heartland into Siberia, the Caucasus, Central Asia and the Far East. The October 1917 Revolution and subsequent civil war not only brought a violent end to the Tsarist regime in Russia, it also deposed feudal and traditional leaders across the whole empire. A socialist government took over, and one with an innovatory, revolutionary approach to the national question. It took a decade to draw up, but the USSR's federal structure made important concessions and gave wide-ranging rights and privileges to more than a hundred peoples and nations in the geographical outskirts of the USSR – that is, within the union republics as they took shape in the 1920s and 1930s and developed more rapidly after 1945.

This is the geographical focus of the book – development in the far-flung spaces of the Russian Empire, the USSR and the post-1991 independent states of this region. In the Soviet period there was a high degree of integration and complex plans were made for economic and other interactions between different republics, co-ordinated by the Communist Party and central planners in Moscow. A single model was imposed on the Soviet Union's periphery, to some extent erasing differences and certainly speeding up its development relative to the richer or more central areas. In the post-1991 period, we see a somewhat different situation. Capitalism and the international financial institutions clearly relate to Siberia, Central Asia or Caucasus as subsidiary regions. At best, they are sources of raw materials (oil, gas, gold, etc.), at worst 'fragile states' that pose a security risk to their own populations and the states around them. Centre and periphery – this is the world of uneven or unfair development, where one region gains ascendancy at the expense of others.

And in the post-1991 period, these harsh realities affected Russia itself. From its position as world superpower number 2 – significantly less powerful than the USA but for two or three decades post-1945 beginning to compete with it – in the chaotic Yeltsin years Russia saw its industries collapse, its science and technology sector fall apart, the dethronement of the Communist Party and the sidelining of the 'people's intelligentsia'. Russia quickly became a second-class power. Wealth was ruthlessly exported and thousands of talented cadres followed the money into new, better-remunerated and better-resourced professional occupations in the USA and western Europe. Indeed, the violence and corruption of Russia in the 1990s were hardly an environment for those who wanted a peaceful and productive career.

Shorn of its political superpower status, running a mafia-type economy, Russia found itself on the outer fringes of global decision-making, increasingly consigned to the role of a raw-materials supplier to more developed countries – in particular Europe. Can these losses be reversed? Could Russia climb back out of the periphery it feels it is in? This is a topic for this book, too.

In looking at these complex issues, I am coming from a particular angle – that of an NGO activist and development programme manager working in FSU for almost twenty years, the last twelve of them based in Central Asia. So my viewpoint is from one of the more distant corners of the former Russian Empire and USSR, a region that was among the poorest in both 1917 and 1991. My book considers what Russia has been able to do for and with these regions in the past and what it might do in the future. It takes a civil society perspective, focusing on the role of social and political actors in the process of change. As someone working mainly with local organizations I am interested in community dynamics just as much as the national or international levels. Thus, the book will explore questions around social mobilization, volunteering and access by women and men from excluded and vulnerable groups to power, resources and decision-making. Very often it raises issues but does not provide answers.

The book has three parts. The first part looks at the heritage of the Tsarist, Soviet and post-Soviet periods and the role of capitalism, the state and civil society in them. In Chapter 1, the development consequences of the transition period are contrasted with the record of Russian capitalism and civil society development on the eve of 1917. Chapter 2 considers the model of state-led development established by the USSR. In Chapter 3, the account moves east and south, into a consideration of colonialism and the Soviet approach to the national question within its borders.

Part 2 of the book takes us out into the different regions of FSU, examining a number of development struggles. Chapter 4 considers political and civil mobilization in Central Asia in the Soviet and post-Soviet period, with examples from the women's liberation movement and coloured revolutions. In Chapter 5, the focus is on government decentralization and the role of civil society within the Russian Federation. Chapter 6 takes us back to Central Asia and gives a short account of the Russian response to political challenges emerging in Tajikistan, plus the now important factor of mass migration from this region to Moscow and other cities. In Chapter 7 we consider the growing opposition to the Putin and Medvedev tandem – new political and social movements in Russia.

The third and final part of the book attempts to sum up Russia's development challenges in today's international context. In Chapter 8, the focus is on NGO campaigns for greater democratization and accountability – making demands on the private sector as well as government at all levels. In Chapter 9, an attempt is made to define Russia as a middle-income 'BRIC' country, reasserting itself with a new development policy and role in the world. My account relies quite heavily on a number of case studies and focuses on particular countries and regions that can be seen as illustrative of more general processes. Thus, in the wider FSU most examples in this book are taken from Kyrgyzstan, Tajikistan and Uzbekistan. Within the Russian Federation, the main case studies come from the middle Urals region and central and eastern Siberia. Some of the examples are quite small-scale, about particular people, organizations, episodes – but I hope that this will add interest for the reader.

The book arises out of my own experience of study, work and immersion in the region, so this is an individual as well as a professional view. I have tried to relate the stories that I can tell to the literature about Russian and Soviet development, but my focus is in reality quite practical – on the realities of Soviet socialism and neoliberal transition. I have used as many local sources as possible in my analysis, hoping to encourage students and other readers to consult the Russian agencies, thinkers and experts who play the main role in defining their country's development priorities today. My references are inevitably selective, tending to focus on independent and civil society sources; indeed, these are often the most interesting ones.

PART 1

THE HERITAGE

1 | CAPITALISM, CIVIL SOCIETY AND DEVELOPMENT IN RUSSIA (TO 1917 AND FROM 1989)

1 Return to the transition

In summer 1995, I got the unexpected opportunity to return to the now 'former' Soviet Union (where I had worked and lived some fifteen years earlier) – that is, the Russian Federation and Newly Independent States – as regional manager within an international volunteer programme set up by VSO under the title 'East European Partnership'. The countries in my patch were Hungary, Czech Republic, Slovakia, Poland, Lithuania, Latvia, Russia and Kazakhstan. I spent the next six years travelling up and down my region, from Budapest to Riga, Moscow to Almaty, researching, recruiting, launching and monitoring a variety of projects in English language teaching, small business development, healthcare, social work and NGO development.

As someone quite familiar with Russia's big cities as they were in the calmer Brezhnev period of the late 1970s, my first reaction to the changes under way in the mid-1990s was simply shock. In a travelogue I began to write down for myself in the 'highways and byways of transition', I described my observations and feelings ... Surprise at being able to visit once closed locations like Gorky – now Nizhny Novgorod – and the Urals cities, even towns located near major nuclear facilities; amazement at seeing so much abandoned farmland or huge factories closed down, rubbish uncollected in the cities and grass growing freely between the paving stones; shock at seeing old people, often with a very respectable appearance, begging in the streets; revulsion at the new, crude advertising in eastern Europe and Russia of the 1990s; amazement at the rate of change – for example, my generation had opposed Thatcher's radicalism in privatizing 15 per cent of the British economy over fifteen years, but the Russians had privatized 60 per cent of their economy in just five ...

The main donor for VSO's programme was the Know How Fund, a new unit created by John Major's Conservative government bringing together staff and resources from the departments for development, on the one hand, and trade and industry on the other. The Fund's main objectives were the promotion of political pluralism and the market economy. VSO had set up East European Partnership (EEP) as a semi-autonomous unit some five years earlier. One of its earliest initiatives was in response to the crisis in Romania's orphanages after the fall of the Ceauşescu regime, sending childcare and social workers to give temporary assistance. It supplied large numbers of English teachers and teacher trainers as countries in eastern Europe began to explore ways of increasing communication with the West after the fall of the Berlin Wall.

The idea was that volunteers from Western countries could work alongside citizens in the former Soviet Union and eastern Europe, sharing skills and developing new ways of working, reforming, re-building their countries. In part this can be called a social mobil-ization, in part a political one. EEP volunteers were people with professional qualifications and experience, typically aged thirty to fifty, who undertook a one-year placement under the management of a local employer. The programme gradually developed two main competencies: 1) promoting civil society, support for NGOs and vol-unteering; 2) social services development, including the move from long-term institutional care to community-based facilities, and the promotion of multidisciplinary and client-centred approaches. In Rus-sia, it had a geographical focus in the Volga and Urals regions, as well as Moscow city and province. In the Urals, this meant the provinces of Perm, Sverdlovsk and Cheliabinsk. Those days are long gone now, but they were fateful ones, for reasons this book will explore.

The term 'transition' itself was annoying to many people, including VSO's partners. I heard this from a local expert on my very first visit to Russia: transition *where*? We don't understand ... And why is everything falling apart? Similar sentiments could be heard all round the region during the 1990s, in any train, airport lounge, shop or workshop coffee break. As the decade came to an end most objective analysts recognized it had been in many ways a disaster, a travesty of the word 'development'. To kick off the discussion about this, let us look at two other big words in the title of this chapter – 'capitalism' and 'civil society' – and recall some main points made by the critics.

A primitive, violent and unfair form of capitalism emerged in

Russia in the 1990s, born of ill-considered workplace privatization and hasty market reform. Banks crashed, the population lost all their savings, millions were thrown out of work or stayed at work but without pay – or were paid years in arrears. Housing privatization led to old people being forced out of their flats by criminals. The oligarchs made millions. The profits of sale of public enterprises to managers and other insiders at knock-down prices were exported to Western banks and offshore tax havens.

Perestroika and *glasnost* had been led by liberal, democratic forces within society, allied with reformers in the communist parties across the region. 'Civil society' was a slogan and banner used by these forces throughout the 1980s and 1990s in their struggle with the state.[1] Unfortunately, ordinary citizens did not gain power in eastern Europe and FSU following the fall of the Berlin Wall in 1989 or the failed putsch in Russia in August 1991. The new political power and space created in countries that gained independence were immediately grabbed by new elites – or old ones using new names. Elections were held everywhere but mostly unfairly. New civil society associations got registered (we can call them collectively NGOs) and did many exciting new things. But they could not halt a harsh redistribution of economic and political power that had brought impoverishment and exclusion to the majority.

All this was a sad end to what had been a very exciting period. The new Russian social movements that emerged during *perestroika* had raised hopes among observers with varying political opinions that Stalinism had not destroyed grassroots self-organization in the USSR for ever. As Arato put it in his summing up to the book *Perestroika from Below* (Sedaitis and Butterfield 1991: 197–213), there seemed to be a real chance of not just market reforms, but increased support for progressive change in environmental policy, national self-expression, the situation of women, workers' self-management and many other areas of life.

The failure of *perestroika* makes for a bleak picture. This chapter can only refer briefly to some important elements of the picture with the aim of asking questions like: Why? How? By whom, to whom? With what results? In part, the answer may lie in the word 'transition', for clearly this was a time of great and uncertain change. Many of the apologists for what happened make big play with this, arguing that Boris Yeltsin had to destroy the previous system, or in Lenin's words, 'you can't make an omelette without breaking eggs', that many of the policy and implementation mistakes were hard to predict in advance, that corruption spoiled a good plan, or simply that several decades will be required to see the positive results from such major transformations. However, these arguments don't impress people in the region very much. The winners and losers are all too clear to them.

1990s capitalism in Russia as a 'grey area' Why did capitalism get off to such a bad start after 1990? Why did civil society fail to humanize it or force it to work within some decent new laws? An early description of the political and economic reforms initiated by Boris Yeltsin notes some of the problems. In the political sphere, Yeltsin was engaged in a huge struggle, first with Gorbachev and his strategy (albeit utopian) for a democratic, devolved socialist transition; and then with the communist opposition. There was little agreement which institutions should replace the old Soviet party and government structures. The president was in conflict with parliament, the regions were in danger of breaking away from the centre and proclaiming their independence, just like the ex-Soviet republics (Lane 1995).

In the economic sphere, Yeltsin's team had two main policy planks: price liberalization and rapid privatization of enterprises. On 2 January 1992, price controls were lifted on 90 per cent of items – resulting in immediate doubling or tripling of prices on most goods – and the resulting inflation wiped out the savings of the population (which had been quite substantial in the Soviet period). It has been estimated that from 1990 to 1992 the percentage of people living in poverty in Russia rose from 2.9 to 27.1 per cent. The failure of market reforms turned the political arena into a bitter struggle in which Yeltsin soon resorted to executive rule – that is, emergency measures without the assent of parliament or the majority of the people.

In his book *The Wild East*, Viktor Sergeyev (1998) provides a detailed account of the criminal aspects of capitalist development in post-communist Russia. He shows how the Soviet crime rate began to climb steeply from the mid-1980s, closely linked to the first steps towards privatization. The legalization of cooperatives in 1987 began the process, while Gorbachev's alcohol restrictions at the end of the decade forced a major traditional business underground. Cooperatives were used to launder money gained from the sale of stolen state resources, creating a grey zone around socialist enterprises reaching 5 per cent of GDP in 1988; co-ops paid four to five times the salaries of the state sector. A struggle for power and resources began between cooperatives, local authorities and the 'red directors' of state-owned enterprises. The lack of clarity in privatization and property matters opened the door to increasing influence from informal elite or mafia circles. In fact, many of the oligarchs (Boris Berezovsky and others) made their fortunes in pre-1991 privatizations.

Another grey zone formed around legislation and the force of laws. In the Soviet period, 'framework' laws were passed laying out a general approach but requiring detailed regulations to be passed later by bodies lower down the administrative ladder. From the early 1990s, this process was disrupted by the struggle between president, parliament and the constitutional council. Hence laws were passed that could not be implemented. A third factor was the increasing anarchy and anti-authoritarianism in public discourse. While crime statistics had been kept quiet in the Soviet period, under *perestroika* the opposition press made a lot of them, focusing on the Gulag, judicial and punitive processes and the violation of human rights. A large number of prisoners' memoirs were published. The tradition of Dostoyevsky's 'man from the underground' was revived, celebrating fighters against totalitarianism and the now discredited 'socialist rationality'. This opened up public opinion to the idea that the criminal could be a hero. The liberal intelligentsia took a lenient view of corruption, arguing that anything was permitted in the drive towards 'primary capital accumulation'. It was particularly difficult to counter corruption when bribe-takers combined jobs in government with jobs in business, as was often the case in 1990s Russia.

Sergeyev describes, further, how the architects of *perestroika* came up with the idea of a 'power buy-out' as a way of dealing with the Soviet *nomenklatura* (elite). In other words, they offered party bureaucrats economic positions in return for their departure from the political scene. This scheme had already been tested successfully in Poland and other eastern European countries. In eastern Europe, the democrats were well organized and the negotiations were relatively peaceful, but this was not so in Russia. At the 7th Congress of People's

Deputies of Russia in December 1992, some truly alarming statistics were made public: 17,000 people had been murdered in Russia that year. A large amount of this violence was connected with the carve-up of new property. The sell-off of state assets went ahead despite the opposition of the population as expressed in the elections of December 1993 and December 1995.

A common form of corruption in the early 1990s was the issuing of licences for the export of Russia's raw materials at ridiculously low prices. It is estimated that US$10–15 billion was exported illegally from Russia in January–March 1992 alone. Another form involved the granting of tax privileges to selected 'civil society' agents – e.g. foundations of Afghan war veterans, or sports organizations. These groups got seriously involved in the alcoholic drinks business. The grey zone in banking was particularly lucrative. For example, Mikhail Khodorkovsky made a fortune in the Menatep Bank before he joined Yukos. By 1993, banks had become market leaders in the development of new forms of criminal capitalist practice in Russia, helped by their close links with officials in the Yeltsin regime.

The public were mostly left outside these schemes. Vouchers had been distributed to the population so that everyone would have a share in ex-Soviet state property. Their market price was US$16, later falling to US$10, and on average, each family received two to three vouchers (according to the number of wage earners in the family). This sum was not very much! The average family was desperately short of cash and many quickly sold their vouchers. The trade in vouchers soon became criminal. The debates and disagreements in the ruling elite created uncertainty and thickened the fog around what was legal and what was not. Another scam bankrupting hundreds of thousands of people trying to get in on the moneymaking act was the famous pyramid schemes of Sergei Mavrodi and Vlastilina. And here the 'New Russians' made their entrance, their main characteristics hubris and an extravagantly luxurious lifestyle.

Many hoped at this time that civil society would act as an antidote to the oligarchs, developing a new type of negotiated, bottom-up, values-bound order, different from the old mechanisms of state control. But new, liberal or democratic NGOs were in their infancy, with limited resources. As Lane notes, the values and traditional culture of Russian people, much influenced by the Soviet period, were in conflict with the new system. Sergeyev concludes that society was not ready for the changes, or at least the rate at which they took place. The decision of the powers-that-be to move ahead without popular understanding or assent led to the criminalization of both state and society.

Some early development projects East European Partnership opened its Moscow office in 1995. Its first director had a previous career a bit like mine – she had majored in Russian language in the UK and had previous experience working as a translator in the Soviet Union. Many early volunteer placements were in English language teaching, a huge new market that the private sector soon moved into. One very successful project was arranged with Oxford-based NGO Opportunity International, which had recently launched 'ethical microcredit' in the city of Nizhny Novgorod on the Volga river. An ex-Falklands War soldier was the volunteer who found a new frontier here – working with considerable flair and energy. Opportunity International had a religious angle, like many transition-period 'explorers' in Russia. So here we can see an attempt to teach the poorer classes to save, borrow and basically live with capitalism.

More numerous were EEP's social sector projects. One placement was located around the corner from the famous Taganka Theatre in Moscow, developing self-help, education and youth activities in this inner-city area. There were a number of very successful placements by UK social workers developing new services for people with disabilities, as well as for medical conditions (e.g. diabetes) or using new techniques (e.g. in physiotherapy). EEP's flagship project at this time was a two-year European Union-funded project for child protection at the Ozon Centre in Moscow.

The Ozon Centre was run by a handful of highly committed Russian doctors, psychologists and social workers who had already made good links with UK charities working in the child rights field. The Moscow city authorities had provided funds to refit the centre, and European Union funds were being used to develop new lines of work, using Western needs assessment and case planning, translating and printing new information and methodological materials. This was a time when there were several scares around child abuse rings in western Europe, and senior policemen as well as social work experts came out to Moscow to explain the approach now being taken. However, the Ozon Centre had a much wider remit – that is, to deal with any kind of psychological, emotional or physical abuse being suffered by children. Their staff still had many collectivist instincts, not fitting so well with the more open and individualistic ethos EEP was promoting. I myself remembered how in the Soviet time children were frequently referred to as the country's 'only privileged class'; problems of neglect or violence in the family were very often covered up. Unfortunately, as Russian families fell apart under the impact of 1990s unemployment and moral/spiritual questioning, the problems were getting worse.

The environment for NGOs was more difficult in Russia than in central Europe. Over the two years of this joint project, we observed what a careful line our Russian partners took between their EU funders, on the one hand, and the city education committee on the other. The work they were doing with foreign agencies was invaluable, but to mention the word 'aid' in Russia was politically unacceptable in a country so recently a superpower ranked on many development indicators among the most advanced countries in the world. Russian NGOs that accepted Western grants often risked losing public funding or rent-free use of local authority buildings.

2 Poverty, survival strategies and the role of civil society

There is by now a large literature on survival strategies employed by both NGOs and ordinary citizens in Russia of the 1990s. For example, an early collection by Bridger and Pine (1998) included examples of NGOs working with international aid (very like the example given above) and women's groups in Moscow trying to find entry points in the transformed labour market.

Urban and rural poverty increased dramatically in the 1990s, both in Russia and the ex-republics, but in very different ways. A study carried out by the Institute of Urban Economy (IUE) shows that, comparatively speaking, major cities like Moscow and St Petersburg prospered in the transition years. Indeed, visitors to those two cities at the end of the decade were often surprised by gleaming new office developments and shopping malls (albeit the majority of the population could not afford the goods in the shops and was hardly to be seen in the hotels and business centres). The picture in other regions was worse, especially in mono-industrial towns and in remote and climatically inhospitable locations like the Far North.[2]

Was it easier or more difficult to survive in a town than in the country during the 1990s? If one looks at income levels, the urban population seems to have done better. However, studies of household expenditure show a different picture. This is because rural dwellers generally had another source of support – their so-called household plot, used by over 90 per cent of villagers in Russia to grow vegetables and fruit – whereas less than half of urban households had access to this vital life support. Growing your own potatoes has often been mentioned as one of the most important survival strategies in the hard years of the 1990s. The overall conclusion of the IUE study was that at the end of the decade, extreme poverty affected about a third of Russia's urban poor.

An EU-funded research project carried out at the same time revealed some of the main risk factors causing people to fall into poverty. First, disability or serious illness of a breadwinner. Second, lack of access to social assistance networks – whether benefits received from the local authorities or from newly set up charitable organizations (money, food, clothes, etc.). Third, the problems of recent migrants – e.g. refugees from the South Caucasus and Chechnya who often arrived without any possessions at all. Fourth, the collapse of a small business (Manning and Tikhonova 2004). The study noted that marginalized groups in the 1990s were forced into individual strategies of self-provisioning, shadow work, underground commerce and hustling. Self-employed people and small traders were highly likely to go bust, losing whatever investment they had made. And newly registered small businesses failed just as regularly. Finally, there were those with multiple dependants. But the researchers noted that being a 'normal' two-parent family with two children was no insurance against social exclusion – over half the households of this kind in their sample were socially excluded too.

Case study: social exclusion and uncivil society in Yekaterinburg in the 1990s The majority of EEP's volunteer placements were not in Moscow but in the Urals region over one thousand kilometres away to the east. In summer 1996, the programme opened a small office in Yekaterinburg, a town named after Catherine the Great, founded in 1723 and renamed Sverdlovsk in the 1920s after the first president of Soviet Russia and now renamed again. In the 1990s Yekaterinburg was beginning to address the uncomfortable fact that Tsar Nicholas II and his family were killed in a house here during the civil war: a new museum and shrine had just opened on this spot. The city stands just east of the boundary between Europe and Asia running north–south down the Urals mountains, and so this is also a small gateway into the Asian section of my book.

The Urals cities had been closed to Western travellers during the Cold War. There were many obstacles to overcome in the placements, most of which were in the public sector – in hospitals, polyclinics, children's homes and the like. They included the language barrier, a lack of equipment, huge gaps in experience, knowledge, and assumptions between the volunteers and their Russian hosts and colleagues. At a time of severe funding cuts and many problems at home, not all local staff were convinced that this kind of assistance (rather than, e.g., money) was what they needed. It took time for the volunteers to prove themselves. Meanwhile they got a chance to see urban poverty first hand, living in standard flat accommodation and being paid the same salary as their Russian counterparts.

It is interesting to compare the EEP experience with another account of Yekaterinburg – also by a visitor from the UK – at about this time. In a detailed study of urban deprivation, Francine Pickup (2002) also examines mafia associations and the newly forming city elite. Her description of the four main criminal groups operating in Yekaterinburg takes the description we began above a stage farther. Thus, the *Uralmash* group was named after one of the region's main industrial enterprises (Urals Machine Building Plant). It had interests in vodka, retail trade, street markets, prostitution and trade in non-ferrous metals from Uralmash ... During 1993 gang leaders shot over thirty competitors and organized a bazooka attack on the Department for Fighting Organized Crime. The *Tsentralny* group, so called because they came from the centre of the city, gained prominence in the early 1990s. Once again, their business had some strange bedfellows: on the one hand, the control of street-corner kiosks, gambling and prostitution; on the other, arms smuggling and an interest in local blast furnaces ... A third group was led by Afghan and Chechen war veterans. They set up a branch of the Union of Afghan Veterans and provided social assistance and employment to 85,000 former soldiers in the Sverdlovsk region, helped by exemption from taxes and customs duties. In the early 1990s, they bought up a large city market ... A fourth group, the *Sinyi,* covered themselves with blue tattoos and had a standard Soviet-Russian ex-offenders character.

In the academic literature about civil society, a lot of attention is given to informal groups or networks alongside registered NGOs. Experts agree that in many societies there is another 'grey area' lying between official or respectable associations, on the one hand, and unofficial or 'uncivil' groupings, on the other. The organized crime groups described above are a good example of this. In almost all of these mafia groups, we can see a Robin Hood element – that is, the championing of certain social or ethnic groups against a hostile or unjust society, by whatever means available (cf. Eric Hobsbawm's work on 'bandits'). The story of corruption in Yekaterinburg was taken up by campaigning journalist Anna Politkovskaya in her book *Putin's Russia* (2004). And she made many enemies with her courageous exposés.

Women faced many new forms of discrimination and exploitation in the transition period. Thus, a case study of post-Soviet dispossession in the Central Asian city of Almaty in the 1990s focuses in particular on 'sexualized strategies', defined as 'finding a good job by responding to employers' sexual demands; finding a wealthy husband; finding a "sponsor", a lover who will support her financially, and sex work' (Nazpary 2002: 90). The violence and stigma associated with these strategies are analysed alongside the new consumerist culture which was beginning to take hold in the cities of FSU, and the way in which other people tried to hang on to their moral sense.

In the concluding section of her account, Francine Pickup comments on the effect of the changing economic situation on gender roles.

The withdrawal of the state from family life resulted in the renegotiation of household roles. Male respondents would try to be the breadwinner, but for those without marketable skills and weak social ties, their ability to do so was very limited. In addition, they showed little inclination to take on an increasing burden of household management and maintenance of kin ties ... Women shouldered the increasing burden of household management – juggling several jobs, supporting dependant kin, maintaining support networks. This made it difficult for them to engage in wider, more influential networks ... Women in kin-based households were likely to draw back from forming marital relations because conjugal interests were likely to conflict with obligations to dependant kin ... Women increasingly relied on kin rather than conjugal relations, which contribute to men's further abdication of responsibility in the home. (Pickup 2002: 310–11)

So Yekaterinburg society consisted of two separate worlds. In the wealthy one, the collapse of the Communist Party plus the new opportunities for enrichment resulted in rapid changes and a fragile peace. At the very top were economic and political echelons hanging on to their control over the region's resources; below them, a fluid layer of newer economic elites, including in the early reform period younger entrepreneurs. This world was gradually penetrated by organized crime groups, forming alliances with state officials. As the 1990s ended, it was becoming increasingly difficult to enter the city elite, as the state tightened its grip over the economy and those on board already did their best to exclude outsiders ...

In the other, majority, world, structural adjustment had not produced the burgeoning private sector that was expected to be the basis for the creation of a large middle class. For the most part, people used whatever resources they had to insulate themselves from the changes taking place around them (ibid.: 312–14).

The crisis of the 'people's intelligentsia' Sergeyev presents what he calls the 'prisoner's dilemma' to explain some important things about the mafia culture that took over large parts of Russian society in the 1990s. The prisoner's dilemma – cooperation or defection – arises when two people who have committed a crime together are interrogated separately by the police. The problem here is that if one of them remains loyal to his mate, he has no way of knowing whether the latter will return the favour. Hence in many or most cases the prisoner will try to deal individually with the interrogator. In the example of 1990s Russian entrepreneurship, he more often than not joined the corrupt system so as to avoid being caught out.

The fault here is indeed with individuals, but also with those who allowed this new system to take over.

And it seems to me that this is one of the main challenges that civil society organizations (CSOs) have to confront in present-day Russia – the cynical and violent culture that grew up in the ashes of the USSR's 'worker-friendly' state. In reality, CSOs are not just competitors with mafia groups, they are one of the indispensable tools for loosening the latter's hold on society. Nazpary calls NGOs and community groups islands of morality in a chaotic, violent world (2002: 88–9).

The mainstream Western view of transition in FSU is that the fall of the Berlin Wall was an opportunity for freedom that many citizens took advantage of by forming NGOs and pressing for democratic reforms. Indeed, many did. However, tragically, this movement – valuable as it was – did not involve, find or support outlets for the majority of the ex-Soviet intelligentsia.

We have to remember that the USSR spawned a kind of wider 'people's intelligentsia' quantitatively, geographically and thematically. The Soviet intelligentsia included technical and public sector workers of many different kinds; indeed, professions like medicine and teaching became significantly more democratic. The Russian intelligentsia per se was supplemented by public, culture, health and education workers in regions like Central Asia and the Far North, where mass literacy schemes had only recently been launched. Tragically, many of these workers got very little if anything from the transition years. This is one of the 'paradoxes' of the time, as Russian sociologist Toschenko puts it in a detailed analysis of the social and psychological consequences of the Soviet collapse.[3]

Recalling the origin of the term in the nineteenth century, when rural teachers, doctors, engineers and others began to play a leading role in development, and the particular resonance of the term 'the Russian intelligentsia' (referring to high ideals, civic consciousness, service to the people, responsibility and self-sacrifice), Toschenko's argument is that in the transition years, the Russian intelligentsia proved unable to live up to this role. The failure of the military putsch in August 1991 seemed to have handed liberal change to them on a plate. Why did they fail to make more of the opportunity?

His answer is that during the 1990s the intelligentsia broke up into four groups. The first was a relatively small number of people who took an active part in the social and political transformations. The second was the main mass of the technical and humanitarian intelligentsia who were left to one side, confused and in despair, caught in 'no man's land between the past and the present'. He accuses this group of political naivety and irresponsibility in allowing the depradation of Russia's resources without mounting any kind of broadly based opposition. Indeed, a third group took a direct part in privatization and ripping off these resources (the author does not mince his words). A fourth set get more respect – the new dissidents who by the end of the decade had disassociated themselves from transition. Some of these formed a strident new opposition to Russian capitalism, while others retreated into their professions or devoted themselves to 'minor issues' (à la Chekhov).

In working with Russian employers and colleagues, EEP volunteers came up against all these types. Often it was difficult for volunteers new to the country to deal effectively with the depth of feeling they encountered.

3 Civil society in Russia: towards a historical perspective

In the previous pages, we have looked at some of the dramatic and contradictory aspects of Russia's development in the 1990s. Soviet socialism collapsed – or a pro-capitalist revolution took place. *Perestroika* broke up the 'people's intelligentsia' and led to the rapid growth of new civil and uncivil groups, pro-democracy and pro-crime elements. The political left resisted and almost broke back at one or two key moments. Meanwhile, those in power were desperately in search of legitimacy and tradition to bolster their positions.

This book attempts to take a historical view of civil society and development in Russia. In this it differs from approaches that in the main evaluate the country against principles or standards imported from outside: a universalist approach that was very common in analysis of the transition countries in the 1990s. Often the aim was to assess the level of success of democratization or development programmes funded from outside the given country, the problems they encountered, and so on. However, studies of this kind often fail to explain *why* things happen or don't happen, nor do they question the adherence to Western models.[4]

The historical approach, by contrast, bases itself on a given country's history and culture. In Russia and FSU, key terms include the *intelligentsia*, to which we have already referred, and the adjective *obschestvenny* ('public'), as applied to people and organizations in the social or political sphere, based on collective, voluntary social activity (Salmenniemi 2009: 105–8). In my work from the early 2000s in Central Asia, this issue about imported terms and models has come up increasingly. And in an ex-colonial region such as Central Asia we have a many-sided battle for influence between the Western/capitalist, Russian/Soviet and indigenous traditions.

In Russia there is a democratic tradition that goes back a thousand years and in which the village meeting (*skhod*) was an important institution in social life. In the Middle Ages, another key stage in the development of democratic structures was reached with the establishment of a *veche* or 'town council' in Novgorod the Great, where issues from street meetings were brought by delegates for a wider joint discussion. Here, as in the neighbouring princedom of Pskov, there was a degree of public space for debate. Much later on, there are periods in which the Tsar made strictly limited efforts to open up government to particular social groups (or 'estates' – *sosloviya*) – such as the *boyars* (feudal lords) in the sixteenth and seventeenth centuries.

Historians debate about how inclusive or effective these native or traditional forms of civil society actually were. Thus the village *skhod*, it is argued, made on occasion important decisions and reflected complex, multiple interests quite effectively; but it did not have any clear rules or structure. Experiments in democratic governance in Novgorod or Pskov in the Middle Ages are interesting phenomena, but they were succeeded by many centuries of state violence and absolute rule. The historians note that many of these bright moments of debate and collective decision-making took place during 'times of troubles' (*smuta*) such as the period 1598–1613. In our search for indigenous bottom-up models of democracy, we will look at another important idea, that of *narodovlastiye*, or 'people's power', in the next chapter. Indeed, an interesting comparison could perhaps be made between these freer, more open interludes in the early history of the Russian state and later periods like 1904–21 or the 1990s ... In between it was mostly 'silent' autocracy.[5] These short periods of liberalization did not take hold or change the nature of the system overall.

The emergence of the intelligentsia in the nineteenth century The origin of the term 'intelligentsia' is in the 1860s, taken to refer to the educated classes, often representatives of the liberal professions rather than government servants. Accounts of the nineteenth-century Russian intelligentsia often speak of key generations of writers, thinkers and 'tribunes of the people', linking each generation to a period of Tsarist reform or reaction. Thus historians began to refer to the Decembrist uprising of 1825 as the heroic first intervention by representatives of the progressive intelligentsia.[6] (Tsar Nicholas I reacted against the Decembrist plot by holding back political reform and restricting access to higher education.) The generations of the 1840s and 1860s, immortalized in Turgenev's *Fathers and Sons*, went down in history as belonging to liberal Westernizers and the landed gentry in the 1840s, on the one hand, and hard-headed revolutionaries from the new petty bourgeois and merchant classes in the 1860s, on the other. Here we can see the same association between the development of civil society and the bourgeoisie as we see in many Western countries. In the late nineteenth century, as the revolutionary movement gained strength, the educated classes came under particular suspicion and surveillance from the authorities, and so to be a member of the intelligentsia meant almost to be a revolutionary or a member of a secret sect.

The term 'civil society' has moved from being a political battle cry in eastern Europe/FSU of the late 1980s to a subject for detailed academic inquiry and debate, partially at least supplanting the term 'intelligentsia'. Civil society departments and studies have opened up across the EE/FSU region. They add modern concepts from social, economic and political science to the 'heroic story' of the nineteenth-century intelligentsia, examining, for example, the legal and institutional environment for early CSOs and the practical tasks and activities they got involved in.[7] But whereas the Soviet school emphasized intransigent opposition to Tsarism, present-day scholarship tends to highlight attempts at reform or collaboration with the authorities. In the following section we give some examples of this.

The Great Reforms and first moves towards local government decentralization The opinion of educated society had a great influence on Tsar Alexander II, ushering in the period of the Great Reforms in the

1860s. In this period the biggest event was the Emancipation of the Serfs in 1861, to which historians in Russia attribute roughly the same importance in the development of civil society as the campaigns for the abolition of slavery in the UK and the USA.[8] The Emancipation of the Serfs represented a major stage on the way to both capitalism and less autocratic government in Russia. It also had an overwhelming economic rationale. No fewer than 23 million privately owned serfs were affected by the reforms, completely transforming social relations in Russia. First of all, one class of people was liberated from bondage to another class. Secondly, in the immediate post-emancipation years, all classes and estates in Russian society had to negotiate how they would interact with each other as employers, employees or citizens in the future. Representatives of the progressive intelligentsia criticized the terms of emancipation, arguing that they were unfairly weighted against the peasantry and in particular that the land plots granted them were too small. The 'Land and Liberty' organization was set up to campaign against these injustices. A new social movement, the Populists, took shape and a generation of young radicals left Russia's cities and universities and went off to work and agitate in the villages.

Early Russian charitable associations and their activities Nineteenth-century Russia was a country without a state social security system, and from the mid-1890s this gap was gradually filled by mutual assistance organizations. Their activities included offering financial or material support to needy groups such as widows, orphans or victims of accidents at work; also 'intellectual assistance' to professional groups (e.g. through the organization of libraries, concerts, literary evenings). Social problems tackled included homelessness, abandoned children, the growth in crime, and so on. An example of the comprehensive approach developed by some of them is provided by the Mozhaisk Charitable Association, whose aims were not simply to feed and care for children, but to teach work skills, find them work, and assist in the development of school education and distribution of textbooks and training materials. Another example can be seen in the Mutual-Charitable Society set up by leading figures from Russia's pre-revolutionary feminist movement in St Petersburg in 1895. This was in one sense a traditional women's club, in another

a vehicle for organizing a wide range of charitable and public activities: from day crèches to night shelters, from soup kitchens to
educational and vocational courses and the campaign for women's
political representation.

In rural areas, the support of *zemstvos* (local authority units set
up in the 1860s reform period) was particularly valuable, both as a
source of grants for the needy and for exchange of experience in
social care approaches. In urban areas, mutual help associations
helped workers and professionals accumulate funds with which to
help victims of accidents at work, to pay for medical care or pensions.
By the start of the twentieth century, similar associations had been
created for writers, artists, higher education lecturers, schoolteachers,
doctors, nurses, dentists, merchants, craftsmen, tailors, bakers and
so on – with members paying regular dues.[9]

After the Emancipation of the Serfs, there was a major issue of
how to negotiate new contracts by means of which now-liberated
peasants could freely work the land. Lev Tolstoy was one of 1,700
'arbitrators' who assisted this process, most of them drawn from the
ranks of the liberal or democratic intelligentsia. As a recent study
(Easley 2009) shows, this was a contested and in many ways unhappy
process. The landlords/ex-serf-owners were not used to negotiations
with their social inferiors. In their turn, the peasants tended to see
the arbitrators as placemen for the gentry and were mostly dissatis-
fied with the allotments given to them upon emancipation. The
study argues that this new institution didn't just represent liberal
(or reactionary) interests, it led to a development of 'public space' in
between the three sectors – society, the state and the economy. All
in all, the number of charitable organizations grew fast at the end
of the nineteenth century – from 1,690 in 1897 to 45,000 in 1905 – as
did savings societies and mutual help groups – from 135 in 1898 to
200 in 1905 – doctors and medical associations – from 100 in 1898
to 130 in 1905 – and other professional and artists' groups (Kruzhkov
2005: 50–5).

4 Capitalism to 1917 and from 1989

The reinterpretation of Russian history reaches all corners of
study, and of course the question is debated: were the revolutions of
1905 and 1917 as inevitable as they seemed to be just a few decades

ago? Could capitalism, elements of parliamentary rule and civil society have entrenched themselves and produced an adequate rate and level of development to satisfy the population? Was the social divide in early twentieth-century Russia – between the aristocracy and new capital-owning middle class, on the one hand, and the tiny but radicalized working class and the huge, discontented masses of the peasantry, on the other – really too big to be bridged? In the past, events themselves seemed to show that no outcome other than revolution was possible. But now, under the impact of the 1990s, there are many who claim otherwise.

Indeed, the Great Reforms ushered in forty years of local citizens' activity of a new type, in *zemstvos* and other socially oriented associations. Industrialization gathered force, the Russian Empire moving east and south, aided by the development of railways at the end of the nineteenth century. A range of political and judicial reforms were instituted. But after Alexander II was assassinated in 1881 by members of the Narodnaya Volya (People's Will) party, his son and successor Alexander III reversed the reforms, beginning a new period of repression. Reform-minded officials resisted as best they could. Thus when the Tsar cut back the *zemstvos*' powers and appointed government officials to head them, local leaders tried creatively to keep the flag flying – e.g. by organizing a 'Banquet Campaign' to celebrate the fortieth anniversary of the Great Reforms (Easley 2009: 53). Many supporters of liberal politics in Russia later joined the Cadets (Constitutional Democrats) party.

In the international arena, not everything had gone smoothly for the expanding Russian Empire. Defeat in the Crimean War in the 1850s was another big reason to implement the mid-century reforms. And at the turn of the twentieth century, the Tsarist regime suffered a major setback, defeat in war with Japan precipitating the 1905 Russian Revolution. In August that year, responding to a countrywide revolt put down only at the cost of much loss of life, the Tsar announced a new consultative assembly. However, this provided only limited representation – excluding women, workers, the rural poor and soldiers – and proved not enough to satisfy popular demands. By the end of 1905 there were forty-five national political parties and movements in Russia, with another 113 active in the outlying regions of the empire, where double oppression reigned – social and national. Indeed, many of these regions had long been home to exiled radicals, while others were affected by revolutionary movements such as pan-Turkism imported from abroad.

By this time there was a new Tsar, Nicholas II. The limited political power of the assembly (Duma) created as a result of the 1905 revolution showed, firstly, the Tsar's unwillingness to share power, and secondly, the inexperience of the new deputies and the weak, inactive social base they represented. The Russian peasantry in particular was still inclined to look up to the Tsar as a kind of god, so the deputies representing rural constituencies and outlying regions of the empire tended to adopt the position of beseeching favours rather than demanding rights or taking their own decisions.

Perhaps the key figure in the reforms, Pyotr Stolypin, was both a nationalist and a liberal. The aim of his reforms was to strengthen the richer, more powerful layer of the peasantry – that is, individuals who had 'expropriated' land from the peasant communes and were trying to expand production and commerce; hence the opposition from the mass of the peasantry to the reforms. Stolypin also proposed significant changes in the *zemstvos*, merging civic and administrative bodies and forcing out traditional estate elements. But the reforms ran into resistance from the Tsar, Stolypin himself was assassinated in 1911, and the regime failed to transform itself into a constitutional monarchy on European lines. Russia's losses in the First World War ignited the 1917 revolution, as similar loss of life almost did in several other European countries. The Bolsheviks took advantage of these weaknesses when they seized power in October 1917; as Lenin later wrote, 'our backwardness moved us forward'.

Democracy development in the 1990s Fast-forward to the 1990s – another time of great confusion and disorientation in Russia, a pro-capitalist 'revolution' that turned upside down the hopes of those who for so many years considered the prospects of socialist revolution in capitalist societies (Kotz and Weir 2007; Kagarlitsky 2000, 2008). The main events in the revolution are already a much-told story. The turbulent Congress of People's Deputies where Yeltsin publicly cocked a snook at Gorbachev. Yeltsin standing on a tank and defying the military putsch in 1991. Yeltsin shelling the White House (Russian parliament) in 1993, his dubious electoral victories over the communists in 1995 and 1996. The failed attempt by parliament to impeach the president in summer 1998. The appointment of Putin as prime minister in 1999 ...

Just three points will be made here that relate to Russia's developing political model. First, the 1990s decade was one in which the centre was significantly weakened in its dealings with the regions (a total of eighty-nine federal 'subjects' or administrative units within Russia). As we shall see in later chapters, Russia's regions took advantage of the anarchy and all-encompassing grey areas at the centre to gain some autonomy in policy-making and distribution of resources. Secondly, as not just the USSR but the Russia Federation itself began to seriously fall apart, it was Yeltsin who initiated the process back towards a centralized system as he strove to strengthen executive power (the presidency) over legislative power (the Congress of People's Deputies, later the Duma).

Thirdly, however flawed or corrupt the political arrangements brought into being in the 1990s, there was an active political struggle both inside and outside parliament between four main groupings: 1) Yeltsin, Gaidar and the neoliberal or capitalist 'Bolsheviks' as they are sometimes called; 2) the left opposition represented in the Duma by Zyuganov and the Communist Party; 3) strident nationalists led by Zhirinovsky's Liberal Party; and 4) a variety of smaller opposition parties (e.g. Yabloko on the centre left and Union of Right Forces on the centre right) that were less successful electorally. Overall, Russians tried to make use of their new freedoms and voting turnout at national elections has almost always been quite high.

When you use the word 'democracy' in Russia, you still get the same kind of hostility from many people as you do with the term 'transition'. Happily, as a term 'democracy' is a lot more understandable to the average person. However, the point the objectors want to make is that it was largely denuded of meaning for the population of FSU in the 1990s. What kind of democracy can rob the population of so many rights, destroying their standard of living, their hopes for the future? Hence the protests on the streets, led by trade unions and political parties from the extreme right to the radical left, and wave upon wave of strikes during the 1990s. Alternatively, large numbers simply opted out of society – through suicide, alcohol and drugs – or joined anti-social groups, as we have already seen.

Capitalism Mark 1, Mark 2 The apologists for transition turn out to have been hopelessly optimistic. What happened in Russia of the 1990s is now one of the main arguments for those who oppose economic shock therapy and unregulated market capitalism – mafia or anarcho-capitalism, as John Gray called it in his book *False Dawn* (2002: 133–65). Unfortunately, the opposition was unable to generate sufficient support or convincing new policies with which to halt the process.

What are the essentials of Russian capitalism in the two periods we have been considering in this chapter? It is interesting to consider recent analyses from the journal *Levaya Politika* (Left Politics) showing the similarities and differences between Russian capitalism in the early twentieth and early twenty-first centuries. Indeed, one can make some clear comparisons between the two main periods of growth (the 1890s and 1907–14) in the Tsarist period, on the one hand, and recent (post-2000) economic growth in Russia. For example, there is the dependence of economic strategy on sales of raw materials on the world market, or the dominance of the government bureaucracy in economic matters. Common factors include, too, the low standard of living of the mass of the population, and the inferiority complex demonstrated by many in Russia's cultural and political elite vis-à-vis the Western countries.[10]

But there are important differences between 'Capitalism Mark 1' and 'Capitalism Mark 2'. Russia is now an industrialized country with an overwhelmingly urban, educated, steadily ageing population, a modern society with a relatively high level of technological skills. In the early twentieth century, the industrial proletariat was a small minority, surrounded by the petty bourgeoisie and the peasant masses. Today the working class is much larger and heterogeneous. Conflicts take place between the mass of the population and the ruling elite on a number of issues, many not just class-based.

Sometimes the term 'restoration of capitalism' is used in relation to the transition period. This term implies the return to a previous model – which is impossible, so the authors of articles in *Levaya Politika* argue. Indeed, there have been attempts to 'turn the clock back' – e.g. discussions about the merits of monarchism, restitution of property to pre-1917 owners, or the re-establishment of the Orthodox Church's dominant position in society. However, these initiatives are not central to the new form of capitalism in Russia, they judge. Russia has changed too much, economically, socially and politically. And to explore these changes we need to look at the country's development during the Soviet period – the subject of the next chapter.

2 | STATE AND DEVELOPMENT IN THE SOVIET PERIOD

1 Development as a contested term

The aim of this book is to consider development in Russia and its immediate geographical neighbourhood in a wider perspective and longer time frame than just the transition period. The rationale for this is that both recent events in Russia and the country's prospects for the future can be better understood if key facts and tendencies in the pre-Soviet and Soviet periods are taken into account. Thus, what are now called the Newly Independent States (NIS) were colonized in Russia's Tsarist period and went through a rapid, forced modernization in the Soviet period. If we take Russia's development to mean the process of moving from feudal to capitalist, industrial and post-industrial society, this process has been going on for four or five centuries at least, at different rates across the post-Soviet space. We can expect to find some interesting similarities between development in these different periods – and, of course, significant contrasts.

All this was quite difficult to think through in the early 1990s, including for development workers. The issues around communism versus capitalism, or indeed Trotskyism versus Stalinism, the hard line and the soft line in Soviet studies, were hotly debated in political and academic circles in the final decades before the 'end of history' was proclaimed, but mostly in a different compartment from 'international development'.[1] Well-established development agencies like VSO took on work in eastern Europe (EE) and the former Soviet Union in a frankly experimental way, to meet what was presented as a short-term need and because funding was available to do so. It took a few years to make a serious assessment of the situation in the region and what Western agencies could achieve.

Development is a contested term. In the Northern/Western, 'developed' or donor countries, a number of arguments go on all the time. Critics abound: some arguing that development agencies work ineffectively; others that the images of aid projects on Western TV demean beneficiaries in the receiving countries; others again that development money would be better spent at home. While the private sector argues for a focus on trade or economic development, the NGO sector replies that economic growth cannot be the only objective. Trade unions are concerned about exploitation of cheap labour in Third World countries, environmentalists about pollution caused by transnational companies. In turn, business and government accuse NGOs of being self-seeking or 'holier than thou'.

In the Southern/Eastern, 'underdeveloped' or 'developing' countries, similar debates can be heard. Some groups are grateful for disaster relief and aid programmes; others welcome external support for human rights or democracy campaigners. But others again view the changes through a political lens, seeing only Western imperialism, the drive for military or political power, and in their own societies cronyism, bribery and corruption of local elites. NGOs are accused of being artificially imposed grant seekers, estranged from the communities they claim to represent. These controversies about international development and aid are heard regularly in FSU just as in other countries and continents.

In a recent book on local government reform in Russia, Simon Kordonsky comments that analyses of the Russian government system don't seem able to answer simple questions like: Is Russia an Asiatic or European country? Are we moving forwards or backwards? And he contrasts the 'real' situation as described by official commentators with the rather different situation that exists 'in actual fact'. Here the word 'real' seems to be being used as in the famous Soviet term from the Brezhnev era – 'real socialism'. His argument is that whatever the government ideology, structures or regulations, those in charge at any level (region, town, village) treat the unit they control like a 'fiefdom'. This word is taken from the Tsarist period, meaning social 'estate'. So Kordonsky is describing Russia as a system of estates under personalized rule. It obviously poses the question: Are we moving forwards or backwards?[2]

This is quoted because indeed it is important to try to look at the big issues – in the nineteenth century they were termed 'damned questions' and many a literary hero (like Oblomov in Goncharov's novel) sank back on his bed rather than think about them (or went out to the next champagne-soaked ball like the characters in Tolstoy's novels). To put my cards on the table, this book takes the view that Russia's development experience has an importance for other countries in two main areas: first, the lessons of revolution and forced change; second, the experience of development in the context of a strong state. If we want to talk about alternatives to neoliberalism, it seems hard to avoid looking at these models and experiences. However, without democratic institutions and an active civil society, revolution and the state run into trouble, as we will see in this chapter. Therefore we have a third important set of lessons from Russia: about the relations between civil society, state and business sectors for common ends – including development.

Development advocates and critics Though this book is written by an international development worker with a professional interest in the topic many of the writers and respondents quoted in it are among the sceptics. The term 'development' is by no means universally accepted in Russia, as a quick review of some of the main schools of thought shows clearly.[3]

Development 'missionaries'. A multitude of institutions have now been built up around the concept of development, operated by dedicated and well-paid staff, so much so that it has been called a modern-day religion (De Rivero 2001; Rist 2008). In the mainstream of this group are the World Bank, the United Nations Development Programme, the International Monetary Fund and other international agencies. Development is equated by these agencies with progress, economic growth, a general improvement in human life: that is, something hopeful and positive. This was the so-called Bretton Woods agenda. However, in the pre-1991 period, Soviet Marxists regularly called into question some of its main tenets, pointing out that the international institutions failed to make a class analysis or to reduce structural inequalities. And in the post-1991 post-Soviet space (PSS), the social and economic crash in the East appeared to disprove the idea of steadily improving standards of living.

Neo-developmentalists. International NGOs and practitioners like the author probably belong within this group – doing their best to promote and implement a different type of development: for example, the civil society, grassroots or bottom-up approaches that will be referred to in this book. But other observers (including many socialists and nationalists in Russia) argue that development programmes have little impact faced with discriminatory measures imposed on poorer countries and communities within today's global economic system. Sceptics in the FSU can easily refer to the problems that the poorer countries around the world have faced in trying to achieve the UN's Millennium Development Goals for the period 2000–15.

Globalists. With the removal of the USSR as the main challenger to world capitalism, the USA and its allies proclaimed a 'new world order' in what Rist calls a time of 'happy globalization'.[4] This did not last very long. The late 1990s saw the successive crashes of the Asian, Russian and Latin American markets and the rise of a new anti-globalization movement. Environmentalism is central to the anti-globalization movement, and ecological NGOs have long been leaders in civil society across PSS. In the Soviet Union, ecological damage was typically presented by the government as a regrettable but unavoidable consequence of building dams, factories and roads. Many citizens accepted this argument, albeit reluctantly, but far fewer are ready to do this now.

Nationalists and localists. Development in its mainstream form seems to assume that the Western mode of capitalist production is universally applicable. However, far from everyone in Russia is ready to accept this argument at face value. Nationalism became the emotional and intellectual refuge for millions in the post-Soviet space after the collapse of communist internationalism in 1991. Much has been written on nationalism in the region, and once again this book will avoid repetition of previous analyses, focusing more on 'localism'. Following recent 'post-development' thinkers for whom local development strategies are often central, we will review Russian social movements that aim for a kind of autonomy from both the state and international agencies through creating political, social and mutual-help networks of their own (Rist 2008: 256–61; also Rahnema and Bawtree 1997).

Crash and recovery As many theories note, development often has a wave or cyclical pattern. In Table 2.1 we show the fate of Russia and other countries inside and outside the EE/FSU region during the 1990s crash and the post-2000 slow, faltering recovery, using traditional development indicators.

TABLE 2.1 Development in Russia, its neighbours and competitors during transition

Country	1990 GDP per head (PPP) in US$	1990 Human development index	2000 GDP per head (PPP) in US$	2000 Human development index	2011 GDP per head (PPP) in US$	2011 Human development index
Russian Federation	8,013	.730	5,950	.713	21,245	.784
Poland	5,966	–	9,895	.778	21,260	.819
Kazakhstan	5,119	–	4,262	.663	13,099	.750
China	794	.495	2,153	.590	8,400	.695
India	873	.410	1,462	.463	3,627	.551
USA	23,037	.878	33,332	.907	48,111	.936

Notes: 1. Income differences are shown as gross domestic product (GDP) per head of the population, adjusted using 'purchasing power parity' (PPP) to reflect currency variations that make comparisons between different countries difficult. The human development index (HDI) brings together a variety of factors including health, mortality, education level, employment, gender and so on, for a more rounded assessment. 2. The chart shows that the both GDP per head and HDI in Russia and Kazakhstan fell dramatically in the 1990s, whereas in the other countries in the table it increased significantly. In 2000, the USA had almost four times more income per head than Russia. However, by 2011 Russia has almost caught up with Poland, at least in income per head. Like India, both Russia and Kazakhstan have almost trebled income per head, while China has almost quadrupled it. The USA now has only 2.5 times more income per head than Russia.

Sources: World Bank and UNDP[5]

2 The strategy of Soviet state-led development

The Soviet period can be described as an attempted 'opt-out' from the capitalist system. The seizure of power by the Bolsheviks in November 1917 led quickly to the nationalization of land and the economy, and the outlawing of private enterprise. Civil war engulfed the country and several regions in the west (e.g. in Ukraine and the Baltic states) were lost as the price paid by the new socialist regime for exiting from the First World War. The Bolsheviks' attempts to ignite revolutions in the Western world gradually came to nothing. And so, at the end of the 1920s, the country began an experiment with socialism in one country in which the role of the state was central.

Some development debates in the Soviet period

Bolsheviks versus Mensheviks. It is easy to view the events of the Soviet period (like the 1917 revolution itself) as somehow inevitable, whether due to the nature of the Bolshevik party (with its 'iron discipline and determination') or the 'backwardness' of Russia at the turn of the twentieth century. In reality, nothing was that simple and major battles took place over development strategy within the radical or revolutionary camp throughout the period. Thus, while in exile in Europe, Lenin was in constant conflict with what he saw as the revisionism of European socialists such as Karl Kautsky and Rosa Luxemburg. Within Russia, the Bolsheviks argued that industrialization was the only way to overcome backwardness, against the very widespread view (led by the *narodniks*[6]) that the collective nature of peasant society could provide a basis for socialism. Lenin regarded this view as romantic and illusory, pointing to the new factories already being built in Russia with German and other European investment, the spread of the railway network, and in general the first steps in economic modernization that were already taking place in late nineteenth-century Russia.

The argument between the Bolshevik and Menshevik factions within the Russian Social Democratic Party in the early years of the twentieth century set out the main choices for Russia's development in the decades to come. The Bolsheviks argued for nationalization in the name of the people, later developing this into the strategy of dictatorship of the proletariat. The Mensheviks argued that a period of capitalist economic development plus the creation of liberal democratic institutions would be necessary to create the social, economic and political base for socialism (a working-class, expanded education system, functioning representative democracy, etc.). They also argued for a more decentralized state, including devolution of power to municipal authorities.[7]

Lenin accused the Mensheviks of excessive 'determinism' – that is, allowing the classic Marxist positions on the stages of development from feudalism through capitalism to socialism to blind them to the revolutionary potential being created before their eyes by Tsarist oppression and a set of disastrous imperialist wars. However, the break-up of the USSR after seventy-plus years of socialist leadership and development provides massive support to those who have long argued that Lenin's 'refusal to wait for history' amounted to a kind of voluntarism or adventurism, albeit led with maximum discipline and single-mindedness by a vanguard party.

Communism and national liberation. In the field of international relations there were other major dilemmas. The first was whether to look east or west. In 1917, there was little argument: the Bolsheviks expected the proletarian revolution to break out in the Western countries – primarily England, France or Germany. Indeed, capitalism tottered seriously under the impact of the First World War and the October Revolution. But gradually it righted itself, suppressing revolts and workers' opposition across Europe. Meanwhile, another section of the communist movement looked to national-democratic transformation in the colonies of the East. The Comintern (Communist International) regularly reviewed its tactics, debating which arm of the movement – the proletarians in the Western countries or the national liberation activists in the East – would achieve their aims first. Which arm would lead, and which follow? Which slogans or actions had precedence, now that communists were trying to co-ordinate strategies? How could they best help not hinder each other?

The left and right tendencies. In almost all the debates of the early Soviet period we can see a struggle between 'purist' and 'realist' factions in the Bolshevik Party. As the prospects for cataclysmic world revolution faded in the early 1920s, the Soviet regime became increasingly isolated. The steady growth of the workers' movement in many countries was of limited practical help to Russia's leaders, confronted with the economic and military might of the major imperial powers and the growing threat of Nazism on their doorstep. Several tactical retreats took place. One of these was the introduction of the New Economic Policy (NEP) with its concessions to capitalism within the Soviet space. Another was the increasingly close alliance with national-bourgeois forces in the East – for example, Kemal Atatürk in Turkey and the Kuomintang (Chiang Kai Shek) in China. Furious arguments took place within the Soviet regime on these points, between the Westernizers/left wing led by Trotsky, and the Easternizers/right wing led by Stalin.

When Stalin's second revolution began in 1929/30 with the drive for collectivization and industrialization, a new 'ultra-left' period was ushered in, accompanied by the repression of the so-called right tendency (Bukharin and others). The violent repression of rightists in the party, along with the attacks on kulaks (rich peasants) during collectivization and the hysteria generated during the purges against any sign of bourgeois forces, effectively removed this option from discussion until Stalin's death in 1953. Thenceforth the reformist line slowly but steadily began to re-establish itself, from Khrushchev's thaw through the bureaucratic but milder policies of Kosygin and Brezhnev up to the dawn of *perestroika*.

All these debates and dilemmas have echoes and analogies in the post-Soviet period. We have already referred to the 'Bolshevik' supporters of capitalist shock therapy, versus the more gradual approaches to economic reform that were available. The choice between a West- or East-facing economic or political strategy still clearly exists today, too, and will be discussed in later chapters. And the issue of how the state should collaborate with the market remains absolutely central in every country of eastern Europe and the former Soviet Union.

The international impact of the Soviet development model The Soviet model was attractive to many throughout the whole period of its existence, as we have noted already, almost sparking a European revolution in the years immediately after 1917; creating and leading an international communist movement in the 1920s and 1930s; inspiring and supporting anti-colonial movements throughout the first half of the twentieth century; defeating Hitler on the crucial Eastern front in the Second World War; creating a base for communism in eastern Europe post-1945 (albeit with much less popular assent); and providing vital political solidarity and economic support for the Chinese, Vietnamese and Cuban revolutions from the 1950s to the 1970s. These successes in the international arena enabled the Soviet regime to present itself as the leader of the socialist 'camp' right up to the time when I was working in Moscow in the late 1970s, in one of the USSR's main media organizations, Press Agency Novosti.[8]

The successes of the socialist model forced accommodation across the Western camp, encouraging governments in the USA and Europe in self-defence to pay more attention to their own working classes and colonized peoples. It posed questions which are uppermost to this day in the minds of radical critics of the current international set-up. That is, how can we tackle deeply entrenched power systems? How can we achieve greater equality within nations and between nations? How can we empower the poor and disadvantaged? In the 1920s, the Bolsheviks coined some very powerful slogans – for example, 'socialism = Soviet power plus electrification of the whole country', or 'let's make cooks our governors' – and not surprisingly these 'maximalist' ideas evoked a big response among the global dispossessed.

In the 1950s and 1960s, the theory of development stages became very influential among European and American thinkers planning a strategy for post-colonialism. It has been noted that Rostow's theory of stages, the key text for a generation of development strategies, was in a sense 'Lenin minus the Marxism'.[9] By contrast, theories based on the idea of 'dependency' focused on a critique of the world economic-political set-up and tried to posit a more equal alternative. This is the approach adopted and updated by Russian critics today – for example, Boris Kagarlitsky's description of Russia's new status as a second-rate power in the periphery of world capitalism.[10] The Soviet attempt to break out of the capitalist system was used (among other important post-colonial models) by Julius Nyerere in his philosophy of African self-reliance; similarly by Fidel Castro (albeit heavily dependent on support from the USSR), and by other 'voluntarist' communist leaders such as Albania's Enver Hoxha and Romania's Ceauşescu. However, a careful analysis of Soviet aid shows that policy-makers had to balance ideological versus development objectives and more often than not the result was support for a kind of state capitalism rather than socialist revolution.[11]

The collapse of the Soviet Union seemed to bring this whole pack of cards toppling down, giving support to all those who argue that state-led, top-down macro-development with its visions of a 'bright future' have failed humanity. Here we are talking not just about free market ideologists like Ronald Reagan and Margaret Thatcher, who induced Gorbachev to continue with his *perestroika* strategy, but a whole range of other, later 'post-development' thinkers who, as noted above, pin their hopes not on government or international agencies, but on autonomous social movements, small local projects and mutual-help networks.

In Russia today, the dominant school of development thinking uses the term 'modernization' to try to link elements of Soviet and post-Soviet economic and political strategy. Parts 2 and 3 of this book will address various aspects of modernization in the transition period. Not surprisingly, alongside this school there are also those who are more disillusioned – for example, writers like Alexander Zinoviev, who began to rethink communism in the late Soviet period, and the publicist Sergey Kara-Murza, who enjoys nothing more than to debunk the Western, capitalist-oriented story of development and its new Russian adherents.

3 Soviet development results

In this section we take two recent analyses of political and economic aspects of Soviet state-led development. The examples are taken from the 1920s and 1930s and are arranged chronologically because this is natural and logical; but they in no way attempt to tell the full history of the period. These are simply some examples that illustrate an argument.

Case study: people's power, Soviet power and party rule Much has been written on the USSR's political system and, as we noted in the previous chapter, on the origins of and prospects for Russian democracy more widely. In researching this book, the term *narodovlastiye* or 'people's power' seemed to me to convey important things about the Russian experience of democracy and grassroots civic and political movements.[12] Also, it is a term that still has currency in progressive and radical social action in Russia today.

We can find many powerful examples of people's power in the

Russian Revolution. One key moment was the period February–October 1917. During this time the famous 'dual power' situation obtained – with Kerensky's provisional government on one side, the Petrograd Soviet of workers' and soldiers' deputies on the other. By the end of March 1917 there were over five hundred Soviets, not just acting politically on behalf of workers but taking on practical functions like public order and the distribution of food. This was a mass political movement representing the demands of a wide range of social groups. On the other side of the divide, the Kerensky regime proved unequal to the task of withdrawing from the disastrous war with Germany or stemming revolution on the home front. However, it did succeed in passing a new local government reform and organizing the first free elections to town Dumas in May/June that year – and these can be seen as another, albeit partial, victory for people's power.

Even more important was the convocation of an All-Russian Constitutive Assembly in the same year. The regulations adopted for the assembly for the first time in Russian history gave all parties the chance to compete by secret ballot under universal suffrage without respect to a voter's sex, nationality or religious belief (including persons serving in the army and navy). The voting system was by proportional representation and several aspects were extremely progressive – for example, the extension of suffrage to women and the absence of property qualifications or residence restrictions. Voting for the assembly took place in mid-November 1917. The Bolsheviks received 22 per cent of the votes cast, other socialist parties 60.5 per cent (of these, 55 per cent went to the Socialist Revolutionaries), and the liberal-democratic parties 17 per cent.

However, as Kruzhkov notes, at this point people's power began to part ways with Soviet power. One of the first, most critical decisions was to reject the results of the election, in line with Lenin's thesis 'The Republic of the Soviets is higher than a republic with the Constitutive Assembly'. In January 1918, the All-Russia Central Executive Committee adopted a decree dismissing the Assembly and soon after the 3rd All-Russia Conference (*Sezd*) of Soviets approved this decree. In so doing they turned away from dialogue with a vitally important section of Russia's democratic movement over the previous half-century – the village communist movement represented in 1917 by Chernov's Socialist Revolutionaries. Popular power in Russia was due to go down another path.[13]

Soviet is another ancient Russian word – from the root *veche* ('speak') plus *so* ('together'). According to Kruzhkov, Soviet power could have become a new form of genuine democracy if it had corresponded to the principles of *narodovlastiye*. But they were weakened as organs of people's power when they were placed at the service of the dictatorship of the proletariat. For the Bolsheviks, the dictatorship of the proletariat was 'the highest form of democracy' – 'a million times more democratic than any bourgeois democracy'. In reality the country's political system fell gradually under the dominance of one party, since, as Lenin put it, dictatorship of the proletariat 'is impossible otherwise than through the communist party'.

The adoption of a new constitution in July 1918 and the formation of a new government – the Soviet of People's Commissars – were crucial steps towards a dictatorship 'with the aim of the complete suppression of the bourgeoisie, the annihilation of exploitation of man by man and the introduction of socialism, in which there will be no division by classes nor state domination'.[14] Among the casualties were the institutions of local government gradually built up over the previous seventy years in the face of Tsarist reaction. In December 1917, the Bolsheviks called on local Soviets to take over all government offices and bodies and use them to consolidate the new socialist regime. In February 1918, the People's Commissariat of Internal Affairs announced the abolition of urban and rural *zemstvos*, dissolving those that had opposed the new regime and calling on those that supported it to subordinate themselves to local Soviets.

A similar fate awaited independent civil society institutions during the next decade. At the outset of revolution, popular activity flowered. The Soviet arts, cultural and scientific avant-garde of the 1920s is well known, somewhat less so the fact that local movements, peasants' and proletarian organizations played a key role in mobilizing the population all around the country. However, to use a word employed by civil society researchers at the Higher School of Economics in Moscow, during the next ten to fifteen years these organizations were gradually 'nationalized' (Jakobson et al. 2011). Thousands were shut down and new associations set up in their stead as part of the government machine.[15] Eventually only the Red Cross and the Children's Fund remained from among the original social assistance groups.

Commentary on the case study. The debate about how to interpret the Soviet period, including important parts of the radical political legacy, is still ongoing in Russia. Kruzhkov's analysis shows how hard it is to achieve or hang on to real people's power. His own conclusion is that Soviet power as propounded by Lenin and the Bolsheviks led eventually to the one-party state. And his redefinition of 'people's power' owes a lot to recent thinking about civil society and development. He argues that true people's power entails a compromise between the majority and the minority; it means equal rights for all citizens, the maintenance of a balance between different interests, not just through civil society but through state agencies, in particular local self-government (2005: 14–21).

Case study: economic policy, Urals regionalism and the road to Stalin's purges A level up in the Russian administrative hierarchy from civil society organizations (CSOs) and local government there are *oblasts* (provinces), groups of *oblasts* and regions. In this section, we offer a case study taken from Harris (1999) on Urals regionalism in the 1920s and 1930s. The case illustrates economic development debates that were uppermost in the minds of the Bolshevik leaders, believing as they did that economics determines consciousness and the rest of life. And it tells an interesting story in the wider historical frame, too.

The Urals region was one of the first in Russia to develop heavy industry, as Peter the Great took the decision to launch iron and steel production as part of his war effort against the Swedish Empire. In 1700, the Swedes inflicted a crushing defeat on the Russians at Narva, and Peter speeded up his plans; within ten years the Urals had become a major metal producer. By 1800, there were over 170 metallurgical plants in the region, most of which were in private hands – but completely dependent on orders and support from the state. It was a profitable business – a *pood* of iron cost 10 kopecks to produce in the Urals and sold for 65 kopecks in St Petersburg; factory labour was provided by serfs. By 1750, Russia supplied its domestic market fully and was even able to export 22,000 tons of iron. It was producing more than England, the home of the Industrial

Revolution, and by the end of the eighteenth century it was the largest producer in the world.

However, the Urals iron industry depended on wood and fell behind its competitors as coal burning took over gradually in the nineteenth century. The Urals industrial magnates were slow to respond to the new techniques pioneered in England. They reinvested very little from their massive profits, enjoying a sumptuous lifestyle in faraway St Petersburg or abroad, rarely travelling 1,300-plus kilometres on muddy roads to their factories. After the emancipation of the serfs labour costs went up by 60–80 per cent. Meanwhile, the Russian state began development of the Ukraine, using its plentiful coal and iron resources to launch an industrial region thenceforth in direct competition with the Urals. The development of Russia's railway system under Witte generated state orders for almost five million tons of rails, but the Urals could supply only a fifth of this amount. The Ukrainian industrialists used their plentiful natural resources and state orders to attract foreign investment, and within ten years they had drawn level with the Urals in total output.

In the 1920s, Bolshevik leaders struggled to reverse the losses in industry consequent on civil war and the removal of factory owners and professional managers. Even during the era of the New Economic Policy many factories stayed closed. Harris's account shows how with the advent of the first five-year plan there came an opportunity to redress the Urals' fortunes. Despite central control, there was a significant element of inter-regional competition (e.g. with Ukraine) for state investments. Industrializing a mainly agrarian economy in such a large and climatically difficult country posed many problems for which no simple solution existed. The left block in the Soviet leadership tended to promote capital accumulation via increased taxes and requisitions in the countryside (with the risk of sparking even more opposition from the peasantry), whereas Stalin and his supporters focused on solutions within the industrial sector. Forced labour using prison camps dotted around the Urals and Siberia was becoming a feature of the economic system by this time.

Many regional leaders gradually found themselves on the side of Stalin and his allies in the Politburo at the end of the 1920s. By now, the Urals region had good rail links with the Kuznetsk coal basin farther to the east in Siberia, and almost half its iron ore was now produced in coal-fired furnaces. They enthusiastically produced plans which showed the feasibility and payback from increased construction and investment (e.g. the development of the famous 'iron mountain' at Magnitogorsk). The Urals region produced plans that would contribute significantly to the national plan – and at the same time compete with Ukraine. Unity among the leadership was essential to the lobbying effort, but in reality there were divisions between the 'revolutionary optimists' and those who feared that the project was unrealistic.[16]

As the negotiations on the first five-year plan reached their climax, the leaders at the centre attempted to cut costs without loss to the tempo of industrialization. Many experts and managers resisted the cost-cutting efforts. Eventually this led to one of the first political trials, the so-called Shakhty affair in the Ukrainian coal basin (Donbas). At a plenum of the Central Committee in April 1928, mining specialists in Donbas were accused of delaying investment programmes, hindering planning, and directing resources to less expensive shallow mines – all supposedly in an attempt to create a fuel crisis in the USSR. These accusations were supported by leaders from other regions keen to show their political colours or gain advantage for their own industrial centres.

Soon a similar scandal erupted in the Urals – the Uralplatina affair. Once again, the arguments revolved around the planned rate of investment and return in major industrial projects. The Urals OGPU (financial police) discovered a group of 'counter-revolutionary specialists' undermining the plans – in this case, geologists were accused of deliberately understating mineral reserves and dragging their feet on surveying new deposits, hence threatening the Urals' claims of equalling or surpassing the plans emanating from Ukraine.

These debates were echoed at the centre, resulting in an intervention by Bukharin warning of the dangers of operating from inflated figures; and then a campaign against the 'cowardice' of the 'right deviation' by Stalin and his supporters. Later that year, the first secretary of the Urals regional party organization was replaced by a proponent of higher investment and production targets. Many of the Urals' targets for its first five-year plan were doubled. Capital investment in the region was more than trebled, thus assuring the future of Urals industry. In the second five-year plan this tendency continued, but the conditions became much tougher – only 100 per cent delivery of targets was acceptable ...

Realizing the danger of adopting unrealistic plans, many in the Urals region opposed the party's Stakhanovite campaigns for increased production – but their resistance was doomed as the period of terror began in the mid-1930s. Eventually the finger of blame pointed at First Secretary Kabakov himself, but not before he had condemned many of his colleagues. In 1937, the Urals Oblast Committee was engulfed in wave after wave of leaks, denunciations and confessions regarding faked production reports, subverted policies, exaggerated reserves, etc. The Stalin regime, faced with the likelihood of war with Hitler's Germany and at the same time falling industrial output (in part due to the economic chaos unleashed by terror), simply panicked, resulting in more and more arrests and the show trials that discredited the whole Soviet system.

Commentary on the case study. The Urals story encapsulates a lot about the achievements of Russian economic development and the human tragedies associated with forced industrialization in the Soviet period. The regionalism of the *zemstvo* movement in the late nineteenth century (see Chapter 1) finds its continuation in the lobbying efforts of Bolshevik leaders in the Urals in the 1920s. The case study reinterprets history to show that, contrary to most assumptions about the workings of the Soviet state, decisions were not completely centralized. In actual fact, Soviet leaders were dependent on ideas, information and detailed plans from the regions for the rapid development of Soviet industry. It shows the origins of the Stalin Terror in the processes that created the five-year plan system, where left and right factions were pitted against each other. In this case study, as so often, politics is tightly intertwined with economics.

4 The golden age of 'real socialism'

The arguments for people's power or a radical, decentralized alternative disappeared or went underground for many years. The USSR emerged victorious from the war with Germany at huge human cost, the country having been occupied and trampled by armies from Brest on the Polish border to Stalingrad on the Volga, not far from where the Central Asia deserts and steppes begin. A new page of history opened with the reconstruction effort, albeit with no political relaxation for ten years until Stalin's death and the 'thaw' introduced by Khrushchev in the mid-1950s.

This was already the Cold War period, with increasing repression of communists in the USA and determined efforts to try to halt the political gains the left had made in post-war Europe. Russian and Soviet studies were dominated by the right, with many an academic journal or research institute funded by the CIA and its various ideological allies. The friendship societies promoted by the USSR across the world reproduced the Communist Party's own orthodoxy. Those in the left or liberal camps who tried to maintain a friendly but independent view were termed 'fellow-travellers' and were not much trusted by officialdom on either side.

Twenty years on from this, the author of this book arrived in Moscow with his wife and baby son on a two-year contract as a translator/editor for the Soviet news agency Novosti, during what is now sometimes called the 'golden age' of 'real socialism' under President Brezhnev. This is indeed a story in itself. Our stay in the USSR lasted from January 1978 to January 1980, just before the Moscow Olympics.[17] These were years of relative prosperity, so the statistics tell us, though even in well-supplied Moscow queuing for basic daily necessities quickly became a way of life. We were provided with a flat in an ordinary block (most foreigners lived in enclosures) and I was paid mostly in roubles (it was more advantageous to be paid in foreign currency). But one of the advantages was that Novosti was able to arrange travel during annual leave periods to different parts of the country; so we visited Leningrad, Kiev, the Black Sea, Georgia and Samarkand, Bukhara and Ashkhabad in Central Asia.

Every day our department in Novosti brought out a summary of the daily press in several foreign languages. The subject matter ranged from economic and political news and analysis from around the country, to detailed coverage of speeches by Brezhnev and official state events. In general, this was a time of on-and-off détente with the West. The Soviet press continued its propaganda wars against internal dissidents, and the USSR's military intervention in support of communist and secular nationalist allies in Afghanistan took place at this time, too.

Twenty years after the exit of the USSR from the stage of history, studies of the social, cultural and political heritage of the Soviet period have become popular in many countries. And not just in Russia, where President Putin made great play from 1999 of his view that the fall of the USSR was one of the biggest global tragedies of the twentieth century. In Japan, Europe and the USA the same phenomenon is increasingly visible in academic and expert circles – albeit, of course, the assessments of this period vary a lot. The reason is not just the nostalgia felt by many – especially the working classes, public servants and inhabitants of Russia's geographical periphery – for the benefits they enjoyed at that time. It is mainly because the positive impact of Soviet-era institutions and reforms is still felt in many areas of life. In Central Asia, for example, many bureaucratic procedures and government structures, plus much of the legal system and the health and educational sectors inherited from the Soviet period and *perestroika*, have stayed in place – frustrating reform-impatient Westernizers but somehow preventing the countries of the region from complete collapse.[18]

What was Soviet socialism? A number of writers have already begun a post-collapse review of the USSR's development record. Moshe Lewin's *The Soviet Century* (2005), for example, is a massive summing-up that my account can in no way emulate. A shorter book by Stephen Lovell (2006) gives a useful list of the selling points of 'real socialism' in the Brezhnev period. He says that the regime maintained popular support not because of its adherence to Marxist ideology but because it represented a 'strong distributive state and some form of social justice'. In the post-1945 years the USSR opened up and the system softened a bit, with the result that more and more groups of Soviet citizens gained a sense of entitlement to housing, vacations, pensions and so on. The regime embodied the commitment to an 'alternative route' towards modernization, including a principled critique of the market economy and hostility to Western consumer culture and liberal democracy. And yet the USSR regularly defined its development level by comparison with the West – and in the Brezhnev era it was moving slowly but surely in the direction of consumerism.

During my stay in the Soviet Union, I spent a lot of time trying to figure out the difference between the structure of a 'producer' society, such as promoted by the Soviet publications I was working on, and the 'consumer' society that I was familiar with in the West. Indeed, the producer philosophy has a lot of attractive points – provided that we can avoid the senseless production of unnecessary goods. And the advantages of a society based around the value of 'labour' (that is, efforts and activities for social need and enjoyment at different levels) against a society built on 'capital', owned by a few and used to protect their privileges against the majority, are also quite clear. In this sense, Soviet socialist propaganda had an argument that is to this day not answered adequately by the capitalist camp.[19]

5 Post-1991: picking up the pieces

Soviet development decisions for distant or 'backward' regions like the Urals, Siberia or Central Asia took place behind closed doors, as a result of production and policy discussions in top government bodies. Thus, after a geological or technical/economic survey, a decision might be made to build a factory near an iron ore deposit or a coal mine. Housing for the factory workers would be agreed according to centrally determined living conditions for particular industries. As noted above, in the pre-Second World War years the infrastructure was often created with forced labour. But from the mid-1950s this gradually stopped and instead mass recruitment campaigns were used to attract volunteers from around the country. Initially the new arrivals were housed in temporary workers' barracks, to be replaced (often many years later) by blocks of flats. Local executive bodies were given the task of delivering housing, transport and communal services. Towns created near a key factory or military unit would commonly be eligible for a 'Moscow budget', with better facilities than the surrounding areas, so that people would travel from afar to buy things in its shops.

The Soviet commitment to industrial and infrastructure development was massive. The environmental movement now criticizes many aspects of this – from the overlying philosophy (aggressively scientific-utilitarian in its approach to natural resources) to the manner of its implementation (Schedrovitsky et al. 2005: 43–9; Yanitsky 2007: 21–7). However, the scale and seriousness of the commitment are not in doubt.

And then it fell apart ... The spectacular fate that awaited many of the giants of Soviet industrialization in the 1990s has spawned a whole literature – from glossy photo albums of decaying factories, to tongue-in-cheek accounts of tractor factories in the previous period.

For those working in the development sector the problems of decaying infrastructure early assumed great importance. Poverty in the FSU in the 1990s was a bit different to poverty in the 'usual' poor countries (i.e. the developing world). Ex-Soviet citizens had quite a lot of material possessions – they were now selling them on the pavement, in all manner of bazaars or flea markets (from books to kitchen equipment, electrical appliances, furniture or cars), and they had high expectations of life – now dashed. And in the infrastructure realm, development projects were typically not digging wells or laying electricity lines where none had been before, or building new houses and schools – they were repairing ones constructed in the Soviet period.

From a social anthropological stance, Caroline Humphrey discusses infrastructure as the base of social life inherited from the Soviet Union, noting how the word echoes the Marxist opposition between 'base' and 'superstructure' – where the economy is the base, and political and cultural life the superstructure it supports (Humphrey 2010: 234–52). Thus infrastructure has a wide resonance in the FSU as the material foundation for all social life, a key condition for the level of civilization that society had reached. People assumed that urban or rural infrastructure would remain in working order.

Repairing Soviet infrastructure – an NGO view But even socialist infrastructure falls apart, as we saw in the transition period ... When, at the start of the 2000s, I left VSO and began work with INTRAC in Central Asia,[20] supporting NGOs working on development projects at community level, it was obvious that our NGO partners and all manner of local groups, especially but not only in rural areas, were continually engaged in a process of infrastructure repair – that is, trying to keep Soviet-era equipment (water systems, electricity generators) and the built environment (bridges, dams, school buildings, youth clubs) from breaking down or collapsing. For this, they gained small grants from international agencies, topped up with voluntary labour and in-kind assistance from their local authority. It is a system that was reproduced across the whole FSU region and many good things were achieved. And INTRAC was working in some of the farthest-flung parts – in south-eastern Kazakhstan, Kyrgyzstan and Tajikistan, next to the China and Afghanistan borders.

Humphrey describes the situation in Ulan Ude, capital of the Autonomous Republic of Buryatia in eastern Siberia, when one of the city's two power stations broke down during a particularly hard winter in 2000/01, with a graphic account of how terrified people were when they saw on TV the cold front hit the city of Krasnoyarsk to the west and realized it was moving towards them (ibid.: 240–1). We experienced the same kind of situation in Tajikistan in the winter of 2008/09. In Tajikistan, the population had been living for several years with just two or three hours of electricity in the morning, the same in the evening, 'if you're lucky'.

While in general the climate is much milder in Tajikistan than in Siberia, the temperature always drops below zero in January, and during the harsh winter of 2008/09 it hovered around minus 20 degrees Centigrade for almost two months, bringing people across the country to breaking point. Central heating systems in Tajikistan have been out of order since the civil war of the 1990s and most heating in the cities is provided by electric fires or even woodstoves reintroduced into city flats. Residents describe their homes as 'icy coffins' when there is no heat and citizens regularly try to take the local authorities to court for 'moral injury', on the grounds that lack of basic services has made it impossible to live a normal human life. The country's National Consumers Association monitors electricity supply across the country and regularly protests against nonsensical commercial and individualized strategies for heating. But court cases and civil society lobbying have had little impact on the overall situation.[21]

Just as working infrastructure is associated by citizens of FSU with the relative stability of the Soviet time (at least post-1945), deteriorating infrastructure post-1991 is often explained as being subject to corrupt practices between the town hall and the newly privatized housing management companies, or simply political shenanigans. Thus, Humphrey describes a high-level political spat between Chubais, architect of neoliberalism in Russia and later head of the country's main power company, and Nazdratenko, governor of the Far Eastern Region (including Vladivostok), at this time. After a major argument about payments and supplies, the regional power company simply cut off electricity across the Far East, forcing the resignation of the governor.

In Ulan Ude (as in Central Asia) many of the people who pay their bills regularly are pensioners (the reason being that heating is a matter of life or death for them, hence they can't take the risk of being cut off). Many others tend to find excuses – 'our salaries are paid late', 'our neighbours don't pay, so why should we?', etc. In larger towns like Irkutsk, consumer groups are strong enough to challenge this situation, but in Ulan Ude the relevant officials have political connections and feel able to ignore the complaints. In Bishkek, some of the worst offenders are new private sector companies (restaurants, shops, etc.).

Psychological repairs or rebuilding 'social capital' This is the other side of development work at grassroots level. In Chapter 1, the consequences of sudden pauperization were described briefly. What measures can be taken to counter them? In general, development agencies used a variety of everyday strategies and solutions aimed at rediscovering collective action and the community (social capital). In this they were helped by another impact of human development in the USSR: good organizational skills among the general population and close to 100 per cent literacy even in distant, isolated rural areas of the region.

A number of excellent examples of NGO first steps and 'first aid' actions are provided in Giffen et al. (2005), including the setting up of NGOs and NGO support centres, work with micro-credit and small businesses, community water projects and conflict prevention activities. Some of the most important factors were described in a study by INTRAC on community development in Central Asia in 2004 (ibid.). In a more practical vein, a more recent note on 'bridging' social capital offers tips for development workers in isolated, depressed communities. The suggestions below give the flavour of the approach taken:

- Try to understand where people's 'passivity' comes from ... Could this be cultural factors or structural ones like poverty, lack of information about their rights?
- Don't neglect local capacity ... For example, existing mutual support groups, family connections, informal associations
- Overcome distrust: listen to people first, organize 'reality checks'

- Move people out of tight (defensive or exclusive) group networks: promote local volunteering, parents' associations, faith communities
- Try to deal with increasing socio-economic disparities: ensure a mix of people in workshops, cultural and other events ... Organize exchange schemes between leaders and activists in different locations ...[22]

The social disorientation and exclusion produced by mass unemployment and the failure of basic municipal services such as those mentioned above produced a large increase in suicide as well as deaths from violence, alcohol and drugs (especially for men, whose average life expectancy dipped below sixty years in Russia and several other countries of FSU). In general, development agencies worked on psychological problems indirectly. However, at an INTRAC conference on community development in 2007, a participant from Azerbaijan gave an interesting example of a holistic psychological approach to the very severe problem of mental health in the region.

In this case study, the director of the Azerbaijan Psychological Association describes how a group of NGOs working with disadvantaged groups gathered together to discuss how to reinforce civil society development in a country racked by war, poverty and unemployment. Their idea was based on the development of healthy citizens who can then make ties between formerly divergent groups, acting together and sharing resources. Civil society 'cannot be imposed top down, but rather must grow from the consciousness of the people', they said. 'Changing laws or courts or constitutions is of no use' if people themselves are not first prepared for citizenship. Short-term projects, the association argued, don't bring sustainable results but rather keep communities dependent on external factors – government, foreign experts, donor agencies and old authoritarian habits. People 'don't see that they can affect the social changes and conditions in their community' and children growing up in refugee camps (e.g. after the Azerbaijan–Armenia conflict of the early 1990s) 'are being raised with similar negative and oppressive attitudes'.

The association went back to the theories of Russian psychologists Leontyev and Stolin, which showed that individuals develop an identity in the group they belong to. In cooperation with professional colleagues in the USA, they designed a long-term project which would support personal growth through group therapy, skills training and the development of a 'core community' made up of psychologists, social workers, doctors and teachers to work in a multidisciplinary way with the target groups. In 2005, they initiated the largest national campaign ever in Azerbaijan to celebrate World Mental Health Day, holding dozens of events all over the country, as a result of which the World Mental Health Federation suggested that this approach should be used as a model in other countries in the region (Cheryomukhin 2007).

More examples of progressive social work initiatives will be provided in Chapter 5. This was one of the several strong suits in EEP's volunteer programme in the Urals region.

Postscript: left political parties resisting shock therapy in Russia

So what happened to the Communist Party and the millions of rank-and-file communists around the country after 1991? The Communist Party of the Soviet Union (CPSU) was banned immediately after the failed military putsch in August that year and millions left the party. In commenting on emerging political pluralism in Russia, many analysts have focused on the performance of liberal or democratic forces. But in reality, the development of a post-Soviet communist or socialist movement is just as important, and in most elections the left vote has been at least as high as the liberal/nationalist vote – usually higher.

As we have seen above, many in the elite of the CPSU supported Gorbachev and his economic reforms – and once the opportunity came, converted their personal political capital into its economic equivalent. However, the majority of middle and lower officials, party researchers or ordinary employees, either did not navigate the rapids of change so smoothly or found themselves in ideological opposition to the path Russia took in the 1990s. During the previous decade, many different strands of 'transition' left thinking had begun to emerge. From these, three main groups came together at the time of the re-establishment of the Communist Party as a Russian party in 1992.[23] Willy-nilly the events of the 1980s had long ago forced Soviet communists to reconsider their positions and the temptation to sit tight and do nothing had become untenable. The first group can be called Marxist reformers (revisionists), most of them internationalist in orientation; the second were more orthodox Marxist-Leninists; while the third group tended towards Russian nationalism (Urban and Solovei 1997).

Some views were shared by almost all of the above groups. First, all agreed that the result of Yeltsin's privatization, shock therapy and pro-Western orientation vindicated what Marx and Lenin had written about capitalism as a cause of mass impoverishment, social polarization and human degradation. Secondly, the mass imports of consumer goods from the West and Asia, plus the export of Russia's raw materials to the West, corroborated what Lenin had said about the danger of Russia being transformed into a colonial outpost of the Western powers. Thirdly, they viewed the dissolution of the USSR as an act of treachery by Gorbachev and Yeltsin – and the Communist Party in particular began to promote itself as the country's only true 'patriots'. There was an important division at this time between those who supported the re-establishment of the Communist Party as a supranational organization working across the post-Soviet space and those who argued for a new Russian party. The nationalists won. Their leader, Zyuganov, from the very start argued for a 'national emergency' approach and for building bridges with other nationalist forces inside the country. This was the 'popular front' strategy that the CPSU had adopted in previous periods of national crisis and calamity (such as during the rise of Nazism and the Second World War); however, Zyuganov's apocalyptic language and conspiracy theories were off-putting to many outside the party's own ranks.

These political developments determined the arena in which civil society could play its role as an agent of progressive change in the 1990s. With democracy in disarray and the left movement increasingly nationalist in character, a situation took shape quite unlike that in the USA or Europe, and one in which Western political assumptions and solidarities quite often failed to work. And the pro-Western ideology of the democrats and the pro-Russian ideology of the nationalists and socialists all tended to ignore the other parts of the old USSR.

3 | MOVING EAST AND SOUTH: EMPIRE AND AFTER

1 Russia's expansion into Siberia: the Tsarist period

The history of 'international development' in the twentieth century is in large part the history of the post-colonial era. Countries that became 'donors' in the new scheme of things very often focused their attentions on countries that had previously been their colonies, building development programmes on foundations and links created in the previous period. Few countries had managed to escape the attention of the colonizers and those that had tended to fare badly (Haiti and Burma spring to mind in this respect). Indeed, development in its modern sense began with changes imposed on colonies in the age of empires.

There are several aspects of the Russian Empire that seem to stand out and distinguish it from other European empires. The first has already been mentioned: the phenomenon of serfdom – that is, a version of slavery in which the rural inhabitants of Russia were held right up until the middle of the nineteenth century. The second can be seen readily from any map of Russia. This was a land empire extending over six thousand miles from the Baltic Sea at St Petersburg to the Pacific Ocean at the easternmost tip of Chukotka. Explorers, hunters and trappers, and settlers of various kinds began moving east from the sixteenth century. This began as a spontaneous movement of people looking for new opportunities or escaping oppression but soon became official policy. When trading took over from simple territorial incursions, fur was the main commodity and it quickly became a strategic one: in the seventeenth century, animal pelts mainly from Siberia comprised no less than 20 per cent of state revenue in Russia (Ablazhei and Vodichev 2009). The main physical barriers were the low-lying Ural mountains chain and thick forest or taiga to the north, steppes and deserts to the south. The Siberian rivers provided a useful means of navigation (mainly north–south), so too the ancient Silk Road trading routes overland to the Middle East and China.

A third difference between the Russian Empire and other empires is historical. Following the first flowering of the Russian state in Kiev, there had followed several centuries when the Russian princedoms fell victim to invasion from the east – the Tatar and Mongol 'hordes' that overran large parts of central Russia and later exacted tribute from them. Thus, the Russian Empire (now with a new centre in Moscow) gradually rose over peoples that had previously been its conquerors. A fourth factor is the harsh climatic conditions prevailing over most of the country. This has turned habitation, travel and economic activity (whether agriculture or industry) into a constant struggle with the elements – and more expensive (in terms of the cost of shelter, heating and so on) than in countries with milder climates. And finally, there is the nature of state-dominated capitalism as it evolved in Russia from the time of Peter the Great. As noted in the previous chapter, Peter was a Westernizer, and his development of the iron industry was largely designed to create the armaments with which to oppose the next-door Polish and Swedish empires. But he did not ignore the east, nor did Catherine the Great, who in the eighteenth century invited Germans and other settlers to join the colonization movement.

The beginning of the nineteenth century saw renewed debates in Russia about what to do with the lands occupied gradually over the previous 200 years to the east and south of the Urals. By this time the population of Siberia had grown to just under six million people and trade in furs had given way to minerals extraction – for example, silver mining in the Altai and Trans-Baikal regions bordering present-day Kazakhstan and Mongolia. Agricultural and forestry activities had begun to develop in Siberia from the middle of the seventeenth century. This and the discovery of gold and silver provided the main stimulus for the Tsar's penal servitude policies in the region. Penal settlements were concentrated in the imperial estates of Altai and Trans-Baikal, along the main highway from Moscow and in the border regions. Troublesome serfs were typically sent into servitude by landlords/owners, and political opponents of the regime soon followed them.

After the emancipation of the serfs in 1861, civilian (that is, unforced) colonization took precedence over penal colonization. By this time, state policy was more focused on the expansion into Central Asia than Siberia in any case. Migration as a whole decreased; indeed, population movements within Siberia assumed more importance as urbanization began to make itself felt. Human settlements in Siberia had been very small up to this time. In 1850, Irkutsk, the largest town in Siberia, had only 17,000 inhabitants, Tobolsk 15,000, Omsk 13,000; and some 90 per cent of the population lived in villages. The development process owed much to the efforts of merchant families in these urban centres. These families had grown rich on monopolies in the fur, minerals and vodka trades and they defended their gains fiercely. Merchants uniting in guilds gradually developed into a commercial bourgeoisie and some began to get involved in educational activities on the side. In Russia as a whole, besides the state, the landed gentry and industrial capitalists, civil society organizations were also beginning to play a role in development. In the nineteenth century, a generation of explorers and orientalists helped drive forward the process of colonization.

Case study: the Imperial Russian Geographical Society The Imperial Russian Geographical Society was set up by two prominent scholars, Fedor Litke and Karl von Baer, in 1846, with the aim of developing a knowledge and love of Russia among its people. Geography was understood in its wider sense (including human and not just physical geography) and promoted in the most open and active way possible within the constraints of the Tsarist regime. Litke was an explorer who had taken part in naval expeditions to the Arctic, Baer a naturalist-embryologist. They reflected the generation of the 1840s, when, in the words of the society's long-time secretary, P. P. Semyonov, 'Russian national feelings had started to awaken among Russian young people, when in harmony with signs from above, progressive young people began to work not only on the rebirth of the Russian ethnic group, but also on the liberation of Russian people from servitude ...'. As in other European geographical societies, the founders and early members included military and government officials and scientists. They approached Tsar Nicholas I and Minister of Internal Affairs Perovsky and gained their support, persuading them that a private society would be able to collect data, coordinate research and popularize findings in a way that the government could not. Through careful lobbying they gained a substantial government subsidy – 10,000 roubles a year.

One of the most important aspects of the Geographical Society was its Ethnographic Division. Both Litke and Baer were particularly interested in studies of the non-Russian peoples living within the empire, arguing in 1846 that 'we see that the life of peoples and their corresponding character is more and more being driven out by western progress. For this reason it is all the more urgent to preserve for posterity, in accurate descriptions the special features of folk life before it is too late.' Early expeditions went to the northern Urals and the Baltic. In 1847, the Geographical Society sent out 7,000 questionnaires to all corners of the empire to collect information on a wide variety of topics: the physical features of the people of Russia; language, dialect and slang; domestic life, including material goods and customs; intellectual and moral features; social life; and folk legends and memories. A huge amount of information was collected by a wide variety of official and unofficial surveyors and scholars.

The Geographical Society thus included elite and popular elements, a top-down and bottom-up impulse. The society had some difficult political moments. One of its activists was Petr Kropotkin – not only an anarchist but a scientist who made several expeditions to the Arctic for the society (as well as suffering bouts in Siberian exile arranged by the Tsar). Litke had pioneered public discussions of learned papers, but the society had to closely monitor these debates and at one moment it seemed possible that it might be taken over by the radical Petrashevsky circle. It also opened a Statistics Division that operated in close accord with government policy at a time when information of this kind was usually kept secret. As Joseph Bradley comments, 'a forum outside government in autocratic Russia existed on treacherous terrain', but the society 'drew in the public and created civic consciousness'. By the end of the nineteenth century, it was probably the most prominent association of its kind in Russia (Bradley 2011: 92–127).

Siberian regionalism Kuleshov and Evseyenko (in Boiko 1998) describe how at the beginning of the nineteenth century the Decembrists group debated two models for Russia's development: one a unitarian state, the other a federalist arrangement in which the main units would correspond roughly to the existing provinces of the Russian Empire. In the 1870s this concept was developed by the Ukrainian

Mikhail Dragomanov, and the radical political party People's Will (*Narodnaya Volya*) included the principle of self-determination of regions of Russia in their programme.[1]

The nineteenth-century *zemstvo* movement was a wide coalition, including both those who promoted regional policies (e.g. the *oblastniki* in the Urals) and those who aspired to greater national autonomy (e.g. Bashkir and Tatar radicals). By the end of the nineteenth century a group of 'regional patriots' had emerged. These were promoters of educational reform, founders of local press organs, students of the complex ethnographic character of the Russian periphery. Within the socialist movement, many activists argued for greater self-government. Thus the programme of the Russian Social-Democratic and Workers' Party, adopted in 1903, contained the demand for local self-government based on universal suffrage, and in 1905 the party supported a number of radical demands put forward by elected assemblies in Siberian towns like Tomsk, Krasnoyarsk and Chita.[2]

After the defeat of the 1905 revolution, the Bolsheviks concentrated on political work within trade unions and workers' cooperatives. The Mensheviks, by contrast, continued to focus on local government. Thus an article in the party newspaper by their leader Martynov in 1910 notes that government diktat is less felt the lower down the administrative hierarchy you go, and that 'workers who have got used to self-sufficiency and organized discussions will naturally begin to set their sights on urban self-government, since even if it is only for urban property owners, this is the only level of government really interested in somehow tackling the revolting conditions that obtain in impoverished workers' quarters ...'. And a leading article written in 1913 about municipal workers' struggles in Omsk stated: 'Making municipal demands on behalf of the proletariat, the avant-garde of workers should, on the one hand, force progressive Dumas to define their attitude to such demands, and on the other, to popularize these demands among the masses and try to organize them on the base of these demands'.[3] In the early Soviet period, the Socialist Revolutionary Party issued a number of manifestos for Siberian regional development that have been described as a kind of 'eastern hypothesis' within development strategies for this period. In other words, the outlying provinces of Russia were no longer seen as simply the frontier for an expanding empire but as regions with their own character, needs and agenda.

2 Siberia in the Soviet period and transition

War, imperialist intervention and civil war in the first twenty-five years of the twentieth century broke Russia apart and led to separatist ideas and movements in many areas. In the previous chapter, we noted what an important role national liberation played in Bolshevik strategy, and how Lenin appealed to the colonized peoples to support the Russian revolution on the side of socialism. Many of their leaders followed his lead and a large number of commentators in Russia and FSU still view the creation of the USSR as a positive step forward in resolving the national question. But in practice there were problems in implementing truly equitable systems. On the one hand, the national republics received huge capital investments from the centre, both in the economic and cultural fields, but on the other, many national elites felt slighted or held back by the one-party regime (Alexeyev 2009: 85).

In the 1920s, the GOELRO[4] plan helped to address these issues, creating large regional units like the Urals *oblast* (province), and the eastern Siberian and Far East *krais* (territories). But these decentralizing trends eventually fell foul of the drive towards central planning, and the new administrative units were disbanded in the 1930s. As we have seen, raw materials processing industries (not just iron ore and other metals, but also forestry) were central to the Soviet Union's development strategy. They determined major population movements from old to new settlements. Siberia's economic space took on a 'ribbon and cluster' geographical pattern in increasingly complex, multi-year industrial and economic development programmes, several of them integrated with the plans for Kazakhstan and Central Asia to the south (Kuleshov and Yevseyenko 1998).

Post-1945 Soviet developments included Khrushchev's 'virgin lands' campaigns to plough up the southern steppes for wheat, the construction of enormous industrial projects like the hydroelectric dam in Bratsk and major oil and gas exploration in Tyumen. Hundreds of thousands of young people were mobilized from around the USSR to work on these projects, joined by internal migrants from Siberian villages. Town dwellers now made up 70 per cent of the population of Siberia. However, these population increases hid a problem which became immediately evident post-1990: the continuing unattractiveness of living conditions in the region.[5] From this point, the region has experienced year upon year of unremitting deurbanization.

Perestroika gave Siberian activists the chance to raise the flag of regionalism once again. In 1990 the so-called Siberian Agreement was signed by political leaders in Kemerovo, and with the help of allies in higher education establishments like the Siberian Academy of Sciences at Novosibirsk they developed a new critique of socio-economic development in the region, arguing that most schemes had worked more to the benefit of the USSR than Siberia itself. In 1993, they aligned themselves with the radicals in Moscow in condemning Yeltsin's shelling of parliament. The work by Boiko and others on a new vision of development in Siberia as a '21st century bridge between West and East' continued all through the 1990s. Resolving nationality and ethnic issues in this very mixed population was a key priority.[6]

Of course, the economic crisis and structural reforms of the time played no small role in forcing alternative strategies. The post-1991 Russian government's priorities had changed dramatically and newly privatized companies had a narrower profit motivation, with little concern for the wider development of towns and regions previously under their wing. Thus critics charged that by the end of the twentieth century the government had abandoned broad-based development in Siberia. The economic stimuli that used to work for Siberia were now working better in Western, more developed parts of the country. Now it is simply a struggle to provide the basic minimum of social protection to the population, an impasse, as Alexeyev and others argue, that can be solved only by a long-term, three-pronged strategy – to link Siberia's raw material resources with labour from China and high technology from Japan.

Reflecting mainstream opinions in Russia, Alexeyev argues that at the turn of the 1990s as the USSR's socialist experiment came to an end, the chance to move to a looser confederation of post-Soviet states was missed. People had become increasingly conscious of their own national traditions and values, and the Union fell apart. In the 1990s there was a period of 'careless sovereignization' of

TABLE 3.1 The Urals, Siberia and Central Asia regions: land area and population

Country or region	Area (1,000s km2)	Population (millions)	Population density per km	Main ethnic groups
Urals region	1,789	14.3 (2002) 12.1 (2010)	8.01	Russians 82.7%, Ukrainians 2.87%, Tatars 5.14%, Bashkirs 2.15%, Khanti-Mansi & Nenets 0.52% (2010)
Siberia region	5,115	19.3 (2010)	3.76	Russians 84.9%, Ukrainians 3.9%, Germans 1.6%, indigenous peoples 5.8%
Central Asia region (five ex-Soviet republics)	4,003	64.7	16.17	Country populations: Kazakhstan 16.6 million, Kyrgyzstan 5.5 million, Tajikistan 7.6 million, Turkmenistan 5.1 million, Uzbekistan 29.5 million (2012)
Kyrgyzstan	200	5.4	26.82	Kyrgyz 70.9%, Uzbeks 14.5%, Russians 9%
Tajikistan	143	7.8	54.50	Tajiks 79.9%, Uzbeks 15.3%, Russians 1.1%

Note: 1) Urals is defined in this table as the 'federal district' created by Putin in 2000, though the latter excludes some areas usually considered part of the Urals – e.g. Perm *krai*. 2) The Siberian 'federal district' extends beyond Lake Baikal but does not include the Russian Far East (which is a bit larger but with only one third of the population of Siberia). 3) Population density in Siberia is less than half of population density in the more urbanized Urals; and the Urals has less than half the population density of Central Asia. 4) The population of the five ex-Soviet republics in Central Asia is double that of Urals and Siberia taken together, and it is growing fast – about 10 per cent overall between 1990 and 2010 – while during the same period the population of Urals and Siberia declined by 5 per cent. 5) The ethnic breakdown of the Asian part of Russia shows the Russians have a huge majority – about the same as the titular peoples of Central Asia have in those countries. 6) The Uzbeks are the most numerous people in Central Asia – about twice the size of the next biggest group, the Kazakhs – and they form significant minorities in both Tajikistan and Kyrgyzstan.

Sources: Wikipedia and others

regions within Russia itself. He argues that Siberia is not viable as an independent unit. 'What is Siberia to do, for example, with its circumpolar territories that objectively cannot and should not shut themselves off for their own interests?' Isolationism or a reliance on market mechanisms alone will lead to disaster.

Alexeyev supports the innovations in the Russian Federation's 1993 Constitution aimed at giving national areas greater rights than 'ordinary' geographical ones. However, he warns that these clauses could cause difficulties in the future, instancing the authoritarian regimes in national or autonomous republics such as Tatarstan, Bashkortostan or Kalmykia and the series of laws adopted in autonomous regions in the 1990s that clashed with legislation at the centre. There is also a degree of inconsistency in the Federation Council (Russia's second parliamentary chamber), where numerically small units ('subjects' within the federation) have equal representation with much larger units. Indeed, the demographic and administrative picture is complex – see Table 3.1 which provides comparative data for Urals, Siberia and Central Asia. Alexeyev sees the future of Russia in large cultural-regional complexes, based on populations with a well-established historical identity and attachment to the region where they live, and whose socio-economic development has brought them to a point where they can withstand the 'destructive processes visible in the political sphere'... (Alexeyev 2009: 87–8)

3 The colonization of Central Asia

Central Asia's association with Russia starts with the Mongol/Tatar invasions of Russia referred to above. In this complex history of tribes and peoples, Central Asia was often at war, itself invaded and overrun for several centuries in what we call the Middle Ages. Islam first arrived in what is now Turkmenistan from the south in the eighth century, but Persian influence was stronger in settled areas in the ensuing centuries. The invasion of Mongol armies under Chinghiz Khan destroyed the cities of Samarkand and Bukhara in the thirteenth century. Russian colonization began significantly later, with expeditions against the northernmost Kazakh *zhuzes* (tribes) under the empresses Anna Iohannovna and Catherine the Great in the seventeenth to eighteenth centuries, but these attempts to settle and educate the nomadic peoples came to little.

Case study: Przhevalsky's expeditions Nikolai Przhevalsky (1839–88) is one of most famous Russian adventurers and explorers of Central Asia and China in the nineteenth century. A lover of hardship and a keen student of fauna and flora in the region, he brought back a total of 7,500 specimens of Central Asia fauna – mammals, birds, reptiles and fish. He was the first European to identify the so-called 'Przhevalsk horse', and he contributed invaluable surveys and maps of the mountains and lakes of Central Asia, western China and the northern Tibetan plateau. Like Siberia, this more southern frontier of the empire was perceived by the romantically inclined as a realm of adventure and freedom, far away from the repressive atmosphere of autocratic Russia. Przhevalsky was a leading member of the Russian Geographical Society, feted by academics, the media and the Tsar himself on his infrequent trips back to the court at St Petersburg. However, another side of the story is the geo-strategic importance of Przhevalsky's expeditions and the explorer's strongly held view that Russia needed to strengthen its southern and eastern borders. Thus, in an 1886 paper, he argued that China had become the 'weak man in Asia' and Russia should expand its influence throughout the region. In this respect he was a man of his time – the period of imperial expansion that came to a nasty end with defeat in the Russo-Japanese War.[7]

Post-colonial re-evaluations 1. It is perhaps interesting to compare the images of Siberia and Central Asia in Tsarist times. The first and dominant image of Siberia, inside Russia as well as outside, has always been of a wilderness, and an especially harsh and cold one at that. For the state and enterprising industrialists, the region was viewed and exploited from the start as a 'resource frontier' for the whole of Russia. Later the images became more complex. For example, after the exiling of the Decembrists and other generations of radicals and democrats, Siberia got a new image – as a zone of freedom for escapees from oppression. And increasingly it was viewed in a more autonomous way, from the point of view of indigenous peoples or even the descendants of Russian settlers, who in the course of several generations developed a quite different identity from fellow Russians in different parts of the country.

Conventional images of Central Asia in Tsarist times included endless steppes and deserts, flocks of sheep or camels, herders and women in bright dresses and the *parandzha* (veil), the noble ruins of Samarkand and famous mosques of Bukhara. As recent publication in the series *Historia Rossica* by a team of experts from the Central Asia department of the Russian Academy of Sciences puts it, the poverty of rural people, ever vulnerable to epidemics, was contrasted with the wealth of the traditional rulers or khans – and above all of them, the 'white' governor-general, a symbol of Russian power ... (Abashin et al. 2008: 313).[8]

In reality, the region was almost as far away for Russians as it was for western Europeans. Little was known or understood about its ancient centres of civilization, Samarkand, Bukhara or Khiva, separated as they were from Russia by the wide-open Eurasian steppes. It was only in the nineteenth century that Russian-language journals began to devote attention to the region – for example, the *Eastern News*, published in Astrakhan, also the *Siberian Vestnik* and *Siberian Bee*, which published accounts of expeditions like Przhevalsky's to the region. Russian readers were attracted by the idea of a rich civilization at the crossroads of the Silk Road. But it gradually became clear that Central Asia was not entirely rich, nor was trade so easy to develop owing to the activities of robber bands among the nomadic peoples of the steppes and deserts. Despite this, from the 1860s Central Asia began to move into the focus of attention of Russian foreign policy. Indeed, expeditions to the region have been described as a kind of 'compensation' to the army for its losses in the Crimean War, a way of expanding Russia's territories and at the same time resisting British imperialism.

The work of the Russian painter Vasily Vereschagin provides an interesting example of artists' engagement with political events in the mid-nineteenth century. At an exhibition of his paintings of Central Asian people and landscapes created during an expedition to the region in 1869/70, a series called 'Barbarians' caused a great stir, with pictures showing plainly the horrors of Russia's military struggle with native populations, and others the brutality and inequality of daily life in the region. In his diaries, Vereschagin described the sangfroid of Governor-General Kaufman as he justified his harsh measures: we have to 'shoot, shoot, shoot' (ibid.: 322). One particularly controversial picture was entitled 'Forgotten' – depicting a wounded Russian soldier left behind on the field of battle. This was not good for imperial propaganda and along with several others it was later destroyed by the artist.[9]

Post-colonial re-evaluations 2: national movements and resistance to Tsarism in Central Asia. Several of the sources already cited in this chapter give considerable prominence to the national question and resistance to colonialism in the pre-Soviet period. Kazakhstan was the first part of Central Asia to be incorporated into the empire. Russian colonization changed almost everything in the region, forcing the move from a nomadic to a settled mode of life, introducing money relations, creating a new balance of power between the main tribes, colonial authorities and traditional Muslim leaders.[10] At first the Russians tried to interfere as little as possible with the traditional elites. However, the introduction of government service and new courts led to a steady reduction in the influence of tribal leaders, who often opted to take up positions in the Tsarist administration.

While outright slavery was outlawed in 1822, economic divisions in the Kazakh community increased steadily. Thus, at the end of the nineteenth century, 12,500 poor households in the Pavlodar *ueszd* (district) of Semipalatinsk *oblast* had between them 63,500 animals, while 800 *bai* (traditional leader) households had between them 172,700 animals. Apparently this was typical for the whole Steppe and Turkestan region at this time. The growing polarization in property status and the destruction of traditional relations led many families to migrate to other parts of Central Asia or the Russian Empire. At the same time, a small working class was forming in the larger towns – estimated as just 60,000 persons across the region in 1917.

Soviet historians took a very particular view of political movements. On the one hand, they were happy to support and popularize any resistance to feudal and colonial authorities; on the other hand they were not keen to promote a new national elite, nor to repeat any stories that might harm the relations between different nationalities (and this included a reluctance to refer to abuses committed by Russian settlers).

In fact it was not only socialist revolutionaries who tried to influence or soften the colonization process pre-1917. After the failure of the 1905 revolution, a generation of middle-class graduates from universities in European Russia, many of them linked with liberal-democratic parties like the Kadets, came back to work in the

Steppe region of Turkestan. Political leaders like A. Bukeykhanov and B. Karataev demanded a halt to mass expulsion of the native population to make way for Russian colonists, government support for national schools, and the promotion of national culture and languages. One current in the liberal-democratic movement was national-religious (taking inspiration from Muslim organizations in Tatarstan), the other Westernizing (modelling itself on the Russian opposition to Tsarism). Representatives of the Steppe and Turkestan regions were active in the State Duma that had been set up by the Tsar as a concession to the 1905 revolution in Russia (ibid.: 277–92).

The Jadid movement that spread across the Turkic-speaking areas of the Russian Empire in the early twentieth century is of particular interest here. The movement began as an attempt to reform Muslim religious education through the creation of 'new method' schools, including secular subjects like arithmetic, geography and history. Later it became more of a social movement, including the local intelligentsia, merchants and entrepreneurs alongside liberal-leaning clerics. Leaders of the movement included Bekhbudi from Samarkand, Munavvar-kari and Khodzhaev from Tashkent, thinkers influenced in different ways by the ideologies of pan-Turkism and pan-Islamism.[11] The Jadid movement was heterogeneous from the start and Muslim reformers, nationalists, socialists, liberals and conservatives could be found within it.

The settler issue was almost the only question on which the Russian Duma consistently paid attention to issues from the Central Asia region. Bukeykhanov and his supporters worked on a land norm for nomad and settled communities, but in 1910 Prime Minister Stolypin proposed new measures to take away 'excess' land from indigenous populations and give it to Russian settlers, and this was approved in the face of Central Asian opposition. The 4th Duma (1912–17) continued this policy; major irrigation programmes in partnership with private businessmen were approved in 1914 in the basins of the Ili, Chui, Syr Darya and Zeravshan rivers (in what are today southeastern Kazakhstan, Kyrgyzstan, Tajikistan and Uzbekistan). A new charter of rules on water use destroyed the traditional system of participatory local decision-making, setting up government organs to deal with them instead.[12]

Uprising in the Steppe and Semirechye regions The Muslim fraction created alliances with a variety of political forces – Kadets, Trudoviki, Siberian regions, Socialist Revolutionaries. At the outset of the First World War, they protested against the call-up of indigenous peoples into the army and called for a halt to continuing settlements in Central Asia. The war led to a 50 per cent rise in taxes raised on the population and forced requisitions of animals, food and clothing for the front. The land under crops decreased but cotton production was held at existing levels for the war effort. Wheat prices had gone up five- or sixfold. The hardship this caused was raised in the Duma in November 1916. However, many erstwhile allies of the Muslim bloc were concerned to support the war and so the progressive alliance split.

Meanwhile, in June 1916 the call-up of just under half a million men aged nineteen to thirty-one to build defence installations in preparation for war led to an uprising in the Steppe and Semirechye regions of Central Asia. The call-up was supported by many in the religious and national elite, including Duma deputies, while the moving force behind the uprising was a mixed grouping of indigenous peasants, workers, craftsmen and hired labourers. The latter invaded call-up stations and destroyed lists of mobilized people, attacked richer villages and destroyed paperwork relating to land sales (in other words the uprising had a wider economic and class character). In the east Issyk-Kul area of present-day Kyrgyzstan, there were clashes with Tsarist army units. The uprising also affected Siberia and the Caucasus, including workers in coal mines and the oil industry, railway and river steamboat workers. But it was mainly spontaneous. The leaders in Semirechye were caught and hanged. Some Slavic (settler) populations supported the uprising, but in east Issyk-Kul the *bais* and nationalists managed to provoke clashes between Russian settlers and the indigenous population.[13]

One of the biggest clashes took place in the Turgay region, northern Kazakhstan, where 15,000 rebels besieged the district centre, led by Amangeldy Imanov. Only a major counter-assault by army forces managed to relieve Turgay, with many losses on both sides. After the uprising the leader of the Trudovik faction in the State Duma, A. F. Kerensky, visited the region. His report put the blame on local administrations. Meanwhile thousands had fled to desert and mountain areas and even China. Deputies protested against the vicious reprisals that took place to suppress the revolt. The author of the section on the 1916 uprising in *Historia Rossica* concludes that it helped create the conditions for the civil war soon to take place in the region (ibid.: 291–2).

Case study: a progressive husband and wife team – the Nalivkins An interesting example of the more progressive Tsarist colonial admin-istrators is provided by the Nalivkins, husband and wife. Vladimir Nalivkin was born into a gentry family and took part in various military expeditions in Central Asia in the 1870s, which he found at variance with his humanitarian convictions. He left military service and took up anthropological studies with his wife, living in the Namangan area of present-day Uzbekistan. In 1907 he was elected to the State Duma in the Trudovik faction and in 1913 published a book called *Native Peoples Then and Now* calling on Russia to make its rule more attractive to local populations. Nalivkin took the Bolshevik side at the time of the Tashkent Soviet, but once again was horrified by the violence engulfing the region and committed suicide in early 1918 (ibid.: 333–5).

Like their counterparts in many a European colony, the Nalivkins collected a lot of valuable anthropological data. For example, one of their studies was on the position of women in the family. They noted that family size was significantly inhibited by the death rate from illnesses. Girls were married off from as young as twelve years old, while boys often stayed at home until they were thirty and had saved enough money to start a family. The youngest son tradition-ally remained with his parents even after marriage. Women used the formal *vy* ('you') to address their husbands and did not sit in the same room as men. They wore the veil (*parandzha*) when in public – but much less often in rural than urban areas. The rules and conditions for divorce were laid down in detail for men and women by Islam. While gender inequality was a big part of Russia's justification for its 'civilizing mission', in reality women had huge influence in the extended family. Nor were they so cut off from the rest of society as was often assumed. Thus the Nalivkins noted: 'Despite the seeming closed nature of women's lives ... the details of most families' lives was well known to their neighbours, down to the most intimate details of material possessions and personal habits.' They even argued that the tyranny of husbands over wives was less than in Europe (Nalivkin, cited in Abashin et al. 2008: 201–3).

4 The Bolsheviks and hopes for world revolution based on the example of Caucasus and Central Asia

The first measures of the new Bolshevik regime in 1917 were in radical contrast to most of what has been described above. Their first constitutional act was the Declaration of Rights of Labouring Masses and Oppressed Peoples. This laid out the objectives of the dictatorship of the proletariat and the principles of Soviet power. The Bolsheviks' draft constitution was presented to the Constitutive Assembly in January 1918, which rejected it. Later that month, it was presented to the 3rd All-Russia Congress of Workers and Soldiers Deputies, and later the Congress of Peasants Deputies, which both adopted it. Among the rights enshrined in the Declaration of Rights of the Peoples of Russia in November 1918 were: 1) equality and sovereignty of the peoples of Russia; 2) rights to self-determination right down to formation of their own self-sufficient government; 3) removal of all national or religious privileges; 4) free development of national minorities and ethnic groups inhabiting the territory of Russia. A call to the Muslims of Russia and the East in November 1917 said plainly: 'Arrange your national life freely and without interference. You have the right to this. Know that your rights, just like the rights of the other peoples of Russia, are protected by the full power of the revolution and its organs.'[14]

The Soviet state, in Lovell's words, 'resisted or sidestepped' one of the main processes affecting the European powers in the twentieth century – decolonization. This author would largely agree with his contention that the Bolshevik revolution and civil war in 1917–20 produced an 'internationalist and multinational state rather than an empire' (Lovell 2006: 68–71). The Bolsheviks aimed for a state that would be able to resist nationalist influences, partly by coercion, partly by concessions to a huge number of newly created nationally defined units. State-building was used to generate new national identities in the Soviet period – especially the new 'Soviet identity'. In the backward regions, a special human resources policy developed local cadres on a speeded-up timetable. This meant everything from setting up new governance units in remote villages to building the consciousness of people as Soviet citizens. Soviet federalism was a highly complex, multilayered system. Among recent Western analysts, Roy and Jones-Luong have shown how this was done in Central Asia and how the new structures stood the test of time in the first fifteen years of independence (Roy 2000; Jones-Luong 2004). The idea was that liberation and development of the most economically backward regions of the USSR would provide an overwhelming spur to revolution in European colonies across Asia and the Far East.

In the USSR, there was no titular nation. However, Russians dominated numerically and culturally and were often referred to as the 'older brother' of newer or smaller nations or as 'the first among equals'. As regards the national question, Lenin had consciously adopted a softer line than with proletarian dictatorship. A new People's Commissariat for National Affairs consisting of national commissariats (Polish, Lithuanian, Jewish, Muslim, etc.) and departments (Kyrgyz, Mari, peoples of Siberia, etc.) was set up and given responsibility for organizing the national republics and working with national cadres, disseminating information about Soviet policies and decisions to the people, and conducting political and educational work at local level. A large number of new bodies sprang into life, many of them with a dual subordination – to the national agencies and to local Communist Party bodies. This caused confusion and by 1922 the national committees had been shut down – despite protest from the regions.

The dangers of nationalism and chauvinism were noted in a special resolution on the national question at the 12th Congress of the Party in 1923, referring explicitly to recent interethnic troubles in the Caucasus. The gap between more and less developed parts of Russia became more obvious, and attempts to deal with this problem led eventually to the creation of a new federal structure – the Union of Soviet Socialist Republics, formally announced in December 1922. The USSR had fifteen federated republics, 'rationalizing' different units inherited from the Tsarist Empire.[15]

From the start there were many doubters – those who asked what sovereignty the federated republics would really have, or the opposite, how unity between them would be maintained (since in theory the republics retained the right to secede from the USSR).

They were reassured by other party leaders that this 'independence' could never lead to secession. In his analysis of the relation between people's power and national autonomy, Kruzhkov quotes a Georgian party leader, K. Makharadze, as saying: 'Comrades, we all know the reality about this self-sufficiency, this independence. After all, we have one party, one Central Organ that in the final analysis determines things for all the republics, even the tiniest, down to the smallest details or the appointment of particular officials.'[16]

The national republics underwent huge changes in the Soviet period. As Kruzhkov notes, many of the main towns in the northern Caucasus – for example, Grozny, Vladikavkaz and Machakalka – 'essentially lost their eastern character' (and there was huge developments in the ancient cities of Central Asia, too) and began to look like any Russian provincial centre. Industrial development in the Russian Federation had boomed to almost two hundred times its 1913 level by 1986; in the Kazakh Republic by over three hundred times; in Armenia by 550 times. It was about to crash. From 1991 to 1995 GDP in the ex-Soviet republics fell on aggregate to 58 per cent of what it had been just before the collapse of the USSR (Kruzhkov 2005: 94).

National cadre policy applied not only to party members but to each and every professional group within the 'people's intelligentsia'. In the national republics education was prioritized to such an extent that, for example, in Armenia there were 300 people with higher education out of 10,000 in 1989; while in Ryazan province in the Russian Federation there were only eighty. In Buryatia, the percentage of indigenous Buryats with higher education was twice that among Russians. Major efforts were made to develop national academies of science, professional associations and the like.[17] Hence Terry Martin's description of the USSR as the 'affirmative action empire'.

The collapse of the USSR. By 1989, relations between Moscow and the regions (as we described above with reference to the Urals and Siberia) had become very tense and strained. At the plenum of the CPSU Central Committee in September that year, Gorbachev proposed to give autonomous republics in Russia new powers equal to those of the fifteen Soviet republics. However, by this time relations with Yeltsin and the Russian Soviet Federative Socialist Republic (RSFSR) had soured, and it was the efforts of the latter to gain more autonomy which brought the whole structure tumbling down. Indeed, the RSFSR itself had many of the same national/structural contradictions as the USSR as a whole – with over twenty autonomous regions within its boundaries, plus a huge number of smaller population groups without their own territorial units.

During the referendum on whether to retain the USSR in 1991, most of the leaders of the national republics sided with Gorbachev against Yeltsin, as did the voters. Meanwhile, representatives of forty-seven parties and movements from twelve republics meeting at the 'Democratic Congress' had in January 1991 called for the resignation of the president, the disbandment of the USSR and the creation of a Commonwealth of Independent States. This movement proved unstoppable and so Yeltsin won.

5 The role of civil society and the intelligentsia in interpreting history

All these issues have taken on a new meaning in the post-independence period. The newly independent states of FSU have returned to their traditions – or gone in search of their pre-1917 heritage. Much of the history of Central Asia, as noted above, was vilified in the Soviet period as a time of brutal rule by feudal despots. And of course the top priority for communists was to stress the positive side of the Russian Revolution as it pertained to the former empire.

Now this restraining hand has gone, local commentators in the newly independent states (NIS) are increasingly critical of the colonization process. Many Central Asia writers are happy to use the terms 'empire' or 'colony', about both the Tsarist and Soviet periods. However, others prefer to make a comparison between the USSR and two other twentieth-century modernizing states in the near Asian vicinity – Turkey and Iran.[18] And as Russia itself returns to its pre-Soviet traditions, a problem opens up in its relation with the NIS. Shorn of the liberation, equalizing rhetoric of the Soviet period, coupled with the tendency of Russian nationalists to glorify the Tsarist empire, Russia runs the risk of adopting once again supercilious or colonial attitudes that are hardly attractive to newly independent peoples.

A fractured historical narrative The break-up of a once unified historical narrative in FSU can be seen in how two neighbouring states now present their relation to the Russian Empire.

Case study 1: Kyrgyzstan. The story of Kurmanzhan Datka is of a Kyrgyz princess from the mountainous Alai region of southern Kyrgyzstan who persuaded her people to accept Russian colonial rule rather than remain in a perpetual state of war with surrounding tribes, with particular reference to the threat from the nearby khanate of Kokand. It is a tragic story because Kurmanzhan Datka's own husband and sons were involved in the fighting, and some of them died. Kyrgyzstan is a small country of 5 million people that achieved modern statehood for the first time in 1991. There was less conflict and loss of life in its colonization process than there was in Uzbekistan, Turkmenistan or Kazakhstan; less of a wound in the national consciousness and hence a greater willingness today to retain the memory of the Russian and Soviet periods (viz. the Lenin statues and Soviet place names that are still on display around the country). During my own years living in Bishkek, the Kurmanzhan Datka legend continued to receive official attention (with the building of new statues, holding of exhibitions and the like), testifying to the government's wish to maintain friendly relations with Russia. But in the south, where nationalism is strong and the *basmachi* (mujahedin) Muslim fighters fought the Soviets until the end of the 1920s, the local authorities in Osh recently opened memorials to members of her family who were more hostile to the Russians, too.

Case study 2: Uzbekistan. The attitude of Uzbekistan to the Russian and Soviet past is very different. With its ancient cultural centres and historical connections with Alexander the Great, Zarathustra, Chinghiz Khan and Tamberlaine, Uzbekistan sees the colonization period a bit differently. Indeed, it took place differently, and the Bukhara and Khiva protectorates (oases of feudalism) survived for several years within the Soviet space. As Russian expert Sergei Abashin has shown, the authorities are determined to assert Uzbek identity against the 150 years of Russian and then Soviet rule (Abashin 2011). This is being done by actively pursuing a 'memory policy' that legitimizes President Karimov and his regime, especially in Tashkent, where there are so many Russian places to rename, so many Soviet monuments to remove, and in the cultural realm where Soviet-era literature, film and music are being gradually squeezed out and replaced by new Uzbek ones. Abashin notes, however, that while Uzbek memory policy is sharply anti-Soviet, most of its communication techniques are inherited from the Soviet repertoire. Indeed, Uzbekistan has become an 'ideological state' just like the USSR, with all government agencies from top to bottom programmed to carry out mass propaganda activity. The main message is the same too: about a horrible past and a bright present and future.

In our work for civil society development in FSU in the 1990s and 2000s, we could at first count on very similar responses from the population of different areas (although they were contradictory, they were contradictory in largely the same way). Thus my own fairly extensive experience with VSO in Latvia, Lithuania or the Urals region of Russia from 1996 to 2001 addressed many of the same problems and brought on board quite similar local people as my later work with INTRAC in Kazakhstan and Central Asia. In the early–mid 2000s, INTRAC's regional conferences and training courses for civil society activists in Central Asia featured emerging differences (e.g. the state's attitude to civil society) but without any difficulties in mutual understanding. Of course, our participants were in the main the Western-leaning section of the intelligentsia, happy to receive funding with which to do something amid the social and economic crisis. Other sections of the intelligentsia, including traditional and cultural groups, were often excluded, and many individuals had turned inwards or back to the past, as we have explained in the pages above.

Indeed, the rise of nationalism in Russia and the ex-republics is resulting in the fracturing of a once common discourse or understanding of history. As an expert at the Institute for Oriental Studies in Almaty has commented, the region needs a more balanced approach free of nationalist or imperialist distortions. It is a matter for regret, she says, that having achieved sovereignty the new states of the region immediately started to construct national myths and ideologies that artificially divide up the region and in which 'their' titular people are suddenly at the centre, ruling over a wide empire, with unique links back to some great warriors or leaders. The Institute rejects this narrow and tendentious view, calling for a regional approach based on a variety of modern historical methodologies (Abuseitova 2011).

Conclusion

In this chapter we have looked at development within Russia's colonial and Soviet periods. As in other empires, there was a mixture of dream, ideology and self-justification in the colonizing period. Russia clearly had economic objectives in its move to the east and south. Imperial ideologues saw it as their duty to help the more 'backward' peoples of the newly occupied regions. Like political leaders in other continents, the Russian Tsars were keenly aware of the competition with other colonial powers – in particular the British. Russian colonial rule was more indirect (through local elites) than in some other colonial regimes.

Interestingly, even a very short account such as my own confirms what Rist argues – that is, many development practices considered new today were in fact quite well known in the colonial period. He gives as examples: the practice of training indigenous staff in the colonial country; the recognition of the cultural dimension; the focus on primary healthcare; the adaptation of education programmes to the context; the concern for women's status and lives; the attempt to maximize popular participation, etc. The Soviet period was, by contrast, quite different from the day-to-day colonialism in other European empires. The next chapter will look in more detail at Soviet development interventions in Central Asia that had a very political – that is, socialist – inspiration.

PART 2

DEVELOPMENT AND STRUGGLE

4 | POLITICAL MOBILIZATION FROM WAR COMMUNISM TO COLOURED REVOLUTION[1]

This chapter is about how people are motivated to join development initiatives. It is about civil and political action – and so it serves as an introduction to Part 2 of this book, 'Development and struggle'. The idea behind the title is that real development cannot take place without some kind of a struggle with the political or economic powers-that-be. Development requires a reconsideration of policies and priorities in whatever sphere it is envisaged, and inevitably this means a new distribution of resources and power. This is particularly obvious when development initiatives aim to give more of the 'pie' to the working (non-propertied) classes in society, or to open up space and access to resources for marginalized and vulnerable groups.

Where civil society is concerned, the struggle for hegemony is hopefully peaceful, through debate between citizens and representatives of the government and business sectors. In Gramsci's terms, civil society is an arena of contention, and if the conditions for free and open discussion are present, the struggle for progressive change can be a 'war of manoeuvre' rather than an assault on the citadels of power – an evolutionary not revolutionary process. But in the examples of political action we will look at first, this was not the case. They are taken from the early years of the Soviet period when war communism and radical people's power were the order of the day. The aim is to see how well the Bolshevik 'theory of change' worked in one of the least developed parts of the empire they had inherited, in Central Asia.

The boundaries (often blurred) between political and civil action are one topic for this chapter. Another is the difference between top-down and bottom-up development strategies.

1 Top-down versus bottom-up development approaches

In the twenty-first century we are witness to an intense concentration of economic and political power. Economic decision-makers in the advanced countries operate through complex market-mediated systems with a daily stock exchange 'show', a corrupted banking system, and enormous struggles for influence by private corporations with individual countries or groups of countries. Following the economic crisis of 2008/09, we could see this in the European Union's struggle with currency speculators over the fate of the Eurozone, and also the struggle waged by the Obama administration to maintain public sector investment as a way of restraining unemployment and to press ahead with health reform for the poorer classes in society. Public opinion in FSU tends to regard problems of this kind in the West as being, however awful, better than the situation they now have in their own countries. The view that concentrated economic power is out of the control of ordinary citizens is very widespread today. But attempts are being made by CSOs in many places to apply some sort of monitoring – even in FSU, as we will see in later chapters.

The state-led development model is often labelled 'authoritarian'. The examples given in the first part of this chapter challenge that view; they illustrate the assault on established elites and traditional institutes that took place after the October Revolution. However, Part 1 of this book has already shown how central planning and the CPSU's hierarchical decision-making systems gradually eliminated the diversity of opinion needed for all-round development in a modern, educated and well-informed society. Post-1991, most regimes in PSS have remained authoritarian or semi-authoritarian. The government set-up in most of these states is presidential, and while multiparty elections have taken place everywhere, there has been widespread abuse of the rules to ensure that the ruling 'party of power' comes out on top.

The main aspects of the top-down or centralized approach to Russia's development during Vladimir Putin's first period of power were summarized by Van Zon (2010) as follows:

In the economy, Putin brought the oligarchs to heel while at the same time operating business-friendly tax policies and creating places for government officials on the boards of strategically important companies. Stabilization of the economy was achieved through increased export of oil, gas and other natural resources, and much-reduced inflation. Politically, Putin presented himself as a 'strongman' holding the balance between three elite factions – the security forces, the free market liberals and the technocrats. At the very start of his regime, he abolished the system of elected governors, gradually building up United Russia as a new 'party of power', with branches across the country and an active youth wing, *Nashi*. Putin has often expressed hostility to civil society groups that he perceives as lackeys to foreign influence. Van Zon describes this as a return to traditional Russian 'patrimonialism' or a 'new symbiosis of money and power'. Indeed, a cult of power came to permeate public life.

From inside Russia all this feels a bit different. Indeed, in the early 2000s many people from all levels of society appreciated their new, energetic and relatively youthful leader. A good example of Russian commentators with a more positive view is the well-known historian of Stalinism Roy Medvedev, whose recent books describe how, during his first two terms of office (1999–2007), President Putin established himself as an excellent communicator, ably presenting government policy and decisions on TV news or through phone-in sessions with the public.[2] Indeed, after the anarcho-capitalism of the Yeltsin years, there were many in Russia who agreed with Putin that the state should intervene more. During the first decade of the 2000s, many pointed to the impressive rates of growth being achieved by the Asian Tiger economies (without any special role for civil society).

But still the question remains: where and how should the state intervene, and how can it respond to citizens' initiatives? Russia is still some way from the model of 'socially responsible capitalism' promoted by mainstream development agencies. This model usually includes an effective welfare state and a place for civil society complementing the role of government by fostering social cohesion and offering a space for the expression of difference and diversity, consensus and even non-violent conflict (Howell and Pearce 2002; Pratt 2003).

Main elements of a bottom-up approach Faced with a capitalist revolution, mafia business structures and what now appears to be an increasingly conservative government in Russia, hopes for a bottom-up approach might appear futile and condemned to failure. In Chapter 1, we briefly described attempts to increase the economic resources of poor people via micro-credit schemes, as well as some new social sector projects for specially disadvantaged groups in Moscow. In

Chapter 2, we featured local mobilization to repair essential local infrastructure – water pipes, electric generators, school roofs – now falling apart across the whole FSU. In Chapter 3, we began to look at how people in Siberia and Central Asia are beginning to recapture their own history and identity. These are some of the building blocks of popular or 'social mobilization' – a widely used phrase in the post-Soviet countries that means almost the same as 'community development'.

They are all highly problematic while the general system of inequality and injustice remains in place. Micro-credit schemes come up against the limitations in the willingness or ability of lenders to lend at low rates of interest, and the risks undertaken by those who borrow. Social sector projects typically depend on government support to succeed – the problems are so widespread and complex. The infrastructure example from Chapter 2 showed how development is sometimes simply an attempt to halt decline and regain elements of local control. And the regaining of a sense of history is inevitably a highly charged political or cultural struggle, located for the ex-republics within a post-colonial or neo-colonial/imperialist framework.

These were the kind of issues that I began to work on with INTRAC, after moving to Bishkek, the capital of Kyrgyzstan, in early 2002. My job was as regional coordinator of a civil society strengthening programme in the five ex-Soviet republics of Central Asia. The aim was to strengthen voluntary associations and help them be more effective in their work. Lots of the activity was at local level, within development projects funded by international agencies. But it also included some other important elements: first, scanning the whole civil society sector in our region through a set of mapping reports and updates; second, assistance to CSOs in opening up channels for discussion with other sectors via the media, NGO networks, and institutional links between organizations; and third, support for advocacy and lobbying around reforms in the political, economic and social spheres.

It is from this perspective that the historical case studies below are offered. They are an attempt to describe, from a civil society development viewpoint, how the socialist revolution and people's power approach worked in the early Soviet period in Central Asia.

Indeed, USSR provides one of the main examples in the twentieth century where a government has aimed at root-and-branch social change by mobilizing the working class and peasant masses.

2 Political mobilization in Central Asia in the 1920s and 1930s

From the early 1900s, Russian socialists had debated the specificities of the 'Asiatic mode of production' and what it meant for development. One of the founders of Russian Marxism, Plekhanov, argued that Asian societies (the main example was China) were not developing from feudalism to capitalism in the same way as in Europe in the sixteenth to nineteenth centuries.[3] This had potentially a lot of importance for development prospects in at least the Asiatic part of Russia. However, despite the theoretical discussion, in reality most of the Bolsheviks' experience of agitation and struggle was in the European part of Russia. The events of 1917–20 showed that they were good at political intervention (the timing and execution of the conquest of power, a first assault on the old order) and had created an effective instrument for this – the Leninist vanguard party. However, this group of professional revolutionaries had set itself the task of building socialism in a society in which large parts had not gone through the stage of capitalism that was supposed to come before socialism in the Marxist scheme of things. Lenin had decided that it could be done, but these were still unfavourable conditions.

In Chapter 2, we referred to the critique developed by Russian environmentalists in relation to the 'instrumental' approach of the Soviet regime, where ecological damage was accepted as an unavoidable consequence of economic development. The same comments could be made as regards the Bolsheviks' use of human and other material resources: they were determined to employ them in whatever way possible (via 'social engineering') within a development strategy often described by Soviet political leaders and writers as the 'speeding up' of history. But having achieved power, in regions that in classical Marxist terms were not ready for it, they faced major practical problems. One of the major challenges was what to do when the working class in Central Asia – supposedly the main actor in a socialist revolution – was still so small in numbers. In the first decade of Soviet rule, the approach taken was cautious, often with the limited aim of retaining or consolidating power. This is how, for example, Olivier Roy describes the Soviets' approach with regard to working with local institutions.[4]

The five post-Soviet countries of Central Asia all achieved independence in 1991. In the first fifteen years after independence, not much was written about Soviet development strategy. Both national governments and international agencies preferred to consider that they were starting from scratch. Hence in my researches I have returned to a number of Soviet-era analyses that I hope the reader will find interesting. One of the main sources for this is Massell's work on how, in the absence of a mass proletariat, the Bolsheviks attempted to mobilize women for social transformation in Central Asia. One of the most interesting things in this account is the comparison of different approaches to social and political mobilization at different times – what he calls 'direct' and 'indirect' social engineering (1974: 57). Massell's view is that, what with civil war, foreign intervention on several fronts and political and economic chaos in Russia itself, it took almost ten years after the 1917 revolution for the Bolsheviks to develop a truly developmental strategy in Central Asia. However, we begin with the class struggle.

Case study 1: Class struggle in Kyrgyz and Uzbek villages An account by Chokushev (1968) illustrates many of the problems faced by the Soviet authorities after the revolution and seizure of power in Kirgizia.[5] On the one hand, the regime declared that only the poor Muslim population could implement Soviet power; on the other, the latter were under the influence of traditional clan and religious leaders – the *bai* and *manap* layers – 'bloodthirsty boars', as the revolutionary poet Toktogul called them in his struggle with local bullies and clan chiefs at the end of the previous century.[6] The first task was to somehow organize the Communist Party. Since many party activists were Russian, one of the first instructions issued by Frunze[7] was for all party members, whether soldiers or party workers, to begin learning a local language. In 1921, the party declared its intention to transfer all administration into the local language.

The country was still recovering from the 1916 uprising (see the previous chapter), and one of the regime's early actions was to encourage Kyrgyz refugees in China to return home. An estimated 300,000 people had sheltered in the cities of Kashgar, Aksu and Uch-Turfan.

Medical and food stations were opened to help the returnees, with resources commandeered from richer elements in the community. Special measures were taken to assist Kyrgyz people who had been sold into slavery in China. Land reform was carried out in 1921/22. This involved requisitioning 'excess' land from rich peasants (*kulaks*) – in particular Russians who had seized land during the 1916 events – and also agricultural equipment, cattle or sheep.

In 1921, the *Koshchi* association was set up to unite landless and poor peasants and farm labourers throughout what was then called Turkestan. The association's aims were as much political as economic. In many villages there was as yet no Soviet or party organization, so *Koshchi* groups represented the new government, helping to provide basic information about its decrees and programmes, collect taxes and redistribute land, equipment and livestock from the *kulaks* to the poor. The land reform process gripped the whole country. Meetings were held in every town and village, led by party officials wherever possible. However, they provided only limited information or opportunities to deal with local problems. It was recognized that the party needed to reach smaller settlements and nomadic communities, so special local language courses were organized for rural development workers. According to Chokushev, from a total of just under 200,000 hectares distributed to poor farmers in Kirgizia during 1921/22, 7.9 per cent was seized from *kulak* and *bai* owners; 11.2 per cent was taken from Russian settlements; 65.9 per cent was apportioned to new settlements created after the 1916 uprising; and 15 per cent was transferred from various non-functioning villages, abandoned huts, etc. He comments that this campaign had a clearly 'anti-colonial' character. Six thousand poor households got land for the first time, enabling them to set themselves up as small producers (Chokushev 1968: 47).

This was a time of armed struggle, too. In 1917, the Kokand Autonomous Government proclaimed itself in opposition to Soviet rule, signalling the beginning of *basmachi* resistance in the Ferghana Valley and the mountains round about. Famously, British agents were said to be actively involved, stirring up opposition to Soviet rule, hampering it in attempts to move southward towards India.[8] Armed resistance on a smaller scale took place all around Kirgizia; for example, in 1919 Russian landowners took up arms in the villages of

Dmitrievka, Belovodsk and Tyup in the northern part of the country, and in 1920 a major uprising was organized by *bai/manap* elements in the highlands of Naryn, with party officials in several towns murdered in an attempt to scare activists.

As Roy notes, traditional leaders in Central Asia were not slow to use the new system to their own ends. A large number of more well-off people joined the Turkestan Communist Party in the years immediately after the revolution, despite the messages about class struggle against *kulaks*, colonizers, *bais* and *manaps*. Indeed, the aim of local elites in joining was often to control and restrict party activities. Political education was at a very low level, often limited to reading the constitution and aims of the party; thus, a meeting in Pishpek in 1921 heard that many Kyrgyz 'having joined the party and being illiterate find it difficult to absorb the ideas of socialist construction and politics in general'. One common method used was to attach trainees to more experienced workers. Two-week education workshops were organized around the country in an attempt to pass on information and improve the quality of political work. A list from 1921 shows fourteen different political and economic topics, with lectures organized in so-called 'red *yurts*' (traditional tents made of felt) and 'red *chaikhanas*' (tea houses). The association *Doloi negramotnosti* (Down with Illiteracy!) was set up.

As early as 1920/21, the party decided it had to clean out inappropriate elements within its ranks. In Pishpek *uezd* (Chui Valley), it had 9,300 members before the purge and just 2,348 members afterwards; in mountainous Naryn, there were 7,000 members before and 1,500 after. Officials admitted that membership had previously been offered to all and sundry, including members of exploiting classes. The regional Turkestan executive committee set up national departments for the main national groups: Kazakh, Kyrgyz, Turkmen and Uzbek. These were charged with developing cadres and information resources and dealing with complaints from the population. Communist youth unions (*komsomol*) were established in 1921, and once again their class and ethnic membership was monitored closely.

By 1924, the party had made some headway in its membership aims. Thus, the Semirechiye party organization counted among its members: hired farm labourers – 1.5 per cent; seasonal farm labourers – 2.5 per cent; previous farm labourers – 9.5 per cent; previous workers

– 6.0 per cent; office workers and intelligentsia – 27.0 per cent; small farmers and peasants – 53.5 per cent. Chokushev comments that this was a sizeable achievement, though still some way short of the targets set by the Turkestan leadership. A recent account by a group of Kyrgyz historians agrees on the main points. For them, the main advances were made in beginning the move of the nomad population into permanent settlements. They note not just the absence of proletarians or hired labourers among the indigenous population, but also the weakness of Soviet attempts to force-start industrialization in the 1920s and 1930s (Chotonov et al. 1998).

Workers' solidarity mechanisms. What were the views and experiences of working-class 'development workers'? When Stalin's second revolution began at the turn of the 1930s, it too required a political mobilization. During collectivization and the first five-year plan, one of the mechanisms created to boost rural development in the cotton sector was mentoring or accompaniment (*shefstvo*) organized by urban enterprises and organizations. In essence this was a kind of state-sponsored volunteering that became very widespread in the Soviet Union, expressing an important political message about the 'friendship' between the working class and the peasantry. Thus, in 1929 the Bolshevik leadership took the decision to send 25,000 model proletarians to help set up collective farms around the country. Some 75,000 people applied from around the USSR and in the end 35,000 were sent, all attending pre-departure training courses. They included many different worker professions: engineers, mechanics, smiths, plasterers, textile workers, and so on ... (Razzakov and Gulmetov 1968).

One of the mentoring arrangements made in support of the '25-thousanders' campaign was initiated by textile factories in Moscow, Leningrad and Ivanovo-Voznesensk. Money was collected in the factories to fund the purchase of tractors for Uzbekistan. Some four hundred model workers set off for the south and the Uzbekistan authorities mobilized over twenty-five local factory workers alongside them. The priority was national self-sufficiency in cotton, and most of the placements had a technical function linked to the setting up of collective farms in this sector. As experienced party activists, however, they were expected to take a political lead in organizing farm workers, setting up workers' management systems in the collective farms and dealing with the predictable opposition of traditional leaders.

Leningrader A. P. Tikhonov arrived in Uzbekistan in March 1929 and was sent into the mountains to assess the readiness of villagers to sign up to the new farms. During his placement he helped to establish three farms, each one drawing members from the inhabitants of ten to twelve villages. He wrote in his diary: 'The conditions were very tough. The *kishlaks* [villages] were separated from each other by distances of 5–15 kilometres. The population was in the main illiterate and there was a shortage of teachers. The *bais* and *mullahs* actively destabilized the situation, turning local people against Soviet power ... The famers lived in poor conditions: mud huts with a fire inside, no furniture, people sleeping side by side on the floor, feet towards the fire. Morning, lunch and evening, we had just one meal – dry bread and raisins. But I have to say that the farmers were very welcoming ...' (ibid.: 80–1).

The textile worker volunteers arrived in Tashkent in time for the spring sowing season in 1930. Organized in 23 brigades, they produced some pretty impressive results for a four-month stay till the end of May: 24 party cells set up, 102 party members recruited, 406 talks given on different themes, 44 collective farms assisted, 27 literacy points created. And this was alongside their technical work in repairing farm machinery ...

Case study 2: Women's emancipation in the early Soviet period The topic of women's rights in the Soviet period has always attracted interest – from the lives and writings of early female activists like Inessa Armand and Alexandra Kollontai, through to later accounts by foreign observers.[9] As we saw in the previous chapter, the tough lives and supposed backwardness of women in Central Asia had been a matter of concern in Russia – as it so often is around the world – from colonial times. This section briefly considers women's mobilization in Central Asia in the 1920s as a development intervention. Women's liberation was a Soviet Communist Party priority. Indeed, the oppression of women in the region was one of the strongest arguments for the Bolshevik assault on traditional elites.

In the words of Nukhrat, one of the first female writers and activists in Central Asia in the Soviet period: 'Before the October Revolution, there was, throughout the vast expanse of Russia, no human being more ignorant, more downtrodden and enslaved, than the Eastern women.' Like many other party activists sent to Central Asia, she made it her business to study local culture, the Koran, contemporary commentaries on shariat law, and the descriptions of ethnographers and other early travellers to the region. Naturally Nukhrat and her sisters/comrades were extra-sensitive to the primitive living conditions, illiteracy and disease that women suffered; and especially the signs and symbols of 'female inferiority' within Muslim society. The key question was: could political agitation around these inequalities and injustices mobilize society against traditional male elites? How much resentment had accumulated in the female half of the population? How much resistance could be expected from men, and would some men eventually emerge as allies in the struggle? How could activists best encourage a sense of women's solidarity and give them the courage and confidence to challenge tradition?

TABLE 4.1 Development of strategies for social transformation

Key aspects of the message – from women's movement activists Nukhrat, Niurina, Zavarian, Moskalev	Communist strategies for social transformation
Women are naturally social creatures – friends and sisters to each other Women are hard-working, a kind of toiling class in themselves	Revolutionary legalism (changing the legal environment) – *revolutsionnaya zakonnost*
There is nothing inevitable about customs – they can be changed if we are determined enough	Administrative assault (shock therapy) – *administrativny naskok*
The old world is departing for ever, and in the new society women will acquire a new sense of personal dignity and consciousness of themselves as human beings Women must become more aware of their rights, will power and strength	Systematic work (people- and organization-oriented development) – *sistematiches-kaya rabota*

The table above describes arguments and strategies that, in themselves, are completely rational and rather up to date. A key aspect of the strategy was the attempt to create a political alliance between women and the poorer sections of the peasant class. It had proved up to this point almost impossible to mobilize poor farmers, labourers or herders against the middle or rich layers; as noted above, the traditional elites were finding ways to subvert Bolshevik agitation and maintain the old hierarchies.

Some women activists went farther. Rather than seeing women as a disadvantaged stratum per se, they identified particular groups of women as specially disadvantaged. These included orphans exploited by other members of their families, girls separated from their lovers by parental diktat and/or forced into unwilling marriage; divorced women, and so on. These women, activists reasoned, would be the most bitter about prevailing norms, and their experiences could be used to fashion a revolutionary message. Nukhrat offered yet another reason why girls and women might become committed supporters: once they had 'come out' (e.g. by joining the Communist Party), they would have nowhere else to go (Massell 1974: 145).

The three main development strategies presented in the table above followed one after the other in time. They are worth explaining in a little more detail. Thus, the strategy of 'revolutionary legalism' was dominant in 1924–28. It included the passing of new legislation and the setting up of secular courts to work in parallel with traditional institutions and eventually replace them; also actions to apply the principle of equality of the sexes before the law.

The strategy of 'administrative assault' meant politically inspired direct action such as the unveiling of women and desegregation of men and women in public places – a kind of cultural revolution. Unveiling (*khudzhum*) was a dramatic and often irrevocable step for women. The campaign had two main stages. In the first phase, party and *komsomol* members (usually public officials) were persuaded to unveil their wives. The second phase was mass action, geographically focused in Uzbekistan, where veiling of women was more strictly observed (as also in Uzbek-inhabited parts of Tajikistan). Tragically this led to the murder of many women by male relatives who considered they had brought disgrace on themselves and their families. The 'administrative assault' approach was attempted at the start of collectivization – in 1927–29.

The third strategy, 'systematic work' or social engineering, was based on the evaluation and coordinated use of diverse courses of action – legal, associational, cultural and economic – for modernization and development; as Massell puts it, 'a pragmatic commitment to relatively patient and systematic social action' (ibid.: 190). This began in the mid-1930s.

3 Social mobilization channelled by the state

As noted in Chapter 2, at the end of the 1920s the Communist Party gradually closed down voluntary agencies across the country, on the grounds that autonomous bodies might become subversive elements opposed to the Soviet system. This applied to the *Koschi* and a number of women's associations in Central Asia. The argument against women's groups was that they might succumb to nationalist ideology or even develop along bourgeois lines, distracting women from the class struggle. They could take women away from the political and social sphere, back into the realm of family and personal issues, in the home.

The advent of collectivization meant new pressures on party members and the general population alike. For senior managers and party officials, the risks were similar to those we described in the Urals case study in Chapter 2. One of the consequences of collectivization was a new famine in the region. The opening of Communist Party and government archives since 1991 has led to new researches and publications on previously sensitive topics like this. An example of this relevant to the present discussion is a recent publication by Batyrbaeva (2010) attempting to read through official statistics in the Stalinist period to see the human toll of forced collectivization in Kyrgyzstan. The author comes to the conclusion that the effects of this major economic and social dislocation were just as catastrophic as the famines in Ukraine or Kazakhstan – every sixth person in Kyrgyzstan's northern Frunze *oblast* died of hunger in the early 1930s. At the same time, the balance sheet of human development also showed huge advances in education and health, especially for the titular population. But the real benefits of social transformation were felt only at the end of the 1950s (ibid.).

Developments in the Zhenotdel The institutional changes that took place from the beginning of collectivization can be seen in the role of the Women's Department or *Zhenotdel*, a structure that operated on several levels within the Soviet administrative apparatus. In 1920s Central Asia, it organized a wide variety of voluntary women's groups

– for example, 'For a New Way of Life' (*Za Novy Buit*) promoting new values, skills and ways of doing things, and 'Down with Bride Price and Polygamy!' (*Doloi Kalym i Mnogozhonstvo!*). Associations of this kind could embrace a number of activities. They would have the usual 'red corner', literacy groups, legal aid and health units and could organize vocational training courses, handicrafts or even small savings banks. These activities were often coordinated by department staff.

In 1929, the authorities moved the *Zhenotdel* out of the Communist Party apparatus into the sphere of responsibility of the elected Soviets. At the same time, they began a move towards the more comprehensive 'systematic approach' to women's issues. This followed a speech by Nadezhda Krupskaya (Lenin's widow) to the Fourth All-Union Conference of Party Organizers among Eastern Women in December 1928 in Moscow, in which she rejected the shock therapy approach as a kind of revolutionary 'reductionism' (i.e. seeing all peoples and regions in the same stereotypical way). The most important aspect of the new approach proposed by Krupskaya was the recognition of complexity in social development issues. While the task of female emancipation did indeed require firm action, Krupskaya argued in favour of painstaking ideological, organizational and economic groundwork. Traditional communities, she now argued, are not organized as a plot to exploit and enslave poor people. They serve certain human needs – emotional as well as material – providing a kind of 'social security' system whereby the individual can find 'moral support' in times of general crisis or personal grief, 'social protection of labour' by way of days of rest and religious holidays, and also the 'emotional outlets' provided by age-old rituals and collective labour habits. In such circumstances, men and women could be mobilized and their loyalty won only if the Soviet system learned to appeal effectively to their self-interest, offering them sufficient alternatives to traditional provision. This is indeed a position much closer to the programme of many development agencies today.

Wartime and post-war mobilizations The voluntary, semi-voluntary and forced movement of peoples within the borders of the USSR by no means ended with collectivization and industrialization in the 1930s. In the build-up to war with Germany, huge numbers of people were moved east for their and the country's greater safety. Whole factories and their workforces moved to the Urals and beyond. Population groups deemed unreliable in the face of Nazi invasion were deported in the same direction. For example, Batyrbaeva's calculations (ibid.: 96–130) show that in 1939–59, the number of Russians living in Kirgizia doubled, and the proportion of Russians in the total population rose from 20 to 30 per cent. At the same time, the republic gave a new home to over thirty thousand deportees from the northern Caucasus, three-quarters of them from Chechnya.

In the post-war period, mobilization gradually achieved a less forced and more professional, acceptable, sustainable character. On the one hand, migration movements were still mostly the result of top-down administrative decisions to develop new areas or industries. Young workers and professionals were typically recommended (that is, directed) to their first job after qualifying. Many were attracted to regions like Kazakhstan or Siberia by the high wages offered in compensation for the isolated location, harsh climate and tough working and living conditions. As Boiko (1998) notes, one of the most important factors in Siberia's development in the Soviet period was the enthusiasm of youth, employed to open new enterprises, build power stations, electric power lines and towns. 'For this the government used simple motivators: romance, a new life, new professions, independent work, a quick career, big salaries, receiving your own flat, improvements in the general material and technological conditions of a territory with difficult natural conditions'. But, he concludes, while these ideas and arguments worked in the political and economic set-up of the time, 'in today's economy they don't work'. Siberia has lost its old attraction (ibid.: 55–9).

In Central Asia, one of the biggest stories of Soviet labour migration was Khrushchev's campaign to plough up the virgin lands of northern Kazakhstan. During the 1950s, some eight hundred thousand volunteers were enticed to settle in the bleak steppe areas around Tselinograd – now Astana, since 1998 the country's capital. A mini-version of this campaign is described by Christine Bischel in a recent case study of Zafarabad, a strip of land pointing westwards from the mouth of the Fergana Valley, where the Syr Darya river flows into Uzbekistan. This is an area that was called from Tsarist times the 'hungry steppe' – a huge desert stretching towards the Aral Sea.

These days, the transfer of very small amounts of territory (e.g. uninhabited valleys or mountain peaks) between the Central Asia states is a matter of extreme political sensitivity. So it is interesting that some years after the formation of the Tajik and Uzbek Soviet Republics, a decision was made to transfer the Zafarabad 'finger', approximately fifty thousand hectares of desert, to Tajikistan. This took place in 1959, and a year later irrigation works began, pumping water from the Syr Darya basin. In 1962 the first state farms were set up. This was a complex development project, including not just canals and fields but new housing, roads, social facilities. International brigades of skilled workers and volunteers from around the USSR did the work, and many cadres stayed on. But the plan from the start was to transfer the core of the new population from the mountain areas of Tajikistan, including the Yagnob area high in the Pamir mountains. Bischel's research shows that the scheme had deeper aims, not just economic development. 'Goodbye Yagnob, hello steppe!' the Soviet banners read, and the propaganda material said plainly: we can't bring civilization to the mountains.

How does this story end? The Yagnob people moved to the steppe. The Zafarabad region was developed, but it required a second recruitment wave in the 1970s to ensure a sufficient labour force for the farms and other facilities. Water has to be pumped into the finger till this day. Not all the mountain people liked the style of life in the plains; some preferred their own stone- or clay-built shacks 3,000 metres up in the Pamirs to Soviet apartment blocks.[10] The history of forced movements of this kind within Tajikistan in the Soviet period is a complex one and researchers have cited it as an aggravating factor in the civil war that erupted in the 1990s. That is, when hostilities broke out, the fact that entire villages were made up of different sets of people relocated within living memory in many cases reinforced antagonisms (on the 'war of the *kolkhoz*', see Roy 2000: 94–6).

International brigades played a key part in the reconstruction of Ashgabat and Tashkent after serious earthquakes in 1948 and 1966 respectively. These mobilizations have some elements in common with international humanitarian aid (the speedy delivery of technical aid and funds after a natural calamity), but also aspects that are different: the numbers of people drafted in and the different political messages too.

Summing up the historical case studies What was it like for a young professional or party activist from the Russian Soviet Federative Socialist Republic (RSFSR) or the other Soviet republics to take on a posting in Central Asia in the 1920s and 1930s? What was it like for women's activists of the kind quoted above? There is a huge amount of material in Soviet literature, art and film on questions of this kind – and to judge by TV in the region, many films still retain their relevance and popularity (while others have been discarded because of their ideological bias or untruth). A visit to the national art galleries in Almaty, Bishkek or Tashkent shows the continuing strength of many pictures devoted to themes such as the 'first village teacher', 'young pioneers', major building and industrial projects, and so on – masterpieces of socialist realism now exhibited alongside modernist art in its various forms. These works convey much of the positive, constructive spirit and energy of those times.

But there were political risks too, for experts and volunteers as well as activists in the general population. A recent article in *Central Asia Survey* focuses on the challenges facing development workers like the '25-thousanders' in Tajikistan. After a description of the physical hardships these grassroots workers faced, we learn that during Stalin's purges of the late 1930s several of them were executed, alongside senior and middle-level communist cadres – much of the 'flower' of the first generation of national intellectuals and socialist activists in Central Asia (Kassymbekova 2011).

The 1920s and 1930s stand out as a period of creativity and conflict, ending in tragedy – all on a grand scale. The methods of the early Soviet period have been described as 'war communism' – that is, the resort to military and coercive methods at a time of foreign intervention and civil war. The limitations of war communism or development at the point of a gun are now a matter of record – but not consigned to history. Unfortunately, they were seen again in the Central Asia region during the communist regime of Babrak Karmal and Hafizullah Amin in Afghanistan. And the question of how much real, sustainable development can be achieved at a time of military occupation and bombardment remains highly controversial today, given the actions of the USA, the UK and NATO in Iraq and Afghanistan.

A visit to the Andrei Sakharov museum in Moscow is quite useful in thinking about the relation between revolutionary politics and development. On the one hand, the Sakharov Museum's exhibits describing Soviet ideology convey well the USSR's undoubted dynamism, modernizing thrust and innovation. On the other, they reflect Sakhorov's ethical critique of the violence and negativity of many communist messages.[11] In the 1970s, Soviet propaganda was still strident, for example, in calling for the 'liquidation' of enemies – as quoted earlier in this chapter.

The comments on the legalistic approach to development, instanced above in relation to women's emancipation, are also relevant today. That is, we have a situation where laws, regulations and standards (including democracy and human rights standards) are exported around the world, with the governments of weaker countries persuaded to adopt them in exchange for funding or credits from the international agencies. But where they have been forced on countries they are rarely implemented. Indeed, legalism and administrative shock therapy are imperfect instruments – as we see from the experience of pro-capitalist revolution in the transition period. In post-Soviet space, the market was proclaimed with all its new procedures and regulations, and simultaneously people's jobs in the state sector were closed down, and their personal savings wiped out. As Massell says in relation to the women's question, the perfectionist (legalistic) approach sometimes deludes its sponsors, substituting itself for more long-term, systematic and transformational approaches. It deliberately induced conflict in traditional society, but was unable to generate the hoped-for social change (Akiner 1997: 261–96).

The next Soviet decade, 1929–39, saw, on the one hand, an increase in administrative shock therapy with regard to collectivization, but at the same time a retreat in matters affecting family and male–female relations. Massell suggests that this is because the USSR could not legitimize itself and pursue its high-level economic and political objectives while at the same time destroying the bases on which legitimacy could be built. An authoritarian system could not safely encourage libertarian tendencies since they might the next day be turned against the regime itself. It could not act at one and the same time as 'insurgent' and 'incumbent'. Indeed, this paradox is very close to the crux of the matter, the double-bind in which the Soviet system found itself.

4 Political and civil society in the time of *perestroika* and coloured revolution

The events, issues and political debates touched on in this chapter are not new in specialist or left circles in the West. But at least some of them are new in FSU, owing to the long years of Soviet censorship and the political sensitivity they still have. A full discussion depends moreover on the recovery of left and academic circles from twenty years of neoliberal dominance. My own aim is more limited: to explore the link between development strategy and struggle in the Soviet and current periods. Too much international development in the 1990s was implemented without a proper historical perspective. As a practitioner, it was uncomfortable working with Know How Fund, World Bank or European Bank of Reconstruction and Development materials with their simplistic pro-market messages, hardly bothering to cover up their attack on the role of the state, full employment and decent social safety nets, and a great relief when more regionally specific and sensitive materials began to emerge – for example, the works of the 'post-socialist' school.

In Central Asia, too few of these issues were raised until the mid-2000s, at least not in the pragmatic circles in which programme staff pass their time. Of course, many international trainers and consultants read history on the plane out to Almaty, Tashkent or Bishkek (whether accounts of the Russian Revolution or spy stories/histories of the John Le Carré and Fitzroy Maclean type). But development material was very firmly fixed on the tasks of the present. Even for regular readers of the Central Asia press like myself, there was almost nothing with a Soviet angle, such was the emphasis on pre-Soviet traditions on the one hand, and the current desperate crisis on the other. However, this is changing fast. For example, a weekly paper in Bishkek has a column entitled '50 years ago today, 70 years ago today', and a lot of the excerpts are indeed about Soviet development programmes. Local exhibitions and advocacy campaigns consciously use Soviet references, phrases and symbolism. Universities, experts and research agencies have woken up to the fact that the twentieth-century heritage matters, and they are full of studies about various aspects of Soviet life that continue to impinge on the present.

Perestroika, *transition and coloured revolution* This book has already outlined the thesis that *perestroika* led to a pro-capitalist revolution in the countries of eastern Europe and the former Soviet Union. This revolution proceeded dramatically in some countries (e.g. the fall of the Berlin Wall and the execution of President Ceauşescu, or Yeltsin's assault on the White House), but in others it took the form of a more long-winded transition. The 'buy-out' of Soviet communists by the neoliberal 'Bolsheviks' alluded to in Chapter 1 did not really work. Many former communists indeed became managers of privatized enterprises, but many of them remained in government, with their old habits and style of work. In Russia, these processes are visible for all to see – thanks to the work of campaigning journalists, but also because of the overall level of education and development in the country.

That the press and political sphere are similarly open in Kyrgyzstan is in part due to its first president, Askar Akayev, an academic and *perestroika* liberal. So in the 1990s Kyrgyzstan acquired the title 'island of democracy' in Central Asia. This was a time when NGOs set up shop on every corner, many of them supported by international funding and capacity-building. It was relatively easy to register as an organization. For the first fifteen years of transition, people were very open not just to Russians but to other European and Western influences. Kyrgyzstan was ready to try all kinds of market reforms and even joined the World Trade Organization. Civil society gradually became aware of itself as a 'sector', alongside government and business.

By contrast, in Uzbekistan the situation was very different. Here we have the top-down authoritarian model pursued by President Islam Karimov, with a focus on maintaining as many as possible of the economic gains of the Soviet period (including advanced industries such as automobile and aviation manufacturing, chemicals and, on the agricultural side, cotton as a cash crop for export). This is quite an achievement when compared with Kyrgyzstan and Tajikistan, where industry was allowed to almost die out completely. And Uzbekistan has tried to maintain the social safety net, with the result that some of its Human Development Indicators are no worse than those of its more liberal neighbours. But in the information field, as noted in the previous chapter, there is nil development. President Karimov announced the policy of 'a strong civil society in a strong state'; but with so few independent, functioning NGOs in the country, this is a slogan, not a reality.

Coloured revolution in Kyrgyzstan x 2 The second thesis of this section (also not particularly original) is that coloured revolution is the continuation, the second or third round of *perestroika*. That is to say, coloured revolution has taken place in countries where a large part of the population and sections of the political elite considered that transition had not worked for them or had been stolen by others. On the political side, their disillusion was expressed in disbelief in or opposition to election results; on the economic side, in opposition to mass poverty arising from corrupt privatization and unfair, poorly managed reforms. Kyrgyzstan has now experienced two bouts of coloured revolution. In the final section of this chapter, we will briefly consider the elements of civil society and political action in the events of 2005 and 2010, from the point of view of a development worker who lived through them.

Similarities between the 2005 and 2010 revolutions. On 24 March 2005, the incumbent President Akayev was deposed after the storming of Kyrgyzstan's White House; on 7 April 2010, the same fate befell President Bakiev. On both occasions the new regime proclaimed this date a national holiday (and later the post-2010 regime decided it was sufficient to celebrate one revolution and erased 24 March from the holiday calendar).

In both cases creeping nepotism and dynastic tendencies were a major cause of discontent. That is, the two presidents were promoting their sons (and daughter in the case of President Akayev) to positions of power and influence. President Bakiev's son Maxim had been made director of Kyrgyzstan's national development agency, controlling most of the international development investments. The proclaimed political agenda for both revolutions was the same: the move from a presidential system of rule to a parliamentary one. The revolutions exposed the continuing north–south divide in Kyrgyzstan. Akayev was a northerner, Bakiev a southerner, the next president – Otunbaeva – a northerner again. The political mobilizations before each event reflected this geographical division. While Kyrgyzstan's active civil society played a role in encouraging people to express their grievances and propose positive solutions to local problems,

CSOs were not in their own right significant political players in the events. Clan, mafia and party leaders called the shots.[12] However, after the 2005 revolution many NGO leaders decided that they had a responsibility to play a more direct role in politics – and stood successfully for election at local or national level.

Differences. The level of political (or quasi-political) violence in Kyrgyzstan increased significantly in 2005–10. Indeed, the 2005 revolution led to a situation where for a while it looked as if criminal bosses would actually challenge the new political leadership (with prison revolts, murders of MPs and top businessmen). President Akayev had decided to flee the country without putting up a fight, but as his successor Bakiev began to run into trouble he declared outright that he would not do the same. The last years of his presidency were marred by the murder of opposition journalists and wavering government officials – and nobody was brought to book for this. On 7 April 2010, a disorganized but armed attack on the White House was met with sniper fire from the roof of the building and some ninety protesters died before the president fled.

The regional divisions took on an extra ethnic character in 2010. Thus, two months after Bakiev fled from Bishkek to his power base in Jalalabad, southern Kyrgyzstan, figures in the new temporary government seem to have provoked the ethnic Uzbek community (who form the majority of the population in this region) to try to dig him out. This led to violent clashes with the local Kyrgyz community (many of whom were Bakiev supporters) and the deaths of over four hundred people in Osh and Jalalabad. These tragic events were a shock to people in Kyrgyzstan, who, while respecting national differences (cultural and religious identities, for example), on the whole considered themselves internationalists. All this meant that while the 2005 revolution had led to widespread euphoria, a flowering of different ideas and opinions, in 2010 there was only bitterness, mourning and a grim determination on the part of the new regime to hang on.

The international situation also changed a lot between 2005 and 2010. The first revolution represented the high-water mark of US influence in the region. Up to this moment the USA had thrown its weight around, with regular statements from its ambassador on different issues appearing in the local press, while after 2005 it became almost silent. Despite the presence of a US airbase at Kyrgyzstan's international airport, Manas, supporting the war in Afghanistan, the USA had fallen out with Akayev in the run-up to 2005, hoping for quicker progress to 'democracy'. In 2010, by contrast, Russia was seen as the main destabilizer of the Bakiev regime. Certainly, on the eve of the April events the Kyrgyz newspapers had been full of stories about Putin's dissatisfaction with the way in which Bakiev was spending the grants and credits offered in the previous year; and the Russian-language press in Kyrgyzstan was always adamant in its protest about the US presence at Manas.

Finally, the role of civil society changed significantly during this period. After 2005, most international donors became much more cautious about supporting radical CSOs; indeed, they stopped supporting the civil society sector as a whole. This had a major effect on capacity-building programmes such as the training that INTRAC provided to NGOs. The donors had started channelling their funds through government, with NGOs engaged in a more piecemeal way as subcontractors in particular projects. After the ethnic clashes in Osh and Jalalabad, a survey carried out by INTRAC's partners showed that the number of active NGOs in these two *oblasts* before the crisis was less than a third of the total five years before. A major difference with 2005 was the role allotted to NGOs in humanitarian aid and reconstruction in the south after June 2010. Indeed, local community activists had been first on the scene during the 'war' in Osh and Jalalabad, working to help each other across the sectarian barricades. This humanitarian crisis stimulated a mini-boom in civil society activity in 2010–12.

Another difference was visible at national level, among the advanced and especially the democracy and human rights NGOs. These had always had a high profile and now they achieved national prominence in the drawing up of the new parliamentary constitution, the formation of a new public broadcasting channel, vetting new judges, in lobbying and consultative groups of all kinds. These NGOs by now had developed their own niches: one focused on election procedures and monitoring, another on transparency, another defended the Uzbek community against post-June 2010 repression by the authorities, another organized crisis centres for women, and so on. That is, the political and professional differentiation within the sector had come on apace. To this day the media in Kyrgyzstan have remained remarkably free and open. For example, there is open discussion of difficult and divisive issues such as whether the soldiers who opened fire on protesters in Bishkek's main square were justified in this (remaining loyal to their oath and obeying orders) or whether the demands of the people had a higher priority; or about the performance of the new parliamentary system that was introduced after amendments to the Constitution later in 2010.

In all this we can see a major difference between the political and civil society point of view. The revolutions of 2005 and 2010 led to a major changeover in political personnel and government officials at all levels. The new leaders claimed that they were kicking out corrupt and inefficient representatives of the old regime; they brought in lots of new people, energetic and committed to their party, clan or regional priorities. From the civil society point of view, work to influence government for wider or deeper development-oriented policies frequently had to start from scratch. Many of the new elected deputies or state officials were often inexperienced in administration matters, others were simply politically biased; it was a moot point whether they were legitimate. In these transition periods it was the weakest sections of the communities which suffered most. As in the 1990s, it was children, the elderly and people with disabilities (to name just a few) who lost out. They lost their benefits, their facilities fell into disrepair and the consultative and political support mechanisms they had built up took last place behind more forceful groups.

Finally, economic issues were more directly important in the 2010 revolution than they had been in 2005. Kyrgyzstan had been hit badly by the world economic crisis in 2008–10, and President Bakiev's decision in late 2009 to sell off the main power companies and simultaneously double or triple electricity tariffs showed he had lost touch with the people. This issue gave the opposition a chance to gain mass support, which they never really enjoyed for their political programme. So here we see the complex environment for development, in its revolutionary or transitional modes, in which political and civil mobilization always play their distinctive and linked roles. And if party political mobilization is dominant, independent civil society activity will often be squeezed.

5 | LOCAL GOVERNMENT DECENTRALIZATION: CIVIL SOCIETY DEVELOPMENT IN THE URALS AND SIBERIA

1 The handover of social services to local authorities during Russia's transition

As we have seen in earlier chapters, in the Soviet period the main economic and social policy decisions were taken at the centre by party and government bodies. Economic units (factories, offices, state farms, etc.) were required to provide for social needs and most of them were accountable to line ministries or comparable agencies at Union level. The individual Soviet enterprise was ruled by a triumvirate: the party, taking political and strategic decisions; the managers, responsible for technical decisions and day-to-day management; and the trade union, helping to organize the work process and responsible for a range of social provisions defined by the state.

The USSR guaranteed two fundamental benefits: 1) employment, 2) across-the-board consumer price subsidies including rents and food. State social policies thus served the interests of the working class. The only type of unemployment that existed was 'voluntary', while social problems like poverty, homelessness and crime were proclaimed to have been eliminated once and for all. Education was mostly free, as were healthcare and cultural facilities. Women benefited from good cash and kind services, including work-based childcare provision. Housing was inexpensive but in short supply. By international standards there were plenty of doctors but they lacked up-to-date equipment and other medical resources.

The system whereby housing, childcare and other social benefits were connected to a person's place of work tended to militate against labour mobility. Indeed, in areas of special economic, political or military importance, the whole town might have an enhanced 'Moscow budget'. This meant social facilities of a higher standard and better access to daily food products and consumer goods. The system was paternalistic in that there was limited opportunity for the individual to choose between services, to influence or help design new modes of care.

In the early Soviet period, communist ideology set out to reduce the influence, responsibility and functions of the family, replacing them with state care. Against this, there was a high degree of popular participation in the delivery of services. Union committees played a leading role, for example, in organizing health points at the place of work, and leisure facilities (workers' and children's rest homes and holiday resorts); indeed, groups of young volunteers, mainly women, often visited retired or sick members of staff at home. From the 1970s, the Soviet regime introduced a number of reforms that softened up the system. Two examples can be given. First, power was given to a number of voluntary organizations such as the All-Russian Association of Invalids to develop information and services for their members, through an extensive national branch system. Second, the 1977 Soviet Constitution stipulated that parents were ultimately responsible for their children; and children in their turn for their parents' welfare in their old age (Deacon 1992). This gave the family back some of its traditional responsibilities.

The collapse of the Soviet Union and privatization of many of the most advanced enterprises meant a sudden abandonment of social responsibilities by employers. Trade unions inherited a lot of the social infrastructure (workplace nurseries, work health units, staff holiday homes and children's camps) but without state funding to maintain them. It was clear that local authorities would have to take many of these services over, but on what financial basis and with what management and technical resources was not so clear.

The dominant ideology of the 1990s was opposed to what it termed 'cradle to grave' welfare. There was an assumption among donors that in any case the countries of eastern Europe and FSU could not afford comprehensive social protection systems. Policy-makers saw their main priority as to create or win over the middle class; the poor and vulnerable would have to wait. Thus social policies emerged much later than marketization or democratization. When they did take shape, they focused on implementing temporary and selective measures for the weakest in society, rather than creating a new universal system of social care. One of Russia's leading social policy experts, Yevgeny Gontmakher, commented at the end of the 1990s that the key to social policy is targeting (*adresnost*) of benefits. He gave child benefit as an example. In 2000, the Russian government took the decision to limit this benefit to families with an average wage per person lower than the official subsistence minimum; this had led to a 30 per cent reduction in the number of those claiming it (2000: 328).

Another problem was that deregulation of the economy reduced the country's tax base. The new rich had shifted their assets and activities en masse into the informal sector, as we saw in Chapter 1. As financial transparency was lost, it became harder and harder to know where to put the emphasis in social policy. Thus the effect of neoliberal economic policy was a reduction in social policy options (Piirainen 1997: 228).

Another major development was the emergence of not-for-profit providers of social care across the region. This was seen as a means of 'denationalization' of state services. However, NGO provision was by its very nature uneven (it took place more slowly in FSU than in eastern Europe and covered cities better than rural communities). This type of provision required an effective local government system to contract out and check services provided by a variety of groups and organizations, but this system was not yet in place in the mid-1990s.

Under the Soviet system, social work was carried out by Communist Party, *komsomol* and trade union workers, as well as public organizations serving women, people with disabilities and so on set up in the post-war years. The development of social work as a profession, with formal qualifications and standards, was one of the most positive aspects of changes initiated in the 1990s. Progressive-minded teachers led the way, assisted by a strong corps of social pedagogues and psychologists. Their work was supported by the adoption of a new law On Social Care for Invalids (1995) and the Family Code of the Russian Federation (1996). By the end of the 1990s, the government was taking a more integrated approach to youth problems, experimenting with multidimensional programmes with social, educational and recreational elements. These often focused on healthy lifestyle and sex education in an attempt to respond to the increasing involvement of young people in crime, alcohol and drugs abuse.

The EEP/VSO programme in social and health services development In Chapter 1, we briefly mentioned an early development 'intervention' in transition Russia – the work of international volunteers working in social and health care. VSO's work in the Urals was particularly challenging because of the severe impact of transition on industry and employment here in the early to mid-1990s. During the Soviet period the region had been closed to foreigners and few people were used to speaking in English, even if they could read it for professional purposes; and they were not used to communication with Westerners. Nonetheless, both grassroots and higher-level work was undertaken in many different areas, as the examples given below show clearly.

TABLE 5.1 Volunteer contributions in the social policy and services area

Perm city and *oblast*	Yekaterinburg city and Sverdlovsk *oblast*	Cheliabinsk city and *oblast*
Social work training	Health information for diabetes sufferers	Social work training
Setting up a hospice for the terminally ill	Community-based mental health units	Development of city NGO resource centre
Work in children's homes and schemes working with young drug and alcohol abusers	NGO-run educational schemes for children with special needs	Management assistance to the *oblast* disabled people's association
Creation of an autism project/unit	Youth outreach work in one-company towns	Health education on HIV/AIDS

There were some themes that were cross-cutting. Thus in many placements standards of social care management were improved by use of reporting, client-focused and multidisciplinary approaches. In the health sector, approaches and specialist skills that were new in Russia included palliative care, and treatment of HIV/AIDS and diabetes. In the social sector, volunteers promoted the transition from institutional care to community care. Within residential institutions (still home to 1.5 million children in Russia in the 1990s), they helped improve approaches to communication, play, and social and independent life skills (see Harwin 1996).

Disability was a major focus of the VSO Russia programme. Volunteer social and health professionals helped establish an early intervention service for children with a cleft palate or Down's syndrome, supporting self-help groups for parents of other severely disabled children that enable them to take care of their children at home. They gave a much-needed stimulus to preventive work for young people suffering from drug abuse and HIV/AIDS, helping establish harm reduction services and organizing awareness-raising campaigns across the Urals region. Hospitals, social services departments and NGOs alike were having to face up to a more independent, less financially secure external environment. Foreign professionals with experience of competition, government budget cuts, marketing and management were a highly prized resource for their Russian hosts.[1]

2 The situation of local government in the 1990s and 2000s

As Gelman notes in his book *Autonomy or Control?*, local government is for many a lacklustre topic; it attracts significantly less attention from political scientists and journalists than, for example, globalization, national elections or the politics of identity (Gelman et al. 2002). On the other hand, government decentralization has huge importance for development programmes and the work of CSOs. It is with this in mind that we introduce a case study from the Urals city of Perm.

There were significant changes in local government in the 1990s, in particular the new Russian Constitution adopted in 1993, declaring in Article 12 that local self-government organs are not part of the state apparatus, and a number of laws passed by the Duma that seemed to many to herald a kind of municipal revolution. However, the results have been less than impressive. Gelman argues that this is largely due to the results of local elections, which have not passed power to political parties or individuals willing or able to exercise greater autonomy from the centre. Municipal budgets continue to depend on central and provincial government subsidies, and they still carry the burden of supporting institutions handed over to them by enterprises at the start of the decade. As a result, some 95 per cent of municipalities were still in the red in 2000.

This is just one of many fields where declarations were not matched by delivery in the 1990s. And there was a huge variation in how local elites implemented the new laws. For example, Tatarstan remained a highly autocratic region, while almost next door the Urals saw several experiments with decentralization, as in Perm.

Case study: Politics, economics and city government in Perm Perm had been a relatively advanced region in the Soviet period, with a well-diversified industrial base – salt and coal mines, oil and gas extraction and refining, machine building connected to the arms industry. In 1990/91, as a local commentator put it, the regional Communist Party elite 'jumped ship' and went off into business, heading up the newly privatized industries. The *oblast* administration soon became the site of almost every issue of concern to the general population. This left the city of Perm (population 1 million out of 2.8 million in the *oblast* in 1989) relatively free from outside pressure for most of the decade. The post of elected mayor was created in 1992 and the first incumbent, Yury Trutnev, while representing commercial trading interests in the city, teamed up with a vice-mayor from the left-centrist Yabloko Party and implemented many of the democratic innovations promoted by Moscow.

The collapse of industry in the 1990s led to the emergence of raw material extraction and communications as the two dominant sectors – with Lukoil and Svyazinform gaining a monopoly position. The provincial authorities provided a friendly tax regime for the 100 most important local companies. It was only at the end of the decade that the leaders of Perm's private sector turned their attention to politics at city level. By the time the city Duma was elected for a third time, almost every deputy had close links to one business grouping or another (Gelman et al. 2002: 200–9).

Unfortunately, once Trutnev got promotion and became provincial governor, he began to reverse the process and the city authorities proved unable to maintain their positions. Hence the authors of the case study conclude that local government achieved only 'quasi-autonomy'.[2] Indeed, in the 1990s a large number of changes were introduced at the same time: new powers for the provincial, district and self-government levels, as well as directly elected governors and city mayors. This caused a level of incoherence – but also gave opportunities to do something new.

By the mid-1990s, NGOs in the Urals region had begun to press local government to create joint programmes with which to tackle social problems and poverty. However, this was difficult for several reasons: first the absence of a federal law laying down a framework for cross-sectoral programmes; second, a lack of clarity about the aim – was it to help fund NGOs, or to tackle priorities identified by local authorities? In Perm, the first steps included the issuing of a guide for local NGOs issued by the Perm Citizens Chamber, then the opening up of government services to tender by private organizations. By this time several NGOs had gained a strong reputation in the city – for example, the Perm Hospice, established with the help of health sector partners in the UK. In neighbouring Yekaterinburg, laws adopted by the Sverdlovsk *oblast* authorities – on charitable activity, on the formation of *popechitelsky* (voluntary sector management) committees, and on children's rights – laid the base for NGO–government collaboration. Youth policy and programmes were among the first areas where practical collaboration was achieved; by 1997 some fifty voluntary organizations had established working links with the Oblast Youth Committee, gaining funding on the basis of a signed agreement (Tomasova 1998: 27–31, 40–2).

Many of the new initiatives and ways of working have stood the test of time. In Perm, the system of 'social orders' has been running for over ten years and NGO representatives play a significant role in designing programmes, approving contracts and monitoring the process. This includes selecting social issues for prioritization each year and promotion of new methodologies of the kind the VSO volunteers helped to introduce in the 1990s.[3] There is an active Public Chamber bringing together the government and civil society sectors. Perm has a local authority twinning scheme with Oxford (city and county level). This has created many avenues for improving policy and services. One practical example in the area of local authority–NGO liaison is the opening of some twenty new community centres with rent-free space for NGOs and community groups, plus a hall for local events. The idea came from exchange visits by Perm local officials to the UK.

Another example of local collaboration is provided by an independent NGO, the Grani Analytical Centre, which specializes in local government reform. Grani has begun working for a variety of local and federal agencies, for example the Ministry of Economic Development, to evaluate efficiency and accountability in government. One study monitored the work of the Federal Anti-Monopoly Service; another piece of work was on land registration services in five regions of Russia; a third was on how well citizens' participation works at municipal level.

The liberal/human rights agenda. During a visit to Perm in July 2011, I travelled two hours northwards through the forests to the biennial 'Pilorama' festival. This gave a chance to see how a coalition of liberally minded individuals and organizations are continuing to promote a rights agenda. The Pilorama event brought leaders from the national human rights organization Memorial, *perestroika*-era politicians and rock stars to former labour camp Perm-36, a small set of one-storey shacks behind wooden fences and barbed wire on the edge of the forest. Over twelve thousand people attended the festival over three days, and heavy rain did not seem to affect the lively discussions held in marquees set up for the occasion. One session was devoted to the government programme to honour victims of repression; another to links between Russia and Europe twenty years after *perestroika*; another to the results of privatization in the Perm *oblast*; others looked at inter-ethnic and civil society issues.

On the cultural front. Another distinctive element of local policy dating from the Trutnev years is the effort to promote Perm as a centre of avant-garde art – the so-called Perm 'cultural breakthrough'. There is a modern art museum in the old river station and a graffiti project commissioned by the local arts committee has covered the fences round the city's empty building lots with some quite impressive decorations. There is a White Nights festival in summer and a musically innovative Diaghilev Festival. The result of this is that almost everyone in Perm (local officials, NGO activists, people in the streets) seems to have a view on modern art – for or against – and this has become a significant factor in the city's perception of itself.

Putin's policies towards local government and civil society In the last chapter we began to look at Vladimir Putin's recentralizing, top-down policies from the early 2000s. If truth be told, the Russian public liked the way Yeltsin's successor began to restore order, bringing the oligarchs to heel, while businessmen and high-earning employees alike were pleased with his tax policies.[4] Over the next few years, the economy began to stabilize, based on export of oil, gas and other natural resources, and much-reduced inflation. Average monthly wages in Russia rose from $95 in 2000 to $395 in 2006. The most blatant crimes were reduced significantly. For example, the Interior

Ministry has estimated that contract killings were brought down from 600–700 per year in the 1990s to just 70 in 2002. During the 1990s, some 70 per cent of legal disputes were settled out of court, via the mafia and private security services. The strengthening of discipline in the state sector, giving governors, judges and police more power, has reduced this figure; but as Van Zon notes, not sufficiently to satisfy the Russian public, who still scored Putin low on many of these issues (2010: 57–67).

One of Putin's most controversial decisions was to abolish elected governors in 2004, added to which he appointed seven super-regional representatives, standing above the governors and giving him a strategic arm for central policy and programmes in the regions. In this way, Putin reversed the centrifugal processes that had become so noticeable under Yeltsin. But at the same time, he was careful not to upset regional clans and power factions.[5] Thus, during the period 2005–08 only twelve out of sixty-seven regional governors left office – and these were mostly governors who had openly defied Putin. Meanwhile, the president and his aides gradually built up United Russia as a new 'party of power' across the country, along with its youth wing *Nashi* ('Ours').[6]

Putin's presidency had a significant effect on civil society development. On the one hand he put serious pressure on NGOs accepting foreign funding, encouraging hysteria in the state media about US imperialism, British spies and unpatriotic Russian citizens working with them. On the other hand, Putin gradually began to put into place a system of Russian government support for the civil society sector – that is, consultation mechanisms and ways in which NGOs could carry out practical work in their chosen areas of expertise and commitment. One aspect of this has already been mentioned – the system of 'social orders' or NGOs contracting for services with the local authorities; the other is the Public Chamber (*obschestvennaya palata*) set up by Putin and approved by the Russian Duma in 2005.

The Public Chamber system has been quite controversial from the start. Critics said it would be 'window-dressing to legitimize the government's increasingly authoritarian policies', 'a phantom, a harmful institution' or a 'wax dummy' (quoted in Javeline and Lindemann-Komarova 2010: 180). The national Public Chamber has 126 members, selected by the president himself, public organizations, and representatives of Russia's regions (one third each). The pro-claimed aim was to develop inter-sectoral dialogue between government, civil society and business. By mid-2009, there were over fifty-five regional public chambers across Russia and many local NGOs have proved willing to give them a try. The chambers are an important part of Putin's strategy to win public support for his patriotic political project and at one time, according to Evans (2006), were planned as a 'single corporatist body'. However, Putin backed away from this. Instead the provision of funding and consultation mechanisms has become one of his 'indirect methods for discouraging independent criticism' by Russian civil society.

Soon after the Public Chamber came two laws that had a direct impact on the work of NGOs. The first tightened up the rules for registration of NGOs and reporting their activities to the author-ities.[7] Legal requirements for NGOs in Russia, particularly relating to financial reporting, have always been onerous. The specialist legal organization ICNL (International Committee for Non-profit Law) later issued a detailed report on the effect of the new law. It calculated that out of the 675,000 NGOs registered in Russia in 2007, some 2,600 had gone into involuntary liquidation that year because of the new requirements. This is not such a large number. However, four out of five NGOs in 2007 did not supply reports in the required format by the official deadline – which left them, too, vulnerable to closure. ICNL surveys indicated that the new law had not proved more burdensome for democracy and human rights groups than for other NGOs. And when NGO leaders were asked to name the main sources of pressure on their organization, the answer 'Not enough money, material resources' topped the list with 59.1 per cent, while government pressure came very low (2.9 per cent).[8]

The second new law boosted citizens' right to participate in local self-government bodies.[9] Javeline and Lindemann-Komarova call this a 'huge stride for Russia in recognizing the value of citizen participa-tion in governance' (2010: 175). But at the same time they note that scepticism remains because many new procedures (such as public hearings and referenda) can easily be manipulated. A lot depends on the experience and influence of individual civil society leaders and organizations resisting official pressure or blandishments.

3 Centre and periphery within the Russian Federation

There are two main areas relevant to this chapter where, in the mid-2000s, it was still difficult to say that Russia's development problems had been solved.

The first was the overall situation with regard to the quality of life in Russia, as evidenced in the 'human development indicators' assessed by UN agencies across the world. Thus a UNDP Russia report by Mikhail Babenko at the end of the 2000s describes how when the HDI indicator was first calculated in Russia, the country found it had slipped from 26th place (out of 126 countries) in 1987 to 72nd place (among 174 countries) in 1995. This was the low point, truly a disaster. Russia made slow progress in real terms in the next decade, but in 2006 it was still only in 73rd place in the world HDI ranking. Babenko argues that there were two main reasons why Russia's HDI dropped so severely in the 1990s: first, the loss of earnings per capita of GDP, and second, a decline in life expectancy. A third worry is the demographic challenge of low birth rates and an ageing population; a fourth – the high level of unemployment and underemployment.[10]

The second development problem we need to mention here is the continuing gap between the standard of living in the capital and a few major cities, on the one hand, and the outlying regions of Russia on the other. During the 2000s, regional disparities increased to such an extent that some 70 per cent of Russia's regions are now recipients of subsidies from the federal budget. It has been calculated that Moscow city, Moscow *oblast*, St Petersburg and Tyumen *oblast* (oil and gas rich) between them account for half of the national gross product. Meanwhile, social expenditure continued to fall disproportionately on local government.

Throughout the last decade, Perm region has continued as an in-novator, trying to get the most out of current political and economic opportunities. As part of this strategy, in 2010 the *oblast* agreed to offer itself up to the scrutiny of UNDP and to collect material for a special human development report for the region. Various things leap out of this report. First, Perm is fully committed to market competition and privatization. On many economic and social indices it seems to have high counts. But life expectancy for men has been very low – around fifty-seven years during much of the last decade (that is, three years below the pension age). The report explains

TABLE 5.2 Some data from Perm's human development report 2010

Indicator	Score
Population	Just over one million. Dropped by 2.5 per 1,000 in 2008
Urban/rural	23.4% are employed in manufacturing, only 4.7% in agriculture
Average income	$16,642 GDP per capita. But 13% of the population have an income below the subsistence minimum
Life expectancy male/female	Male – 59.3 years; female – 72.5 years
Child mortality up to five years	2.8% in 2008
Unemployment	3.5% (registered); 11.8% (ILO method of calculation) in 2009
Access to drinking water	77.9% have running water in their home; 72.8% are connected to the central sewerage system
Emission of greenhouse gases	Several industrial towns in Perm have an air pollution index of 7–15 points against a safe level of 5

this in terms of dangerous working conditions in the raw materials extraction and processing sectors. Another detail that catches the eye is that water, sanitation and sewerage conditions are poor in lots of districts. Another that the health risks from a polluted atmosphere are rising year on year. The gender data are less impressive than one might perhaps expect. While women live significantly longer than men (with a life expectancy of seventy years), they earn only 63 per cent as much as men on average. There is only one woman out of sixty deputies in the parliament for Perm *krai* (territory). In-migration to Perm has stopped. The population is declining ...

Spatial studies of the Russian Federation: expert views When considering the relation between the centre and periphery in Russia today, it is important to remember that the country's spatial/geographical configuration changed completely in 1991. First of all the country became smaller – the space occupied by the Russian Federation is approximately three-quarters of that occupied by the former USSR

– and for political leaders who were used to thinking big, this was a serious blow. Secondly, the country became even more Moscow-centred than it had been before, because it lost important republican centres like Kiev, Tashkent, Minsk and Riga – which now became capitals of independent countries. Thirdly, Russians were separated from next-door Slavic populations in Belarus and Ukraine that they had for centuries considered part of Russia itself; they even lost their former capital Kiev.

As Oleg Yanitsky shows in his book *Ecological Culture* (2007), the break-up of the USSR destroyed not just the geographical 'logic' of the previous seventy years, and not just all the links painstakingly constructed between mines, factories and other economic units, it also affected a kind of natural/human ecosystem that had gradually formed by the end of the 1980s. That is to say, urban and rural development had begun to follow an identifiable pattern, so too migration flows within the USSR. After losing the other fourteen republics, Russia itself experienced a drop in population of 1.8 million in the decade to 2002. And at the same time the country became more ethnically homogeneous: whereas Russians had previously accounted for just half of the Soviet population, they now made up 80 per cent of the new nation-state. For Yanitsky, this necessitates a search for a new vision of Russia as an ecosystem. In particular he emphasizes local knowledge – about history, culture and the environment – arguing that only this can protect the country from the forces of capitalist and oligarchic globalization.

The economic and social development challenges arising over twenty years from *perestroika* were outlined in a collection of articles by Petr Schedrovitsky and a group of co-authors, entitled *Formula of Development* (2005). This book emphasizes the increasing importance of regional (or spatial-locational) studies of the twentieth century in Russia. On the one side, there are the forces of globalization, choosing their sites for development (i.e. profit); and on the other, governments or societies that want to retain their special character or autonomy. Regionalism can thus be seen as a kind of compromise between globalization, on the one hand, and nationalism or localism on the other (ibid.: 9). Much of the book is given over to detailed analysis of how the broken connections and patterns of development from the Soviet time can be replaced – bearing in mind that the industrial bias of the Soviet economy has yet to fully come to terms with the post-industrial age.

Domestic critics (like Kagarlitsky and other analysts in *Levaya Politika*) of Russia's dependency on exports of oil, gas, timber and other natural resources frequently refer to the country's unadvantageous position in today's world capitalist system. They argue (along with Schedrovitsky) that unless Russia develops modern industry and services including the IT, communications and biotechnology sectors, it is doomed to lag for ever behind the most advanced countries. This is undoubtedly true. An additional problem is that within the post-Soviet space itself today, there is a clear centre–periphery pattern. This has several 'rings': 1) an outer periphery – the less developed areas within ex-Soviet republics/Tsarist colonies; 2) a middle periphery – backward or isolated areas within the Russian Federation; 3) an innermost periphery – that is, socially excluded groups within Russia's cities. This inequality and unevenness of development poses a major challenge to policy-makers today – or should do. And it is one of the main subjects of my book.

The argument being advanced in this book – that bottom-up and local development can and should play a crucial role in Russia – is backed by Schedrovitsky. First, he argues that cities play a key role in modern development. In 1991, when the planned economy fell apart, it was the town/city that had to pick up the pieces. One of the consequences of this was the tendency of municipalities to create all kinds of new associations, as discussion platforms within which to tackle the new problems (ibid.: 43–58). After the 1998 financial crash, when neoliberalism reached its lowest point and some of the most rapacious adventurers lost fortunes, Schedrovitsky notes that it was once again local government which held things together – though he complains that federal and provincial organs of government still 'just can't see' this fact. Local self-government is the key to winning the trust of citizens, he writes. But will its representatives and wider civic associations be able to stand up and argue as a new political force in the country? Or will they settle for lobbying parochial interests and making deals with central government behind closed doors? (ibid.: 73–9).

Unlike Yanitsky's book, this volume is much more comfortable with the mega-programmes now being proposed by the Russian government. It argues that a new 'cluster' approach to development has to be found. While dubious about attempts to revive famous Soviet projects like the Baikal–Amur Mainline,[11] it proposes instead a new set of regions forming around raw materials extraction, industrial production and the human and intellectual resources still remaining in the Russian Federation. Some of these regions may feature integrated economic development, others a variety of network arrangements.[12] And of course many of the strategies demand a wider solution working hand in hand with Russia's ex-Soviet neighbours (see analysis in Bykov 2009).

Autonomous areas and the 'middle periphery' The first chapter of this book described the problems of urban communities faced with the crash of the Soviet economy, noting how the intelligentsia (being mainly workers in the public sector) suffered as much as the working class. These groups can be called the 'inner periphery' of post-Soviet society. In Chapters 3 and 4 we began to look at issues affecting populations in the 'outer ring' of the FSU periphery. And here we need to look at the middle layer of the excluded – using the example of smaller autonomous areas that remained within the Russian Federation after 1991.

While on visits to Perm in 2011/12, I took the opportunity to ask about something that had caught my attention when reading about the region – the disappearance of the Komi-Perm autonomous area on modern maps of Perm territory. NGO colleagues explained that in the early 1990s the number of federal 'subjects' in the Russian Federation diminished (from eighty-nine to eighty-three) and Komi-Perm was one of the national units that disappeared. This was in 1993, after a vote in a local referendum to merge the autonomous area with the rest of Perm region, i.e. to bring it on to the same level with other districts. However, as things have turned out, my informants told me, some parts of Komi-Perm remain extremely depressed, and the population is disappointed with the results of the reorganization.[13] Big questions remain about how far the Komi-Perm language can be preserved. Youth and the national intelligentsia both have areas of complaint about cultural development, since it seems that not all the promises made at the time of incorporation have been delivered. Indigenous Komi-Permyaks attend international meetings of the Finnish-Ugrian peoples to which they belong, and some feelthat they gave away their autonomy too easily (Kolmogorova 2010).

Komi-Perm is one of the smaller national units within the Russian Federation, with a population of just over 110,000, of whom 59 per cent are Komi-Permyak, 41 per cent Russian or other. By contrast, the Republic of Buryatia, mentioned in Chapter 3, is significantly larger – with over 970,000 people (30 per cent Buryats, 66 per cent Russian, 4 per cent other). The Buryats are guaranteed the opportunity to stand up for their rights by their 'titular' status and representation in the Federation Council in Moscow. But not so the Komi-Permyaks.

A recent article on the position of 'globally superfluous' smaller peoples in the Russian Federation describes a history that is not so far from what we have seen in Central Asia. During the period of Russian colonial expansion, the peoples of the far north avoided contact with colonists and missionaries insofar as this was possible. Inter-cultural communication was difficult and the Tsarist authorities often ruled through traditional leaders. Many of these peoples showed no particular desire to take part in the forced leap to Soviet socialism, either. Many retained an allegience to traditional shamans or tribal leaders. The sale of alcohol and the high-handed behaviour of local officials affected the indigenous peoples badly. The grand industrial and raw material extraction plans of the period were designed to transform these regions, but said little about the risks and losses involved: 'ecocide accompanied by elements of ethnocide', as one critic put it (Dobronravin 2010).

Post-1991 'piratization' and 'predatory modernization' have continued to impact negatively on indigenous people. The strategies of the latter have been much the same as in the previous centuries, a choice between: 1) passive accommodation, often leading to alcoholism and total social exclusion; 2) economic integration, often with support from environmental NGOs or businesses offering minority groups a role in development projects as junior partners; 3) continuing the struggle for national rights and culture, often via community groups based in Russia's cities and using networks of 'exiles' to support their homeland in the north and east. The article comments that the network strategy seems the one most likely to succeed; otherwise the smaller peoples are 'doomed to social and economic degradation' (Dobronravin 2010: 251).

Two areas stand out as exceptions to what has been written above – the Khanti-Mansi and Yamalo-Nenetsky Autonomous Areas (*okrugs*) in natural-resource-rich Tyumen *oblast* (see Table 3.1). These areas are very likely to stay 'autonomous' since any attempt to change their status would threaten the interests of the oil and gas companies that run them. Their size and economic power are such that they could become full *oblasts*, but any moves to national sovereignty would be fraught with political risks for the powers-that-be.

4 Assessing the impact of social development interventions in the 1990s and 2000s

The example of smaller peoples, whether from the far north or other parts of Russia, shows that the involvement of civil society will be vital in addressing development issues such as equality or access to jobs and services for excluded groups. Campaigning will be needed, and it is not just a matter of extracting a few concessions or privileges, but creating new policies and explaining them to the Russian public at large.

Our historical approach has shown that civil society is by no means a new feature of Russian life dating from the fall of the Berlin Wall. With origins in village meetings and the peasant commune, it developed as a set of citizens' organizations emerging along with capitalism in the eighteenth and nineteenth centuries, in a complex negotiation with Tsarism. The attempts to introduce people's power continued in parallel, with peasant revolts and the activities of radicals (anarchists, liberals and socialists) who challenged absolutism and led the 1905 and 1917 revolutions. The beginning and end of the Soviet period are both remarkable for the flowering of different ideas, activities and organizations in the cultural, educational and political realms. Russian researchers are gradually extending their view of modern civil society development back from the 1980s into the post-1945 period. At the beginning of this chapter we mentioned the advances made by disability associations in the 1970s, and this goes for war veterans' associations, youth and ecological groups, too.

The 1990s themselves saw a complex set of processes. At first there was euphoria about the political changes, with citizens' 'initiative groups' and wider social movements alike eager to press forward with their agendas. The economic crash disillusioned some and forced many others to occupy themselves with survival. This was a period when new NGOs relied almost exclusively for funds on foreign donors; indeed, some slavishly copied ideas, experience or models from outside. This is a much-criticized fact now, but any balanced view will agree that Russian NGOs helped open up a public debate on issues such as feminism, domestic violence, disability, military service and the environment (Laxter and Halperin 2003; Hemmett 2007). The farther you went from Moscow and St Petersburg, into the small towns and villages where over a third of the population still live, the more likely citizens' action was to be informal, small-scale, well linked into local government and often building on associations created in the Soviet period (White 2004).

Indeed, there was often an element of hostility to NGOs or to anything considered foreign. Some of this was political, for reasons that are readily understandable. But writers on civil society quote other frequently heard views that simply register exhaustion or confusion: e.g. the statement 'we were all volunteers in the Soviet Union and what good did it do us?' or a generally felt desire to retreat from the political sphere after the ideological battles of the Soviet period. Luckily other reactions were more positive.

Regional NGO programmes in Siberia With over three million people, Novosibirsk is the third-largest city in the Russian Federation. Situated on the Ob river quite early in its long journey to the Arctic Sea, this is a major centre for machine building and the automobile industry – and home to the Siberian Civic Initiatives Support Centre, one of the first NGO resource centres. Set up with US funding in the mid-1990s, SCISC coordinates a network of support organizations in eleven administrative regions across Siberia.

In 1996, SCISC received US$600,000 from USAID to organize one of the first small grant competitions for NGOs in Russia. In one of the most outstanding success stories of fund-raising development during the transition period, the Centre used this money to open negotiations with the Novosibirsk authorities – eventually gaining an agreement to match the US contribution dollar for dollar and so opening up the way for local government funding for NGOs. Ten years later, grants awarded by Novosibirsk *oblast* and city totalled 18 million roubles, and the annual funding pool has topped 35 million roubles (US$1.1 million) since then. The collaboration is not just about grants. Thus, in 2010, Novosibirsk's city authorities adopted a long-term support plan for NGOs, including the opening of local resource centres, public consultative committees, territorial councils and local volunteer schemes. In the *oblast* the same process can be seen, although it is a bit slower.

Another regional NGO, *Golos* (Voice), operates in the democracy field. It too was set up with US funding, to organize election monitoring activities in Novosibirsk, spreading later to nine regions in Siberia and the far east. *Golos* was one of the NGOs targeted for multiple police checks after the passing of a law against NGOs described as 'foreign agents' and the closure of USAID's Russia programme in autumn 2012. But by this time the democratic mission of both *Golos* and SCISC had many supporters among Russian citizens in the region; they are bound to continue in one way or another.

There are of course significant variations in civil society development around Russia. And it is not always the big cities like Moscow and St Petersburg which lead the way. A study by Mersianova (2008), for example, gave the highest ratings to northern regions like Arkhangelsk, Vologda and the Komi autonomous region, and South Urals ones like Chelyabinsk and Orenburg.[14] Feelings about safety and security, or involvement in volunteering, varied significantly from region to region – some areas giving results almost twice as good (or bad) as others. The organization types that Russians know about are very varied, too. Among the most cited were trade unions, garden and *dacha* cooperatives, veterans' associations, disabled people's NGOs, consumer unions and residents' associations. And after all of these came charities per se.

The Public Chamber system is now providing a vehicle for across-the-country analysis of the work of CSOs and local government. Thus, a study commissioned by the Public Chamber in the Siberian federal region (*okrug*) in 2010 reports on the number of registered NGOs, analysing them by type and sector, and devotes whole chapters to the activities of political parties, youth movements, trade unions and veterans' associations. The report shows that civil society development in Siberia is as uneven as it is across Russia. For example, anti-corruption committees were reported to be active in the Siberian cities of Omsk, Krasnoyarsk and Irkutsk. Budget hearings and citizens' audits took place in several areas – for example, in Altai region in the discussion of a new federal law, 'On the Police'. By contrast, there is still no public chamber in the Autonomous Republic of Buryatia.[15]

According to the umbrella NGO Association for Social Information (ASI), public chambers should be seen as a kind of bridge between the government and the people.[16] They are 'invited spaces' with a mainly top-down function – but they can be used, for example, to lobby on environmental issues with private sector companies. An example of this can be seen in Siberia, where quite suddenly a broad coalition came into being to oppose a new oil pipeline being laid on the northern shore of Lake Baikal. Victory in the campaign 'Baikal is More Important than Oil' against proposals by Russian oil company Yukos and its successor Transneft was due not just to the citizens' and environmental groups who organized meetings and collected thousands of signatures to oppose the plan, but also to local government leaders who decided to support them. In April 2006 Putin responded to local pressure by ordering the rerouting of the pipeline.

Health and social sector programmes in the Urals VSO's volunteer programme in Russia closed in 2003. In nine years of work in the country, ninety-five volunteers completed one- or two-year placements in as many Russian partner organizations. In addition, some thirty young people completed shorter assignments as project assistants in twenty organizations. By this time, so VSO reasoned, Russia was beginning to recover from the worst of the crisis; and poverty in Russia, while serious, was not as deep as in other countries of the world where the international volunteers were working. The funding for eastern Europe and FSU was drying up, too; in the UK, the Department for International Development and Charity Know How had reduced commitments significantly, in Russia the Ford and Soros Foundations did likewise. The Bearr Trust, a coordinating body for British NGOs working in Russia, which had given professional support to many a placement and project in Russia, was also feeling the pinch.

On the programme side, there had been considerable frustration among both VSO volunteers and staff with the slow pace of change at some placements – especially the big-city and provincial hospitals in the Urals with their bureaucracy and Soviet style of working.[17] It was also an expensive operation – almost all the volunteers required the services of a translator to deliver training sessions and engage in technical discussions with their Russian colleagues.

How does one assess the impact of social and health programmes such as those described in this chapter? Achieving results and then measuring them was a challenge and a dilemma for almost all the development agencies working in Russia at that time, because of the complexity of the political, social and economic changes going on at the time – and the sheer size of the country.[18] One way of expressing the dilemma is to say that foreign-funded programmes had two choices: either they focused on Moscow and never reached the provinces; or they piloted innovation in the provinces but never conquered the centre ...

And yet there were significant changes. Three years after the programme closed, I myself visited several organizations where VSO volunteers had served. In Cheliabynsk, a visit to the city NGO resource centre which volunteers helped to set up revealed that it now employed more than ten staff and worked mainly with disability groups. Relations with the authorities were good and in 2006 the city for the first time organized its own grants programme for NGOs. An HIV/AIDS project where British volunteers once provided staff training and health education for young people had expanded significantly. It was about to open a drop-in centre with a flat for HIV sufferers funded from local sources.

In Yekaterinburg the story was similar. Thus, the NGO Global Family Centre was able to quote benefits from a volunteer placement in community development approaches and the creation of a resource library. Like many in the first generation of NGO activists, the director was now in an influential position – as chair of the city's NGO forum. This body had 100 member organizations and was actively involved in partnership discussions with the authorities; she was pleased that lobbying had led to the inclusion of work with civil society in the city's strategic plan to the year 2015.

Just as encouraging was a meeting at Sverdlovsk Oblast Hospital

No. 1, where a large number of international health volunteers served over a period of more than five years. A senior doctor here called the volunteers 'precursors of reform'. They had trained lots of young nurses but, she admitted, once the nurses went back to the wards it was hard for them to fight the old systems and habits. In her opinion, one of the most important issues raised by volunteers was how to improve communication with patients. She herself had just published a booklet for the Health Ministry as guidance on this topic – based on VSO materials – that would be available all around the country. She was now piloting the family doctor system (another institutional innovation based on international experience). Owing to progress in decentralizing Russia's health system, most health authorities in the Urals region had been able to go ahead and open family practices – many of them in newly equipped units.

Conclusion

The analysis and case studies provided above show the importance of development work at local level. Indeed, for many of the protagonists the practical benefits are all that matter; they are cynical or agnostic about politicians and what goes on at the centre. But if we look at the broader sweep of things, we can see that the work of civil society, even if on a small scale and indirectly, can help to build the base for a more democratic and just society. By enabling citizens to meet, exchange ideas and organize collectively, it builds trust and mutual assistance mechanisms. In the 1990s, the work began with individuals, helping them to regain confidence and interest in society around them, assisting them in setting up a wide range of new organizations. In the 2000s, we see the development of networks and wider associations, the adoption of new laws and government mechanisms without which higher-level gains cannot be achieved.

How can the gap be reduced between advanced and less advanced elements in civil society or in government? Or the inequalities that we have seen above on poverty and human development indices? This is a complex issue. One example from the NGO material above: a coalition called 'Regions' has recently been set up to campaign for more attention to organizations and issues outside Russia's two biggest cities; representatives of the coalition are now actively lobbying for equal access to government funds. Seemingly in response to concerns expressed, the government announced in April 2010 the creation of a new fund for socially oriented organizations. But the problems are much deeper, and often individuals and communities have had to resort to protest action or campaigns that go to the heart of the system. This is a topic for later chapters in this book.

6 | DEVELOPMENT CHALLENGES IN AN INSECURE NEIGHBOURHOOD: TAJIKISTAN

In Chapters 2 and 3, we looked at the Eastern- and Western- facing aspects of the 1917 revolution and Bolshevik policy in the 1920s and 1930s, noting the importance of Lenin's national policy and the commitment to extensive infrastructure and industrial development in the most distant parts of the USSR. The huge efforts made by the populations of Central Asia before the Second World War were beginning to pay off in terms of social and economic development by the end of the 1950s. However, at the same time bureaucratization had set in across the union republics, with party and national elites feeling increasingly comfortable with the privileges they had accumulated. Gorbachev's *perestroika* challenged this. At the same time, nationalist and anti-socialist movements gained strength in many parts of the Soviet Union, especially the Baltic states and Caucasus. In Central Asia, the process of disintegration proceeded more slowly (though we saw in Chapters 3 and 4 that Russian colonialism and Soviet 'administrative assault' had their opponents here, too).

The sudden collapse of the Soviet state in 1989–91 led immediately to bloodshed in the farthermost parts of the union – including areas that had not been in the vanguard of anti-Soviet nationalism. Armenia and Azerbaijan found themselves at war over the enclaves of Navchivegan and Nagorno-Karabakh;[1] and Tajikistan suffered the most serious internecine violence of all, during the civil war of 1992–97 in which 70,000 people are estimated to have lost their lives.

This chapter is about development issues in Tajikistan, the poorest of the ex-Soviet republics, about the role played by Russia in Tajikistan since 1991, about civil society, economic crisis and migration from Tajikistan to Russia today. What has happened in Tajikistan says a lot about Russia's influence in its traditional 'backyard' in the new political and economic environment. Indeed, we will argue that finding a common approach and understanding with its Central Asian neighbours is essential for Russia's own modernization strategy.

1 Tajikistan and Russia in the 1990s

In the first half of the 1990s, the five ex-Soviet republics of Central Asia did not figure highly in Russia's political priorities, certainly lower than the Slavic republics or the Caucasus. In fact, with the exception of Kazakhstan (because of its large ethnic Russian population), Russia seems to have tried to ignore Central Asia, possibly in the hope that the USSR's previous commitments (subsidies of up to 40 per cent of GDP in Central Asia) would no longer be required. And in general, the 1990s was a decade when the view that the Soviet Union had been 'too generous' with its aid to foreign countries and its poorer neighbours within the USSR became very prevalent.

The pro-Western trend dominated in Russian politics at the start of the 1990s, but with a huge diversity of opinion on economic, social and military issues. It was only after the political elite realized that sufficient support was not going to become available from the USA or Europe to solve its multiple crises that they turned their attention back to the post-Soviet space. Russia's priorities at this time included the need to find a new defence strategy together with whichever of the ex-republics was prepared to join one. This imperative gradually overcame the preference of the *perestroika* elite not to work closely with the Central Asian states because their leaders were not in the 'democratic' camp. Indeed, apart from the democratic/Islamic opposition in Tajikistan and President Askar Akayev in Kyrgyzstan, all the leaders in the region were closely associated with the previous communist regime.

Another reason advanced for collaboration with the conservative, authoritarian regimes of Central Asia was the need to prevent 'old enemies' from gaining a foothold in the region (e.g. the Turks and British). This argument gained support from groups which were otherwise not much interested in Central Asia – e.g. the Slavophile wing in Russian politics. The debate about what to do with Central Asia reflected the ongoing discussion about whether Russia was part of the European world or a Eurasian state attempting to bridge West and East.

In the early 1990s, Russia's strategy for the newly created Commonwealth of Independent States (CIS) was quite vague and reactive. Yeltsin's government concentrated on creating bilateral relations with its neighbours, ignoring calls for restoration of complex Soviet-era economic links or requests for more aid (though significant debts incurred by the republics in the Soviet period were written off). Apart from economic questions, three other issues weighed heavily on the minds of Russian policy-makers: first, how to ensure the security of ethnic Russians living in those countries; second, how to prevent the spread of terrorism and drug trafficking from Afghanistan, where following the Soviet pull-out in 1989 Russia's ally Hafizullah Amin lost out to the Taliban in 1996; third, and linked directly to this, a fear about the spread of Islamic extremism.

How to respond to political Islam had become an urgent issue for Russia's leadership with the outbreak of civil war in Tajikistan in 1992. Sviagelskaia (1995) divides Russian approaches to this problem at that time into three main schools. She describes the first group as 'alarmists' – those who saw the whole of Central Asia as a breeding ground for militants and all Islamic movements as 'fundamentalist'. Both Slavic-Orthodox nationalists and pro-Western liberals or Atlanticists could be found in this school. A second group was made up of 'rejectionists' – those who argued that Central Asia was so deeply secularized during the Soviet time that any re-Islamization would take a long time. This blended well with the view that Russia could afford to let the region go its own way.

The author herself belonged to a third category that she called 'realists'. This group included orientalists, historians and ethnographers, who in her words

> do not see anything tragic in the apparent move of the Central
> Asian republics towards the Muslim world, do not consider
> Islamic fundamentalism to be the only and inevitable alternative
> in the development of the local societies, are far from ascribing
> to Islam anti-Russian or anti-Orthodox moods that are alien to
> it, and do not see Russia as an outpost of the Christian world
> advanced into the enormous world of Islam, rightly pointing to
> Russia's own Christian and Islamic character. Muslims in CIS total
> some 60 million; in Russia 13 million ... (Ibid.: 11)

The 'realists' did not immediately get the ear of the foreign policy decision-makers. Indeed, Russia was experiencing difficulty in letting go of its 'imperial visions' and – after the Gorbachev détente period, which seemed to have led to national disaster – it was extremely difficult for people up and down the country to get away from the feeling that the country was surrounded by enemies. Key elements of Yeltsin's foreign policy doctrine reflect his unhappy experiences during the 1990s – from the country's marginalization in key international forums, to the West's bombing of Serbia in the face of strong Russian opposition.

The foreign policy concepts drawn up by Yeltsin were not substantially changed by Putin – although the latter's manner of speaking is more hawkish. Russia has a complex or dual position on many key issues – e.g. friendly to the European Union (with which it early on signed a partnership and cooperation agreement) but hostile to NATO, while both these organizations are expanding into the ex-Soviet space. After 9/11 Putin took the decision to cooperate with the US-led invasion of Afghanistan, allowing NATO to overfly Russia and to set up US airbases in Kyrgyzstan and Uzbekistan for the movement of troops and supplies into Afghanistan. Petrovsky (2007) refers to a secret document adopted in September 2002 at the Russia–NATO Council on the political aspects of international peacekeeping activities in Central Asia. It is clearly in Russia's security interests that the situation in the region is not destabilized, and if the USA and NATO were willing to pay for the war on the Taliban there was likely a cynical view in the Russian military that they should be allowed to try. But others would argue – this author among them – that the Afghanistan war has been a disaster and a destabilizing not stabilizing factor throughout the region.

Russia, Islam and the Tajik civil war Try as peace lovers and 'realists' do to argue against it, we have in FSU, as in the West, a coupling of the terms 'security problem' and 'Islam'.[2] This is despite many factors in the history of Islam and Christianity in Central Asia as elsewhere that demonstrate the potential and actuality of peaceful coexistence between the two religions. Thus, the Muslim conquerors of Central Asia some 1,400 years ago belonged to the Hanafi school, considered one of the most moderate currents in Islam. From the start, the impact of Islam varied greatly – more in urban settlements, less in nomadic communities – but none of the feudal regimes in the region ever adopted a theocratic mode of governance. Nor did the Russian conquest of Central Asia in the eighteenth and nineteenth centuries have a missionary purpose; indeed, the Orthodox Church followed the soldiers and administrators into the new colonies, but its role was mostly to serve the settler communities rather than to win new believers. The Russian Tsars preferred not to interfere in the mosques or in Islamic culture and educational life. As we have seen above, Islamic ideas continued to evolve during the Tsarist period, producing reform movements like the Jadidists which had an important potential in Russia (Sagdeev 2000; Roy 2000: 143–60).

The Bolsheviks were more radical in their attack on religion and largely succeeded in controlling Islam through its official leaders and representatives.[3] However, a parallel 'folk Islam' existed alongside official religion, in families and communities, through a kind of *samizdat* of religious texts and sermons. After independence, there was an 'Islamic boom' across the FSU region, just like the 'Orthodox boom'. A split between traditional and radical Islam had begun to take shape in the 1980s as the Central Asian republics gradually opened up to the Muslim world through a variety of cultural and educational exchange programmes. The Tajik civil war saw thousands of young Muslim oppositionists go into exile in Afghanistan and Iran; also the creation of the Islamic Revival Party (IRP), which first went into government with the ruling elite, then – through its military arm – led the opposition during the main hostilities. But still, Akbar Turanjonzoda, the country's leading cleric, has often repeated that the IRP has no intention of creating a theocratic fundamentalist state.

Owing to civil war, development in post-independence Tajikistan began several years later than in the other countries of Central Asia. The war had proceeded unevenly but with huge loss of life and destruction to infrastructure and property. In the first phase of hostilities, an alliance between Democrats and Islamists was able to mobilize opposition to the communist authorities and even to present a popular presidential candidate for the elections in autumn 1991. His failure to win the election did not prevent a steady escalation of protests, including a two-month rally outside the Communist Party Central Committee building in Dushanbe in spring 1992. Reconciliation talks that summer could not prevent a breakdown in law and order, the formation of a variety of criminal groups, the collapse of municipal services and the beginnings of armed clashes. The Democrats and Islamists were strong in the centre of the country (e.g. the city of Kofarnikon, home to Akbar Turajonzoda), in the high-mountain region of Gorno-Badakhshan in the south-east, and in Garm in the north. The government forces, now reorganized as a Popular Front with Russian and Uzbek support, dominated in urban, more industrialized areas like Leninabad in the Ferghana Valley, Dushanbe and the southern region of Kulyab. The man who came to be president at the end of the peace process, Emomali Rakhmonov, a former collective farm director, was from the town of Dangara in Kulyab region; and from this time, many say that a Kulyab elite (or mafia) has controlled Tajikistan.

Tajikistan was ravaged by civil war all through the second half of 1992, until the Popular Front forces reconquered areas held by the opposition and forced hundreds of thousands into exile. A peace-keeping force was created, led by Russian troops, and talks began in Moscow in April 1994. However, progress towards the setting up of a Council of National Accord was slow – seriously denting Russia's claims to effective leadership in the CIS. During the negotiations, field commanders of whatever affiliation did their best to clear 'their' terri-tory of opposition elements and consolidate military and economic gains from the war. Key factories such as the aluminium plant at Tursunzade were a fierce battleground as different factions tried to gain control. By the time a General Accord was signed in Moscow in June 1997, seventy years of Soviet development in Tajikistan had gone into reverse. As Sviagelskaia wrote in a typical comment that year, civil war 'has hurled Tajikistan back economically, socially and culturally ... [It] has practically been pushed back to the stage of semi-feudal relations' (1997: 26). Meanwhile many foreign commentators looked forward to the beginning of a new 'great game' in Central Asia (Rashid 1994, 2002). That is, to a new competition for power and influence in the region on the part of outside powers.

Military assistance from Russia to Tajikistan since independence has been critical at several stages. For example, in 1999/2000 this included repair of Zenit rockets that had fallen victim to scrap metal hunters during the civil war years. In 2005/06 Moscow gave Tajikistan US$26 million in military aid, including M1 helicopter and warplanes. In 2007, a large part of the famous 201st Motorized Division (long stationed on the country's southern border) was transferred to the Tajikistan army.[4]

Islam and political struggle elsewhere in the Russian Federation: a comparison. In the 1990s, the Yeltsin regime faced a number of challenges to the continued viability or existence of the Russian Federation. We have mentioned the pressure for regional autonomy in Urals and Siberia already. If we look at areas with a Muslim population, two examples have a special significance. First, the Tatars were once again in the forefront in the struggle for national self-determination and religious freedom. In fact, they won a referendum on sovereignty early in Yeltsin's rule, which their leader, Mintimer Shamiev, used to lever significant rights in domestic policy within Tatarstan (he also managed to sideline the republic's main radical Islamic party). The Tatars in this way managed to come to an accommodation with the federal authorities in Russia.

In Chechnya, by contrast, the struggle between traditionalists and radicals was more bitter and violent. The colonization of the northern Caucasus region during the nineteenth century was extremely bloody, and in the Soviet period Islam was held down in Chechnya much as in other parts of the USSR. The republic's bid for independence in the 1990s led to the 1st Chechen War, when nationalist leaders appealed to the wider Muslim world for support and millions of dollars and significant numbers of young fighters arrived in the northern Caucasus, significantly altering the balance in favour of radical Wahhabi sects, such as the one led by Shamil Basaev. After huge destruction and loss of life, Yeltsin made a deal to stop that war and Russian money began to flow into Chechnya for rebuilding programmes – but large amounts were diverted to the insurgents. The 2nd Chechen War, launched by Putin after Basaev's incursion into neighbouring Dagestan and explosions in several apartment blocks in Moscow, was just as bloody as the first. It also led to further splits within the Muslim camp in Chechnya, where leading cleric Ahmed Kadirov led the traditional wing (until his assassination at a May Day parade). And then his son took charge.

2 Tradition versus modernization in Tajikistan after the civil war

Secular and civil society forces are engaged in a long-drawn-out moral, ideological and political contest for hegemony with conservative Islam in Tajikistan. As part of the National Accord that ended the civil war, Rakhmonov's National Democratic Party became

TABLE 6.1 Some statistics from Tajikistan human development reports

Indicator	Score
Population	7.3 million (2009)
Urban/rural	26% urban, 74% rural
Average income	$2,200 GDP per capita. In 2006, it was only 85% of its level at the start of the 1990s
Life expectancy male/female	67.1 years combined; 63.9 years men, 70.5 years women
Child mortality	37 deaths per 1,000 children (2012)
Unemployment	2.4% officially. Large numbers employed in subsistence farming
Access to drinking water	58%
Pollution	Main problems around aluminium plant at Tursunzoda which accounts for 40% of the country's exports

Note: If we compare this table with the figures for Perm (a 'typical' Russian *oblast*) given in the previous chapter, we see 1) a major difference in the breakdown of urban and rural population; 2) life expectancy in Perm is slightly lower than in Tajikistan, but its child mortality is one tenth of Tajikistan's; 3) GDP per capita in Perm is eight times higher than in Tajikistan.

the main political force in the country, with the Islamic Revival Party a coalition partner assured of 30 per cent of official positions at all levels in government. The IRP's position in government is unique for a religious party in FSU, but nonetheless the party has found it hard to develop coherent economic and social policies and programmes with which to face the ruinous position Tajikistan found itself in after the war.

Indeed, it is tragic that fifteen years after the signing of the peace accord the situation as regards social and economic indicators is still so difficult in Tajikistan. In a recent paper, Saodat Olimova from the Dushanbe-based research agency Sharq noted some of the main economic and human resource problems: 1) Decline in the education system – in length of schooling, attendance rates (especially for girls and children from rural areas) and the quality of services offered. The percentage of GDP spent on education was 9.7 in 1991; over the next twenty years the percentage was halved; 2) Deindustrialization

– only 20 per cent of factories operating in Soviet times are left today. Changes in the structure of the economy mean a reduction in sectors where highly skilled workers are required and an increase in those requiring fewer skills (services, the bazaar); 3) Deurbanization – as wages disappeared, families returned to the countryside to engage in subsistence farming. The percentage of the population living in urban areas has dropped from 33 to 26; 4) Demographic growth, leading to huge pressure for school places. All in all, there is a serious decline in the human capital available for development (Olimova and Olimov 2014).

From the late 1990s a huge humanitarian effort began, bringing food, medical and other essential supplies into Tajikistan, and agencies from the USA, Europe and elsewhere began to play an important role in the country's reconstruction. The author began work with INTRAC's civil society development programme inside Tajikistan in mid-2002. In the first five years, training was offered to a range of NGO resource centres and research organizations around the country; in the second five years, the focus was on a smaller number of local NGOs working on poverty reduction and gender equality issues. The following are some of the main effects of civil war and economic collapse as seen from the civil society sector:

- Demoralization and passivity among the population. Some say that dependent, passive attitudes were engendered by the Soviet welfare system; others argue that they were encouraged by the distribution of free food and other goods during and after the civil war. Or indeed by payments by international agencies for labour on development projects that might otherwise have been contributed voluntarily via traditional mutual help mechanisms.
- Increasing isolation of individuals, families, villages and regions from one another. The heritage of the civil war (old enmities, clan allegiances, lines of defence and solidarity) is not always visible to foreign aid workers and the Tajik population prefers not to talk about the war – except in their own tight family circles. Professional and secular networks were weaker in Tajikistan than in other, more developed parts of the USSR, and in the 1990s they declined fast. Instead, kinship and money-based networks took over.

- Another security problem worries the development agencies – no less important than the question of violence and war: food security. As the strategy moved from emergency aid and reconstruction of damaged houses, hospitals and schools towards longer-term economic development, the question in the majority of rural areas was – what kind of agriculture to support? Agencies like Christian Aid, Oxfam, Mercy Corps, CARE International and others invested large sums of money in agricultural diversification – that is, supporting *dekhan* (small) farmers in growing fruit and vegetables on their family plots or other land rented from the local authorities. Comparatively little attention seems to have been paid to other major players in agriculture – the old collective farms, engaged mainly in cotton and wheat production – except inasmuch as most international agencies lobbied hard for land privatization (that is, the breaking up of the farms and the cotton monopoly).

- A slow rate of civil society development. Ten years after the civil war ended, civil society organizations faced a number of challenges. Many of them are stuck in the role of subcontractors to the international agencies, providing jobs and outlets for the professional skills of the old Soviet intelligentsia but unable to develop a strong local membership or constituency. There is criticism of the artificial or externally implanted nature of some NGOs. Meanwhile, the development agencies have found other mechanisms for social mobilization around the country – including village committees with links to traditional institutions like the *mahalla*, mosque or councils of elders; or to local government institutions such as the *jamoat*.

- Environmental security risks. With half of its land 3,000 metres above sea level reaching up into the Pamirs, Tajikistan is highly vulnerable to avalanches, landslides and floods. The fear is that climate change could increase the country's vulnerability as hundreds of large and small glaciers gradually reduce in size. International agencies have invested increasingly large amounts of money in a variety of schemes to plant trees, reinforce riverbanks and inform the population about the dangers.

- A serious energy crisis. With only a few hours of electricity and gas a day in most parts of the country, Tajikistan is suffering from increasingly high prices for imported energy, the gradual deterioration of the old regional energy grid, and the hostility of its neighbour Uzbekistan to proposed new hydroelectric projects. Meanwhile development agencies are trying to promote alternative and renewable sources.

Many of the development projects in the areas listed above are quite small-scale. Indeed, local or bottom-up initiatives directly involving citizens' groups and communities are often the most effective form of development assistance and cooperation. But two observations can be made about the wider context in which they sit. First, development projects are increasingly subject to the security and foreign policy concerns of donor governments and the policies of multilateral international agencies such as the UN and World Bank. Second, the world of 'international development' seems to exist in a completely different box to the contributions made by non-Western governments to Tajikistan. The efforts of Russian soldiers guarding Tajikistan's southern border, the investments made by Iran to build a tunnel through the Pamirs from Dushanbe to Khojend in the north, the armies of Chinese labourers improving the country's major roads – all these efforts exist in a different space from Western-funded development programmes. Is there cooperation, coexistence or simply geopolitical competition between the donors? From a practitioner's viewpoint, it is hard to tell, since we never see the protagonists in one room together.

Governance issues and risky initiatives If we go back to the global critique of the development industry, we will remember the point that programmes come and go, even some economic growth is recorded, but the inequality between rich and poor nations does not seem to reduce. The impression grows that the roles of donor and recipient are there for ever; indeed, it suits both sides to maintain the status quo (De Rivero 2001). Thus, donor governments can show their generous nature and abundance of good advice and practice, while the developing countries make a long-term resource mobilization strategy out of their problems. This analysis applies to both Kyrgyzstan and Tajikistan.[5] In 2007, Tajikistan had to accept an official downgrading of its status from 'transition' to 'developing' country. That is to say, it fell out of the company of those attempting a short-term adaptation to the capitalist economy, into the larger group of countries fated to struggle longer and harder to get out of the mess they are in.

Anna Matveeva (2008) has charted in detail the path taken by President Rakhmonov and his government since the end of the civil war. While this remains effectively a one-party, one-man regime, there are other aspects that deserve attention. The coalition with a legal Islamic political party is one of them. So too is the success of the regime in limiting armed incursions from the south or insurrection from within. The president came through a presidential election during the civil war and a referendum in 2003 allowing him to stay in power for two seven-year periods (winning again in late 2013). His government escapes more serious criticism from the international agencies because of its location and geopolitical importance next to Afghanistan (Heathershaw 2010). External or internal critics from the democracy or human rights lobby notwithstanding, a kind of agreement has been made at a very high level not to rock the boat.

Observing all this on regular visits over ten years to Tajikistan, it is clear that – as in Kyrgyzstan – national government has limited room for manoeuvre. This is not to excuse the cronyism and corruption that undoubtedly exist on a large scale, but simply to state the underlying weakness of the government's position. Two examples may illustrate this point. The first concerns the proposed hydroelectric dam at Rogun. Given the dire energy situation facing almost all households in Tajikistan, this is potentially a vital and popular project. Not only could it meet consumer and business needs, but Tajikistan could also sell energy to its neighbours. Like any big dam in a region subject to earthquakes, it is an environmentally sensitive project – but to the country's credit you can find articles written by experts arguing both ways on it in the local press.[6] Several years ago, President Rakhmonov[7] organized a public campaign to sell shares in the Rogun Dam – in fact he forced the population to buy them (via deductions from their pay and other measures). But then, after pressure from downstream Uzbekistan and Kazakhstan, Rakhmonov was forced to allow an international environmental assessment of the dam. So here one can see a high-risk strategy – the active promotion of a major development project that could be cancelled or delayed indefinitely.

A second example once again shows attempts to set the national agenda and the problems involved. Rakhmonov and his ministers are involved in a long-drawn-out battle to limit the influence of Islam in society. This has many different angles, from military actions against Islamic militants infiltrating the country from Afghanistan, to the registration of mosques and restrictions on what is preached within them, to the campaign for a secular-style school uniform and against Islamic headgear for girls. On almost all these issues there is an opposition – both among secular and religious elements. The manner in which the initiatives are posed is often quite provocative (as were measures imposed a few years ago to limit the number of people attending weddings and funerals[8]). There are in fact very important principles at stake here, and in some cases one can agree with the president. But it is questionable how effective bans like these are in changing public opinion, and these are risky moves in a political system that is not truly democratic.

3 Economic crisis and migration as a safety valve

The conclusions of the analysis in the first part of this chapter are not so encouraging for supporters of modernization and people-oriented, secular development. It is clear that from 1991 not enough time or money was invested in Tajikistan to meet the country's problems.[9] The president and Islamic opposition both deserve credit for their peacekeeping efforts, but the ideological stand-off between the secular and religious authorities is unresolved. Only a stronger civil society including active religious as well as secular associations can help reach common ground on key points. Tajikistan is in a geographical cul-de-sac and destabilized by war on its borders. In the economy we see development in reverse.

The financial crisis in the Western capitals in 2008/09, as a leading Tajik economist put it, 'laid bare the negative consequences of economic reforms in the post-Soviet space ...'. The reforms continue to this day, but he and many others consider that they were wrong from the start, comparing the devastation of the FSU economies with Vietnam and China, where the state has maintained a more ordered, rational development process; or even with countries like Bolivia, which have had the courage to turn away from dependence on Western-dominated economic institutions and policies. Left-leaning analysts have a different view from that of the neoliberal international agencies. They argue that rather than being too state-controlled, Tajikistan is more vulnerable to global financial processes than the USA, the UK, etc. (see Umarov 2010).

At the end of the 2000s, many people were still experiencing alienation, unhappiness and a loss of bearings in Tajik society. While official statistics report growth at around 5–7 per cent annually, the population sees only economic deterioration or collapse. Sociological surveys report that people feel that luck is more important now than hard work; that they are being forced to do things that they don't agree with. Their family and local community are still the most important institutions for more than 85 per cent of the population – no other institution gets more than 10 per cent of votes. Ten years after the end of the civil war, around 50 per cent of the population was still seriously affected by poverty. The market economy had made inroads but the level of technological and daily operational change was still quite limited for the general population. For example, only 5 per cent of people had a bank account or credit card. Some 60 per cent still depended on a household plot for part of their weekly food intake.[10]

Men and women in Tajikistan came to their own conclusions about the economic situation long before the policy-makers and donors. As soon as civil war ended they began to vote with their feet and move out of Tajikistan in search of work (and the refugees among them even earlier). And their main destination was Russia – Moscow, St Petersburg, Novosibirsk, Yekaterinburg and other urban centres. From 2000 until the economic crisis in 2008, sharply rising oil and gas prices produced strong year-on-year growth in Russia, creating huge demand for migrant labour from Central Asia's poorer republics.[11]

On current estimates, there are close to 700,000 migrants from Tajikistan working in the Russian Federation, alongside similar numbers from Uzbekistan and Kyrgyzstan, though it is hard to be exact because so many enter the country though informal channels. From the development angle, migrant labour has made a vital contribution to stabilizing the economy in Central Asia itself. Thus in the period 2005–08, remittances (money sent home by migrants to their families) were reckoned by the IMF to account for half of all poverty reduction in Tajikistan. There was a real worry that the world economic slowdown would badly affect migrants in Russia – with employment sectors like construction especially vulnerable. Significant reductions in remittances would indeed have had a serious effect back home in Tajikistan – but this didn't really happen ... On the contrary, remittances to the three Central Asian 'sending' countries in 2011 rose by more than 20 per cent above the previous year, and were predicted to rise by another 13 per cent in 2012.[12]

As in western Europe, immigrants in Russia are filling the gap caused by a gradually ageing population. Predictions regarding the rate of decline vary, but according to the World Bank, Russia faces a deficit of 25 million workers by the year 2025, despite the pro-natalist policies pursued by Putin's government.[13] Russia's Federal Migration Service emphasizes the need for skilled workers, but many of those arriving from Central Asia are less qualified.

A portrait of Tajik migrants in Moscow A study carried out in Moscow in 2009 (Zaionchovskaya et al.) showed the contribution that Tajik migrants (estimated as 100,000 people) make to the economy and the multicultural character of Russia's capital. The survey revealed that the overwhelming majority of migrants had come to Russia to work. They chose Moscow because of family or friends already living in the city, believing it would therefore be easier to find a job. One in six had Russian citizenship. Some 80 per cent had registered for work while 20 per cent were illegal migrants. Experts interviewed for the study gave the opinion that there was a positive tendency towards registration at this time.

According to the Federal Migration Service, some 40 per cent of Tajik workers in Russia in 2007 were employed in construction, 15 per cent in the wholesale and retail trade, 10 per cent in housing departments, the rest in agriculture, transport and other sectors. A common feature is that migrants work in jobs demanding considerably lower educational and vocational qualifications than they possess (ibid.: 177–81). Almost half those who had been in Moscow for a longer time had experienced discrimination or prejudice in searching for a flat, and a similar amount on public transport, but less when looking for employment.

How should migration be organized, to ensure the best results for the receiving community and migrants themselves? Should it be done officially via a planned approach (*orgnabor*)? Can it be left to private sector employment agencies? In 2011, trade union representatives estimated that fewer than 5 per cent of migrants working in Russia had come through official channels – that is, work opportunities posted in colleges, employment exchanges, health centres and the like. Most still use family links or the services of an informal co-ordinator or *brigadir*. And the reason, they argued, is simple. Poverty makes people migrate, and poverty means that at home in Tajikistan they are busy earning enough for their next meal, supporting their family and gathering the minimum resources with which to travel.[14] Undoubtedly the system needs to be improved. Some local authorities in Russia are creating their own channels to attract labour from Central Asia, filling jobs in particular industrial sectors, with housing guaranteed. And NGOs are involved actively on the sending side, particularly with regard to health issues and employment rights.

Language is a big issue – not so much for the older generation, who even in distant or rural areas of FSU tend to have sufficient Russian, but definitely for younger migrants. The position of the Federal Migration Service in Russia is that the language learning should begin before the migrant leaves Tajikistan; in 2012, attending classes in basic Russian language became compulsory. And representatives from legal aid centres in Dushanbe agree: without a knowledge of Russian, the migrant is locked into the closed world of the diaspora and 90 per cent of migrants experience exploitation within this world.[15]

Indeed, the exploitation of migrant labour and the conditions under which migrants work are also big issues in the sending and receiving countries. News items with titles like 'Modern slavery' are standard in Central Asia: for example, a typical article claims that thousands of people have been lured from Tajikistan to Russia by false promises and have become victims of exploitation, both in the cities and in seasonal agricultural work in the south.[16] Corruption in the law enforcement agencies complicates efforts to monitor the situation and punish the traffickers. Russian trade unions complain about wage undercutting by unscrupulous employers, plus the poor safety conditions in construction and other sectors.

Violence against Central Asian immigrants is a very worrying phenomenon in Russia, fitting into a pattern of racist attacks on other ethnic minorities (from the Russian far north, Caucasus, China, Africa and so on). Harrowing stories have been reported in detail in the Tajik press, and the consular departments of all the Central Asian countries in Moscow and other cities are under great pressure to monitor the situation, help victims and their families, and put pressure on the Russian authorities to clamp down on the skinheads and far-right extremists who are responsible for many of the attacks.[17] The problem of racist violence and inter-ethnic tension reached the national level in Russia after the disturbances between football supporters and national minority groups in Manezh Square in central Moscow in 2011. Both Putin (then prime minister) and President Medvedev made statements condemning the violence and calling for greater understanding. At local level, state grants are being awarded to NGOs working on tolerance issues. The media, too, have a big role to play – for example, the CIS-wide TV company Mir.

Zaionchovskaya's study asked migrants whether they intended to take Russian citizenship and stay longer. An important point here is that until quite recently most citizens of the former Soviet republics had the right to take up Russian citizenship (it is a situation quite different from that facing ex-colonial peoples migrating to the European Union, for example). Most respondents in this study intended to stay only temporarily, but those who had already been in Moscow for three to five years were slightly more inclined to remain longer and bring their families out to join them. A survey carried out three years later, in 2012, revealed that now more than half of migrants from Tajikistan plan to stay in Russian permanently, but low pay delays families from reuniting. Only 7 per cent of respondents were earning more than 30,000 roubles per month, with 15 per cent being paid less than 15,000 roubles per month (US$1,000 and 500 respectively).[18]

The conclusion from this study was overall a positive one. Yes, Tajik immigrants suffer poor living conditions and some hostility from the host community, but many of them have gained an education or new work experience and skills. They have improved their standard of living, mix freely and make friends with Russians, are open to mixed-nationality relationships and try to use the cultural benefits of urban life. They send back vitally needed money to their families in Tajikistan and keep their country on its feet. This is what we mean by describing the migration to Russia as a 'safety-valve'. It has taken some of the pressure off the Tajikistan government, which otherwise might have been faced with serious social unrest.

4 Prospects for development in Tajikistan today

There are many areas of life where Russia has an institutional base and huge influence in Central Asia. Among these are the education and health systems, built up in Soviet times and run by staff that understand and respect Soviet-era practice. Russia's own higher education system still offers some opportunities to students from the ex-republics. The Russian language enjoys a privileged status in most countries of FSU (it is the working language for many international development programmes too). In law and public administration the Russian and Soviet heritage is still very strong – the basic framework in many of these areas has survived surprisingly intact since 1991, and new laws and regulations have to fit in with it – even in new areas like registration or freedoms for NGOs.

However, this heritage is under attack from many quarters – quite simply, it faces strong competition from other regions and countries in the globalizing world. The view of Olivier Roy in *The New Central Asia* was that the states of the region will gradually delink from Russia, and that this is partly because the Soviets made no attempt to establish a permanent Russian elite in the region (2000: 105–7).[19] There were almost five million Russians (along with large German and Ukrainian communities) living in Central Asia at the end of the Soviet period, but they have gradually gone home, leaving huge gaps in many industrial and professional sectors. In Tajikistan the proportion of Russians in the population declined from 7 per cent to less than 1 per cent by 2010. Roy concluded that Russia has failed in the task of setting up a modern sphere of influence, owing principally to a lack of economic tools or reliable allies among the political parties operating in Central Asia (ibid.: 195–7).

The role of regional associations in CIS Roy's first book came out in 2000. Has the situation changed since the early 2000s? Against Roy's view we need to consider Russia's attempts to set up regional associations within its FSU 'backyard'. Any form of wider association is of potential use to Tajikistan in its cul-de-sac situation, hemmed in by unhelpful Uzbekistan to the north and warring Afghanistan to the south.

The overarching collective institution in FSU is the Commonwealth of Independent States (CIS). The experience of post-colonial situations around the world suggests that this kind of organization can indeed play an important political/cultural role and provide entry points to the Western metropolis. However, the CIS is certainly not a driver of development yet. Judging from the press in FSU, most observers are of the opinion that their new Commonwealth is too bureaucratic and top-down in its approach, unable to mobilize popular support despite the clear message from public opinion surveys that ex-Soviet citizens would like to stay connected with each other.

According to Russian foreign policy expert Vladimir Petrovsky (2007), to gain more public confidence, the CIS would have to give its parliamentary assembly and executive organs more power. Greater integration within CIS is unlikely unless issues of identity, culture and education, and free movement of peoples across borders are dealt with more directly and energetically. At present, CIS declarations on rights are not followed up by actions, so the Commonwealth has not become the 'common home' for its peoples that was originally envisaged. Petrovsky stresses the importance of the human dimension and a greater focus on personal security of citizens, based on new social policy and network cooperation with all sectors. Perhaps, he says, a 'group of wise men' could help move the CIS forward ... (ibid.: 77).

On the economic side, Tajikistan was from the very start in 1996 involved in discussions around a possible customs union in FSU and the development of a Eurasian Economic Community. However, the results of this are quite modest to date (Bykov 2009: 72–9). More has been invested in new collective security regimes in the region. Thus, the Organization for Collective Security (OCS) provides a mechanism for Russia to liaise on military matters with both Tajikistan and Kyrgyzstan. All three countries cooperate actively with the Organization for Security and Cooperation in Europe (OSCE) and the Shanghai Cooperation Organization (SCO) – the latter with China as a major partner. However, from a human development point of view the problem with security-based associations is that they tend to play to the rules and stereotypes that the armed forces and military-industrial complex have lived by – from the time of the Cold War right up to today. The security approach works against both civil society and multicultural integration.

How do these issues look in the Russian-language press in Tajikistan? An on-and-off inspection of newspapers like *Asia-Plus*, *Biznes*

I Politika and *Vecherny Dushanbe* suggests that there is a core of experienced Russian-educated local commentators who strongly oppose US policy around the world and support Russia's role in Central Asia. Most commentators express scepticism about the progress of the war in Afghanistan. A variety of articles and analyses are devoted to other players – China, Iran, Malaysia, the Arab states, etc. – reflecting the regime's attempts to gain support wherever possible. Tajikistan appears to be significantly closer to the Islamic world (especially the Farsi-speaking countries Afghanistan and Iran) than any other country in Central Asia. Relations with FSU countries are covered regularly in the Tajikistan press, with deep concern expressed about the continuing dispute with Uzbekistan. Despite its influence in both countries, Russia has been unable to resolve this dispute.

Civil society in a fragile state We can freely admit that civil society has not been able to challenge the state in Tajikistan. We can also admit that CSOs are in many cases still consigned to cleaning up the mess created by current development policy or economic globalization. A good example of the latter is the work of NGOs around migration. In Tajikistan, NGOs are not only active in informing migrants of their rights, about health risks and administrative issues of all kinds: they run a whole range of programmes to support the families left behind. Migration has contributed to an absolute reduction in the number of marriages and an increase in the number of divorces. There are inevitable problems for families that split up when the male migrant starts a new family in the receiving country. NGOs are also working hard to find ways to use remittances not just for family subsistence but for longer-term investments that would ensure sustainable livelihoods in the sending community.[20] There is increasing contact with diaspora and local NGOs in Russia's cities working with individuals and families in the receiving community.

An INTRAC report (Zharkevich 2010a) summarized the challenges facing civil society in Tajikistan in recent years. They include not just the problems of creating a proper constituency of local supporters and moving beyond the subcontractor role allotted them by international agencies, but also the problem of working with corrupt government officials and government bodies made unstable by constant personnel changes and reorganizations. CSO capacity is quite weak, and it is very difficult to sustain wider networks of the kind that could, for instance, monitor government programmes or the observance of basic citizens' rights. On the positive side, when CSOs work within the existing legal framework and focus on practical changes in legislation or services, some advance is possible (ibid.: 37–45).

If civil society is weak in Tajikistan, does that mean that the state is strong? On the one hand it seems strong – it has survived some very difficult years and the population still has some expectations that government will provide for it. On the other hand, the trend towards more authoritarian, 'strong' rule can be seen as a sign of underlying weakness. This seems to be the dominant discourse about the Central Asia region these days – that of 'fragile states' and the paramount need for maintenance of security, conflict prevention or post-conflict peace-building. Jones-Luong (2004) considers that competition between regional elites within the countries of Central Asia has been more influential than bottom-up pressures from civil society. The account we gave of events in Kyrgyzstan at the end of Chapter 4 tends to support this view; and the tensions between President Rakhmonov's Kulyab clan and the elites representing Sogdh in the north or Gorno-Badkahshan in the Pamirs are clearly very significant for Tajikistan. So it does not follow that if civil society is struggling, the state is necessarily strong. Events are moving ahead fast as the USA gradually withdraws from Afghanistan. The prospects for Tajikistan are quite unclear here, that is, whether peaceful trade to the south will open up, or whether increased instability in Afghanistan will spread north.

The issue of migration seems to sum up some of the development opportunities and challenges for Tajikistan and Russia today. Yes, migration policy and programmes have a rather tactical character, in that neither the government systems nor the population in either country was fully prepared for the changes mass migration has brought. But immigration looks like a long-term necessity for Russia, and we see the beginnings of a response to the political, social and economic challenges it raises. The question for Tajikistan is more difficult. Migration robs the country of some of its most active and ambitious people. If it was part of a development package agreed with Russia that guaranteed all-round development, perhaps this would be worth the price. But it is rather too early to say that this strategic direction exists in reality.

7 | BEYOND ALIENATION: SOCIAL MOVEMENTS AND PROTEST IN RUSSIA IN THE 2000s

1 Democracy protests on the move

The protests and demonstrations organized in Moscow and other major cities autumn 2011 and spring 2012 were some of the largest, boldest and most challenging for the political system in Russia since *perestroika*.

The demonstrations began to gather force during the election campaign for the Duma, scheduled for December 2011. This fight had a number of well-established protagonists – political parties that were already in parliament and would likely get back in, and some more marginal parties struggling to reach the threshold for entry. The dominant force was United Russia, the 'party of power'. And the Duma elections had become a prelude to a second major struggle, the presidential elections due in March 2012. During the previous year and a half, the question of which member of the Putin–Medvedev tandem would stand for president, representing centre and centre-right opinion around the country, had occupied the minds of many. Putin's decision to run again disappointed those who hoped for a more liberal line from Medvedev. While Putin's fan club (e.g. the *Nashi* youth movement) was exultant, for many others the prospect of a third Putin term, albeit legitimate in constitutional terms, raised the spectre of a long period of stagnation with few new ideas on hand.

The demonstrations against Putin and United Russia gathered force during the winter and spring. The Moscow locations for the main showdowns – Bolotnoe Square, Sakharov Avenue – are now part of the legend of protest in Russia. An estimated 60,000 turned out on 10 December, almost the same number two months later. The main message was 'Russia without Putin', with posters showing their target aged as he might be after two more six-year terms as president. Many of the slogans were home-made and as funny as they were angry. Thus one declared, 'I didn't vote for these bastards', against the symbol of United Russia, and below: 'I voted for some other bastards'. An alternative line addressed to the conventional majority of Russia's population said '*Vy dazhe nas ne predstavlyaete*', which has a double meaning – not just 'you don't represent us' but 'you can't even imagine us'. If the forces of law and order were amused they rarely showed it: the demonstrations were marked by heavy-handed policing which some said was designed to provoke violence from the protesters.

While the main direction of the protest was pro-democracy – that is, for fair elections and a new political course – it rested on a temporary coalition of liberal, left and nationalist forces. The leaders included many from the old guard (from Boris Nemtsov and Gary Kasparov on the liberal right, to Gennady Zyuganov on the conservative left) but also some new faces who achieved national prominence at this time, among them the radical left leader Sergei Udaltsov and the nationalist anti-corruption campaigner Aleksei Navalny. The protesters called for an end to what Dmitri Furman has called 'imitation democracy' across the FSU region. The regime deployed large numbers of police while at the same time claiming that the sanctioning of the marches showed the reality of political freedom in Russia. Despite ten years of official media attempts to slate coloured revolution in neibouring countries, many hoped it might just happen in Russia itself.

Nationwide polls showed that United Russia was always likely to win the Duma elections with the communists in second place. The official result was that United Russia got 49 per cent of the vote, while some independent experts have put the figure as low as 34 per cent. Well-organized election monitoring in urban areas and across the Russian heartland ensured that fabricated figures were not significant enough to affect the overall result. Independent observers were affronted and angered by an improbably high turnout for the elections in some outlying parts of Russia – e.g. 99.5 per cent in Chechnya, where 98 per cent of the votes went to United Russia. But the opposition could at least celebrate the fact that the party of power ended up with significantly fewer Duma seats than its 70 per cent of seats in 2007. The distribution of seats for the next four years was: United Russia (UR) 239, Communist Party (CP) 92, Just Russia (JR) 64, Liberal Democratic Party (LD) 56.[1]

The Duma victory put Putin in a commanding position for the

presidential election. However, he was still vulnerable on the more personal level; that is to say, the decision to stand again suggested to many of his fellow countrymen that Putin was not able to let go of power, that he and the people around him had too much to lose, and that there was no real formula for letting a true political contender get into the driving seat. Nonetheless, when asked by TV reporters whether he was really ready for a third term, Putin replied simply: 'I can do the job, cope with the workload', comparing himself with Franklin Roosevelt and his four successive terms as US president. Noting the continuing economic crisis, Putin said, 'Russia's recovery needs stability' and that his presidency would provide this.[2]

The opposition call for fair elections on 4 March maintained its temporary, fragile unity. A Levada Centre poll in mid-December showed that 44 per cent of the population supported the protests – a very high figure indeed. But with fabled Russian fatalism, 67 per cent said that they would abate before long. So it was a major triumph that demonstrations and debates continued right up to the vote. The candidates were Putin (UR), Zyuganov (CP), Mironov (JR) and Zhirinovsky (LD) – all of them old guard – plus a newer face, the millionaire businessman Prokhorov. This in itself enraged many, especially younger voters and the middle-class populations of Moscow and St Petersburg looking for a change. The result of the presidential election was Putin in first place with over 50 per cent, so he did not have to fight a second round.

For those concerned with the technical failings of electoral politics, the main result of the 2011/12 elections was a decision by the powers that be to loosen up the rules so that more smaller parties (such as Yabloko, Union of Right Forces, etc.) can reach the threshold for entry to parliament. Proposals for this were brought forward at the end of 2012. At the same time, splits and reshuffles began to take place among all the main parties.

2 Critiques of the Putin–Medvedev modernization agenda

We do not have to look very far to find the ideology of the post-2000 Russian elite – whether this be its more liberal or corporatist factions. It is called 'modernization', and for this book it is important to consider to what extent this term is the same as 'development'.

In a recent textbook edited by Arinin (2010), modernization is defined as the 'effective self-renewal of the political, economic and social systems in accordance with the needs of the time', with comprehensive and stage-by-stage changes in the whole system of social relations. It is a planned process in which professional competency is a key factor. Internal reasons for modernization are defined as: inefficient management, overdependence on raw materials production, lack of innovation in the economy, society not ready to take on self-management or self-organization, inadequate health and education systems, poor housing, etc. External reasons are: not competitive internationally, unable to respond to a changing situation and balance of forces on the world scene or to economic crises.

This is a top-down technocratic agenda, with a focus on the ruling classes as the main driver of change. Refreshingly, the authors immediately note that up to now the majority of the Russian elite 'have been serving their own selfish and clan interests'. They have to understand that if things go on in this way, they will lose everything they have. They have to share some of their wealth and power – that is, give some away (ibid.: 11–17).

Among the various critiques of Russia's modernization strategy, we will consider just three, for the sake of argument defined as 1) systemic, 2) developmental, and 3) internal.

The systemic critique of Putin/Medvedev modernization has been developed by a variety of Russian experts. A good account of the field from idealistic positions is available from two young Urals-based political scientists, Martyanov and Fishman (2010), using Wallerstein's notion of the moral collapse at the heart of capitalism as the starting point. Their chapter on 'political discourses of the periphery empire' features a number of writers who theorize about an exit by Russia from the world capitalist system. One well-known and prolific popularizer of this approach is Sergei Kara-Murza. His view is that the Putin regime ignores Russia's 'civilizational character and path' and tramples on the Soviet heritage, in which a leading role was given to working people in society. In his book *The 'Putin' Project* (2011), the author constructs a typically head-on assault on current policies.

First, the destruction of the social welfare net. The author challenges the arguments about the need to move away from Soviet 'paternalism', arguing that the modern state needs to provide assurances (ibid.: 9–17). Secondly, deindustrialization: he points out that in the 1990s Russia lost approximately ten million working-class jobs. Kara-Murza defends the Soviet industrial record against post-1991 criticism of several economic mega-projects from the previous period. For example, commenting on a serious breakdown at one of the country's largest hydroelectric dams (the Sayano-Shushinskaya power station in central Siberia), he argues that mega-projects are not bad in themselves. The 2010 emergency was due not to inherent faults in the original design, but to the failure to adapt them to a different pattern of use in the market economy (ibid.: 31–2). Thirdly, deregulation: for example, the destruction of the state service Gosstandart and the abandonment of the Soviet 'people's control' function, the deterioration of technical-hygiene stations (local offices responsible for hygiene, water purity and services, health and safety and anti-epidemic measures), the reappearance of diseases (e.g. smallpox, malaria) that Russians thought they had got rid of for ever (ibid.: 91–109).

This is a self-consciously 'Eurasian' view, arguing that Russia is a mix of European and Asian elements. Kara-Murza attacks remarks by Putin's ideology adviser Surkov regarding the 'Asiatic' nature of the Soviet regime (ibid.: 32–3) and he is fond of quoting from articles in the *Financial Times* in attacking the City of London, Western governments and international agencies in their promotion of neoliberal reforms in Russia. He notes that Putin has consistently promoted privatization (e.g. in a talk to the nation in 2003 in which he declared that 'the private entrepreneur is always more efficient than government') (ibid.: 50).

Another example of this approach can be found in the journal *Left Politics.* The editorials and articles in this journal attack Putin by name less often, focusing strictly on the system of 'Capitalism Mark 2' as described at the end of Chapter 1 of this book.[3] Alongside articles on political and economic themes, the journal gives considerable coverage to social policy issues. For example, Ochkina's analysis of 2000s employment policy focusing on the role of women in the informal economy argues: 1) official statistics do not tell the whole story (unemployment is much higher than stated), 2) the realities of the informal sector are not fully understood or taken into account, 3) throwing oil revenues money at the problem (e.g. for short-term job creation) is no substitute for real economic programmes – that is, sectoral strategies and permanent jobs.[4] *Left Politics* also gives regular prominence to social movements and trade union struggles – as we shall see in the next chapter.

Some environmental critiques are also, it seems to me, systemic – that is, they challenge the whole system. This too is a topic for the next chapter.

The developmental critique of top-down modernization by Van Zon was briefly described in Chapter 4. This approach focuses on the problems of poverty and social exclusion – which appear to be necessary by-products of neoliberal reforms. It stresses the multi-sided nature of development, in particular the human dimension, promoting decentralization and municipal reform and posing the question of how to create a 'three-sector' approach fully involving civil society and business in decision-making.

In this mode, Pavlenko argues, 'we have had growth but not development'. We need an economic model reflecting Russia's democratic traditions and history. Modernization needs a popular mobilization going far beyond the Duma. Private capital needs to work in the interests of society as a whole. The market is not a sacred cow and vital public services should not be run on market principles. Social justice means reducing the current income inequality through discussion between the main sectors of society (Arinin 2010: 169–72). Bukhvald comments that municipal reform has been implemented from above with few indications of much demand for it from the masses. This kind of reform proclaims lots of noble aims (e.g. equal access to municipal services for citizens in all regions of the country) but in reality the only winners are state officials (ibid.: 129–36).

Van Zon gives a long list of those whom top-down development has let down: apartment owners defrauded by building associations; small business unprotected from racketeers; pensioners who lost their in-kind benefits; workers still waiting for the government to rebuild key industrial sectors such as textiles and machine-building; local taxpayers suffering from *chinovniks*' (government officials') personalized rule and informal fiefdoms. The deficiencies in Russia's development strategy include: deteriorating health, education and physical infrastructure; poor performance in modern technology sectors; the brain drain and flight of private capital; business groups operating like clan networks, siphoning off profits through shell companies with the connivance of corrupt public officials; the aversion of the authorities to transparency, accountability and feedback from civil society. The result is a big gap between the state and society, the elite and the people (ibid.).[5]

The internal critique is represented largely by ex-officials and ex-ministers from the Yeltsin and Putin period – Kasyanov, Kudrin and others. These officials mainly take a neoliberal line and are popular with Western commentators. The critique is 'internal' because it comes from within the heart of the business sector that is in command of the economy, especially in its dominant global capitalist formations. Some of their arguments are close to those of the developmental group. For instance, a key issue for 'insider critics' is the growth and prospects of the new middle class. Thus, Van Zon quotes the complaint of popular soft left journalist Kostikov that the middle class is 'literally suffocated by the domination of the state officials, local authorities and the criminal racket'.[6]

The public pronouncements of the Putin and Medvedev regime in the 2000–09 period are described by Martyanov and Fishman as a kind of 'palliative ideology' (2010: 81–103). The word 'development' is used frequently (*razvitie*) in annual presidential addresses and other major speeches, as are 'efficiency' and 'freedom', but denuded of any political content. Indeed, the analysis shows similarities with official rhetoric in many another country we could mention.

3 Overcoming alienation: from isolated individuals to collective action

At the very start of this book, we highlighted the problems facing 'paradoxical', confused or alienated man and woman in the 1990s. Russian and European research studies at the turn of the millennium were quoted on how 'social exclusion is gradually taking hold of more and more people who were well-off only a few years ago' (Manning and Tikhonova 2004). The main factors causing individuals and families to fall into this situation were illness, disability, lots of children, death of a breadwinner, unemployment or collapse of a small business; indeed, 'normal' families were by no means 'excluded from the excluded' in what we later called Russia's 'inner periphery'.

When you take a problem in Russia and examine its spatial distribution, it very often turns out to look like an archipelago, to use a famous metaphor. This is very true of urban poverty and deprivation, affecting not just marginalized groups in the booming cities Moscow and St Petersburg during the transition years, but also the working classes in mono-industrial towns around the country. And then there is the population of smaller towns and settlements, in which 1990s 'transition' once again seemed to mean regression. In the study of life in Russia's small towns quoted earlier (White 2004), the geographer Rodman is quoted: 'The backwoods are not only not catching up with the capital, but, in many respects, actually moving in the opposite direction. Pre-industrial, pre-market, feudal relations are reviving: subsistence farming, usury, hoarding of valuables, slavery. It seems that the modernization of the centres is taking place at the expense of the archaization of the periphery.' Indeed, depressed workers' settlements with a mainly ethnic Russian population in the Siberian forests are as much a part of the 'middle periphery' that we have defined as struggling ethnic minority autonomous districts and regions. Of course, it was not all the fault of the 1990s; even in the Soviet period, small towns were recognized as suffering from unemployment, sluggish trade, poor transport and amenities.

Nonetheless, even in the remote and depressed backwaters of Russia, some cultural and community life remains today. As White notes, while people started withdrawing from official cultural activities from as far back as the death of Stalin, participatory rituals like *subbotniks*[7] continued to play a useful function (as across FSU). In post-1991 Russia, she found that members of the local intelligentsia were still disproportionately active compared to other social groups in collective or community activities (e.g. art and music teachers, doctors, librarians). One new factor was the increasing activity of the Orthodox Church, gradually taking back its church buildings from the state (under which they had often been in community use, which sometimes caused some tension). She discovered that local newspapers had continued to play a useful role. People felt strongly about their local newspaper, civic activists of different kinds helped to produce it, and the results helped develop a local identity and independent public opinion. The author concludes that though NGOs per se were weak, there was a lot of community spirit (White 2004: ch. 7, on civil society and politics).

Countering the ideology of despair There are lots of explanations and apologias in Russia about why people don't take part in community or political action, or why they are so 'long-suffering'. We can see discussions of this in great nineteenth-century novelists like Gogol or Dostoevsky, and also in a range of philosophical and political works. In a recent book on propaganda, media and the relation between the authorities and the people in Russia, Yakovenko takes a similar line, defining Russian culture as 'anti-Greek' because of his fellow-countrymen's lack of adherence to key aspects of the ancient Greek democracy, such as respect for the dignity of the individual or private property (Yakovenko 2009: 43). His argument is that while one can see bursts of political activity throughout Russian history, there comes a moment when key social elements renege on their political subjectivity – that is, the masses fail to fully enter or to take responsibility for the political process. He refers to the heated internal party debates of the 1920s, eventually squashed by Stalin without sufficient resistance from the people; and in the post-1991 period suggests that efforts to introduce self-government decentralization have foundered on the failure of social groups to seize on and develop them from below.[8]

Whether or not this is true, one thing is certain: there are many counter-examples of people trying to push democracy and social justice forward and suffering repression for their efforts. Indeed, *perestroika* saw a big wave of protest action – from miners' strikes in Russia's far north, to the independence movements in the Baltic states and Caucasus, to the ecological and grassroots or 'non-formal' movements that grew up across the whole USSR. The 1993 clashes in Moscow after Yeltsin arrayed tanks against parliament are another example, put down violently, after which there were several years of deep depression in the opposition movements. The next wave of popular protest came in 1998/99 with railway workers' strikes and factory occupations opposing asset strippers up and down the country. However, most attempts at workers' control and self-management floundered in the harsh conditions of Russia's new economic system.

The pro-democracy struggle of autumn 2011–spring 2012 belongs to a third phase of popular radicalism that began in 2005 with the pensioners' protests against monetization of benefits, followed in late 2006 by a wave of workers' actions, notably in the automobile industry. Udaltsov, Navalny and a host of other leaders who came to prominence in 2011/12 have their roots in civic actions from the previous five years.

For the thorough documentation of social movements in the mid-2000s we owe a lot to Carine Clement and her colleagues, sociologists in the Institute of Collective Action. The massive product of their labours, *From Bystander to Activist* (2010) charts detailed stories from: 1) the nationwide pensioners' campaign against monetization of benefits; 2) auto workers' disputes (Ford workers in Vsevolzhsk and AvtoVaz/Lada workers in Togliatti); and 3) struggles for self-management and proper maintenance and repair in the housing sector.[9] In the following pages these stories will be supplemented with observations from my own travels and meetings with activists across Urals and Siberia in 2011/12.

Clement's three cases are all interesting in their different ways. To understand the anti-monetization campaign we have to go back to the Soviet period and the long list of in-kind benefits that workers, mothers, old people and others were entitled to. They included free transport, subsidized rates in factory or other canteens, subsidized entrance to leisure and cultural facilities, and so on. In the 1990s, social policy experts in government discovered that only a limited percentage of old people (for example) were using these services, and they concluded that other forms of social assistance would be more effective – for example, giving pensioners money payments instead of free bus passes and the like. The experts seriously miscalculated the situation. There were angry mass demonstrations around the country and the authorities had to backtrack (though the new policy was not completely withdrawn). Political action opposing monetization successfully appealed to cultural and historical strengths in Russia – respect for the older generation, the high official status of their sacrifices in the Second World War, and the solidarity felt by other vulnerable groups who similarly appreciated the pensions and privileges awarded to them in the Soviet period.

The auto workers' struggles documented in Clement's book involved long-drawn-out, often unofficial action in a situation where the trade union movement had been very negatively affected by unemployment. Overall, the 1990s exposed the weakness of workers' organizations in Russia, their lack of experience in organizing independently of the Communist Party. Workers were used to depending on factory managers for social benefits – and after 1991 many a 'red director' tried to keep as many employees as possible on his payroll, even if there was little money to pay them wages. The strikes featured in Clement's study show how individuals conquered the demoralization caused by widespread unemployment, drops in real wages and the inability of official unions to defend their members.

The process by which people move from apathy to activism is analysed in detail in Clement's study of housing activists in Astrakhan, a large city and provincial capital located in the river delta where the Volga flows into the Caspian Sea.[10] The starting position here is the across-the-board privatization of state housing in the early 1990s; hence the sudden disappearance of social housing in Russia's cities and a situation where local authorities had no money to pay for capital or communal repairs and maintenance (since nobody was paying rent any more ...). It might sound good, to get your flat for free or almost free, and it was about the only thing you did get in the 1990s! But there were many abuses[11] and one of the ongoing problems was the private sector management companies that local authorities contracted to take care of hundreds of thousands of blocks of flats around Russia. Astrakhan is built on marshy ground and some 14 per cent of the housing was deemed to be in dangerous condition by the early 2000s: the usual problems, Clement writes – rusty pipes, flooded basements, stinking entrances to the flats, lifts out of order for years.

Because of the almost universal dissatisfaction with the housing management companies, Astrakhan had become a leader in self-management by residents' associations. The case study describes, step by step, how committees were formed in different blocks. The concept of 'reframing' is used to explain how people's self-image, feeling of solidarity and their reputation in the eyes of others changed during the process of setting up self-managing groups. Much of this will be very familiar to workers in the community and development sectors. Clement's analysis stresses elements like struggle, collective decision-making, relations with the public authorities (housing units, electricity and other service companies, etc.), planning issues and the new Housing Code. A big step for many in the housing movement was from the position (frame) of 'situational' or one-off activist to the position of 'confirmed' or long-term activist. Mutual trust and ratification of steps taken by committee members by their neighbours was essential in achieving sustainability, both for their individual roles and for the solutions proposed.

Modes of action at street level In the analysis above, we are talking about social movements pursuing claims, with a coherent strategy and a 'repertoire' of actions (Tilley and Tarrow 2007: 1–24). These movements express the views and hopes of sections of the population that are not satisfied with the status quo and aim to challenge the ideological hegemony of society's ruling groups (Cox with Schechter 2002: 100). Their strategies and actions can be, in the jargon we so often use, 'institutionalized' or 'non-institutionalized'. When speaking of protests we mean mainly the latter, and they can be active or passive in character; if active, they can be violent or non-violent, organized or spontaneous. The more society can develop permanent mechanisms for discussion and negotiation (such as we discussed in Chapter 5) the less chance there is of violence or conflict.

During visits to Siberia in 2011/12, the author got the chance to speak to civic activists linked with the Institute of Collective Action in campaigns on a wide range of issues. For example, a pensioners' leader in Novosibirsk described his part in a campaign to force the city authorities to adopt a more flexible system of free/subsidized travel for pensioners on public transport (a local follow-up to the monetization struggle described above); a campaign to stop the cutting down of trees to make way for a new hotel in a city park; and an anti-corruption action against the management of a major cement factory. All this involved unofficial action. My informant had personally been involved in dozens of court hearings in the past year! Indeed, the restrictions on street protests in Russia now are such that it has become necessary to apply officially for any picket or street demonstration. He and his friends, many of them also retired, had succeeded in making contact with a wider constituency during the upsurge of political activity the previous winter. On one occasion almost seven thousand people assembled for a demonstration around the elections. But within a few weeks the younger people disappeared and it was back to the 'regulars'.

In defending people's rights, the official or institutionalized route is also vital. Also in Novosibirsk, a lawyer described his work in an alternative trade union centre that defends workers through a variety of means, including court appearances and direct action via pickets, strikes and meetings. Union activists spent ten years negotiating the new Labour Code, he told me, but still regard it as ineffective. He works closely with a law centre in the city, advising housing associations and residents of employer-managed hostels. Another client group are pregnant women and mothers on maternity leave. Either the employer denies them their rights, or when the business downsizes or goes bust, they are the first to suffer. His law centre belongs to a national network giving advice to small, inexperienced NGOs.[12]

Present at the meeting with trade unionists were representatives of the NGO Golos, specializing in electoral and democracy issues, and a local activist working on similar themes. Together, they commented on the recent wave of protests and their experience of election monitoring in 2011/12. The demonstrators had made a number of important demands on government but, they admitted, there haven't been any real results yet. 'Except there is some evidence the government is listening – for example, the introduction of video cameras in election rooms.' In Novosibirsk region, 700 volunteers came forward to fill 300 monitor positions, in many cases paying for their own petrol to travel to remote polling stations. In general the election process in Novosibirsk had been fair. Where there were problems, written complaints were made and followed up.

Some 1,250 kilometres to the east, in Irkutsk, the editor of an independent local newspaper, *Narodny Kontrol* (People's Control), described efforts to highlight and uncover local corruption and malpractice. He sees his newspaper's main goal as being to mobilize public opinion and influence government. The latest issue of the paper had just come out with an increased edition of 200,000 copies for circulation around Irkutsk city and *oblast*. 'If I can help people to get a sense of what is going on – in their own head, in their courtyard, in the city as a whole – then I have achieved my aim,' he told us. One of his close allies is a housing movement leader, a retired teacher living on the eighth floor of a block in an enormous Soviet-era housing estate in the hills above the Angara river. She described the fight to create a housing association for her block – uniting some two thousand people – one of the first in

Irkutsk to gain legal status. This work is indeed without any end in sight, a constant battle with the maintenance services for the estate and now a struggle with private sector builders of a new block right opposite. But there are some small victories: after two fatal accidents involving children crossing the main road to school, parents won a new set of traffic lights.

Information dissemination is vital for any campaign. Here, Russia's strong technical expertise in information technology and modern marketing skills often make themselves felt. Internet and email are widely available and used. A local example: in Irkutsk we were told about a new childcare movement led by young mothers called *38mama.ru* – they are very active and use a variety of informal means, including new/social media, to gather support. Their issue is very topical these days, since one of the consequences of the federal government's pro-natalist policies is an increase in the birth rate locally, with some twenty thousand families now on the waiting list for nursery places. A national example: Navalny's anti-corruption movement has raised money via credit card contributions, with two interactive websites, *RosPil* and *RosYama* (literally Russia Scam and Russia Hole), where supporters can supply information about government and business malpractice, and potholes in the roads (and suchlike) respectively.

Can unofficial street actions and long-term collaboration with the authorities be combined successfully? In Yekaterinburg, officials at the ombudsman's office gave an example of the Soldiers' Mothers Committee. This NGO has gained huge influence around Russia since its first campaigns during the Chechen Wars to ensure better conditions for young conscripts. The Sverdlovsk *oblast* committee meets regularly with the military top brass; at the same time, individual mothers' groups are not constrained from protesting energetically in individual cases of victimization, injury and so on.

In summer 2012, President Putin's response to mass demonstrations around the Duma and presidential elections was to impose much heavier penalties on those organizing or just taking part in unsanctioned protests.[13] In Moscow and St Petersburg, youth and anarchist groups have already experimented with all kinds of tricks that make fun of the authorities. In St Petersburg, one group blew up an enormous phallus to draw attention to government shows of macho power. In Moscow, the now world-famous Pussy Riot organized a (very short) rock concert in the Cathedral of Christ the Saviour to protest at the ever closer links between the presidency and the Orthodox Church. They gained even more publicity for this than the topless Ukrainian girls have done for a variety of causes. However, my own favourite to date is the action of civic activists in Nizhny Novgorod, who, after the tightening up of rules on notifying the authorities about planned actions, announced that they were organizing a march to the shop to buy a loaf of bread. In Belarus, experiments with mass, invisible demonstrations began some years ago.[14] All this shows that adversity can bring out creativity not only in literature and art but in protest, too.

Volunteering in Russia today There are many points of contact between the social movement analysis referred to above and studies into Russian civil society carried out by institutions like the CS Unit at the Higher School of Economics (HSE) in Moscow. Indeed, the latter now has sufficient funding to carry out major sociological surveys on all kinds of topics: types of civil society activity, relations with local government, charitable giving, and so on. Since volunteering has been a theme running through several sections of this book, it may be worth mentioning their findings on this mode of activity.

Experts at the CS Unit define volunteering quite strictly, distinguishing it from social activism of the kind featured in the examples given from Siberia above. Volunteering, they argue, is a work not a leisure category, and does not include activity arising from a person's membership of or paid employment with an NGO. A 2008 study found that just over 60 per cent of Russians had engaged in some form of unpaid socially oriented work in the last two to three years (this could be at the workplace or in their community). However, this is mostly unorganized or simply an individual decision to help someone outside their immediate family. And a more recent study showed that while many people contribute to sports, leisure, cultural and religious activities, less than 5 per cent of the population contributes to CSO activities as volunteers.

The advantage of volunteering is that it can be quite unbureaucratic, independent. But there are complexities here too, as a short case study from the Institute of Collective Action shows.

Case study of a volunteer firefighter. In the summer of 2010, Moscow and several other cities were seriously affected by smoke from peat and forest fires sweeping through thousands of hectares in north and central Russia. The website *rabkor* interviewed the leader of a volunteer group, AB, a young man living in the town of Orekho-Zuevo, not far from Moscow. AB had become distressed by the heavy clouds of smoke hanging over the town for days: 'I was feeling desperate, I just had to do something!' He used social networks to put out a call for fellow-helpers. Some five hundred people answered the call over the next few days, but the numbers of actual volunteers grew more slowly: from seven to ten in the first phase, to thirty and then fifty, not just from his home town but all around the *oblast*, Moscow itself and farther afield. People came with their own cars and equipment to put out fires threatening whole villages and towns. The group worked closely with the Ministry of Emergencies, but the ministry itself was short of equipment and water to fight the flames.

Eventually the group got help from a fund called 'Just Aid', run by a civil society activist calling herself Doctor Lisa and linked with the party Just Russia. This solved their equipment and water problems. However, in his interview AB raises lots of questions about the way in which different political parties (in particular the ruling party United Russia and their youth movement *Nashi*) used their involvement in the emergency action for political and PR purposes.

Members of AB's group have stayed in contact with each other, 150 people in all. Lots of them have good organizational and management skills and are ready to help again. As he commented, there could be lots of calls for volunteer emergency assistance in future years, such is the problem not just with forest fires, but decaying infrastructure like electric power stations, water purification units, industrial plants. There was no investment in them during the oil boom so it is unlikely they will be repaired during the economic crisis – and problems are inevitable. He sees the problem as political in the broadest sense. 'If we don't develop mechanisms for self-organization, the core of a new society built on principles of mutual help and personal responsibility for its future, and not on parasitism and indifference like society today, then in ten to fifteen years we will cease to exist as a country or a society at all.'[15]

Analysis of social movements and civil society From what social groups are volunteers and activists drawn? The results of HSE studies on volunteering correspond quite closely to Clement's findings on protests – that is, protesters are mainly from the middle layers that make up two-thirds of the Russian population, while the 'socially vulnerable groups' that make up the bottom 20 per cent, and the elite/top 15 per cent, are less well represented. Indeed, we could say the same for the participants in many development programmes, despite our efforts to draw in the poorest, or indeed the rich.

The 2010 report by the Siberian Public Chamber shows how these new bodies are carefully monitoring the situation with protest, too. Analysing public opinion surveys on citizens' dissatisfaction with the government, it notes that the main causes for dissatisfaction are price rises, unemployment and housing problems. Some 32 per cent of the population defined themselves as 'poor' and only 43 per cent were prepared to describe the current economic situation as 'positive'. Some nine hundred protest actions were recorded in the Siberian region in 2010, with a total of 75,000 participants, the majority of them organized by political parties. But the report also notes examples of more spontaneous protests. One of these was the campaign for kindergarten provision mentioned above.

The firefighter story shows that not just CSOs but individual volunteers can be caught up in or manipulated by political parties in Russia today. It was a similar situation with the mass protests in autumn 2011; they brought together a very wide collection of individuals and organizations and one of the key questions was how long these different political forces could really live with each other. This issue is particularly acute with regard to racist or neo-fascist groups, of which there are quite a few in Russia today. Should democracy or social activists attend meetings or share platforms with radical nationalists or racists? This question is debated regularly on social movement and pro-democracy websites and is of huge significance given the increasing number of migrant workers and their families now living in Russia. Many of them are Russian citizens, others are members of trade unions, and yet they are very poorly represented in both civil society and labour movement activity.

Clement's book discusses the main terms used in social movement analysis, in particular the 'resource mobilization' theory, according to which leaders play a key role in helping others reach a better understanding of the situation they are in – for example, by overcoming cultural stereotypes or reconsidering their attitude to generally accepted forms of behaviour. Poorer groups in society have few material resources, so the moral position and mode of behaviour of the leaders and activists among them is a major resource – also their contacts, sources of information and so on. While people in the movement may be inclined to admire and praise their leaders, the best leaders are very conscious of the responsibility placed on them to empower others. Their commitment to horizontal communications runs counter to the usual vertical lines in society.

After the explosion of interest in Russian social movements during *perestroika*, the events of the 1990s killed this theme almost stone dead. Hence Clement and her colleagues found relatively little in Russian sociology to assist them in their analysis. There is an increasing amount written on *obschestvenniye organizatsii* (public associations), but on the whole this term does not capture the more critical or anti-establishment meaning of the term 'social movement'. Public or politically committed sociology is quite weak in Russia, the authors argue. The implication is that civil society discourse in Russia is dominated by liberals and right-wingers, and here we see the effect of history – that is, civil society's association in FSU with opposition to the Soviet regime and socialist ideas more widely.[16]

4 Conclusion: struggles in the 'three peripheries'

The four chapters in Part 2 have in different ways all tackled the issue of civil society and political action and the often unclear boundary between them. Indeed, development is often a struggle. The social movements described in this chapter face the challenge of how to coordinate their activities, combine different viewpoints, and communicate more effectively with the general public. By contrast, NGOs involved in social issues at local level have put energy and ideas into setting up consultative groups and grants contests, ensuring transparency in awarding contracts. These are the two wings of civil society in Russia today – one is out on the streets protesting and demanding rights; the other trying in a hundred practical ways to make services work better for people. In reality both sides are needed. They need to be aware of one another, when to do what, and how to build on each other's efforts and contributions.

The historical episodes and case studies in Part 2 have focused on the experience of rank-and-file activists, NGO and development workers. They show the need for commitment and good leadership; for a clear analysis of the changing economic and political situation; and for alliances and networking. I have tried to show how vulnerable and excluded groups can through involvement in a variety of activities and movements become conscious of themselves and active, not passive, in relation to the problems that confront them.

But Part 2 has ranged wider, comparing current struggles with mobilizations in the Soviet period, counterposing evolutionary and forced development, class struggle and coloured revolution. Finally, we have considered 'three peripheries' or zones of poverty and exclusion. The 'inner periphery' – populated by the millions of the urban poor and *budgetniki* (civil servants and others whose salaries are paid from government budgets) in the 1990s – has its own hierarchies. As some groups have climbed out of poverty in the last decade, they have been replaced by other groups, notably migrants from Central Asia and Caucasus making their home in Moscow, Yekaterinburg, Novosibirsk and other cities. In the 'middle periphery', we have the depressed zones within the Russian Federation hit hard by deindustrialization and the loss of Soviet subsidies, a mosaic of different national areas most of which are comfortable within the Federation, but within which there are still war/crisis regions (such as the northern Caucasus) and for all of which there are complex identity and institutional issues that require constant attention; and finally the 'outer periphery' of the CIS.

Are the administrative units or regions that remained within the Russian Federation better off than those that received independence in 1990s? Probably they are more stable as members of a major power in today's world, that is more able to create jobs and provide benefits for their population. But less free to take the kind of chances that, for example, Kyrgyzstan has done, during two revolutions, or Kazakhstan – as we will see in the next chapter, a major regional player influencing Russia in the development of Eurasian policy and institutions.

PART 3

THE INTERNATIONAL CONTEXT

Russia cannot produce a development model in isolation from the rest of the world. If it wants to influence other countries, it needs to create a long-term strategy, a set of objectives and possible ways of achieving them that can be communicated to other countries, partners or stakeholders in development. Most likely, the model of development that Russia will promote around the world will be built on what it has achieved or wants to achieve at home. Thus it was in the Soviet period with the state-led development model; thus it was with the models of transition promoted in the post-Soviet space by the USA, European countries and others who offered advice (sometimes wrong advice, as we have already commented).

But at the present time, many experts are of the opinion that Russia is stuck in a raw-materials-oriented economy, with an authoritarian or semi-authoritarian political regime. Probably, external commentators slightly underestimate Russia's achievements in correcting the problems that it had accumulated at the end of the 1980s and 1990s, and little is known outside the country of the government's efforts to create new social policy, rescue depressed regions and so on. Sometimes it seems as if the winds of cold war are beginning to blow again, and this is bad for objectivity. That is to say, hostility between East and West will tend to give people on both sides a distorted and incomplete picture of each other.

This chapter is about development alternatives being produced in FSU. They are all citizen-driven or citizen-based – because it is independent people and organizations that tend to produce or advocate for new ideas. Their proponents are mostly not opposed to the state or business sectors as such, though they are properly critical of what goes on in those sectors, challenging both state and business to work more effectively and with better regard for generally accepted principles and values. Examples are given from three sectors: 1) the environmental movement in Russia; 2) the anti-globalist movement in Russia; 3) NGOs monitoring the activities of banks and transnational companies in the oil, gas and mining sectors in the FSU region. Geographically, the examples are once again focused on Urals, Siberia and Central Asia. The chapter looks at the links between development programmes and campaigns organized by activists at three levels – local, national and international.

1 The local dimension in Russia's environmental movement

Russia's environmental movement is made up of many strands, each with its own history, social base and focus. Developing out of a range of informal and student groups from the 1960s, from independent scientific thinking in higher education institutions and the Academy of Sciences, from cultural movements like the Village Writers school, it gradually developed international links through organizations like the United Nations and UNESCO and began to put forward alternative strategies – for example, the 1970s movement for a new urban ecology.

In the 1980s, environmentalism became one of the most powerful strands in *perestroika* and *glasnost*, mobilizing thousands of citizens to protest against nuclear pollution after the Chernobyl disaster and various industrial mega-projects – for example, the proposal to divert the waters from Siberian rivers south towards Central Asia. Henry (2010) defines three main types of organizations active at this time: grassroots associations, professionalized organizations, and government affiliates. Local organizations and clubs are extremely various, most of them quite small, focusing on practical tasks like nature conservation, greening the city, and environmental education for children and youth. For many observers, the early 1990s represent the peak of ecological consciousness in Russia, as for the pro-democracy movement as a whole.

Environmental NGOs have engaged with the state in a number of ways. Like other NGOs described in earlier chapters, they have a variety of strategies and ways of working, including complete independence from and close collaboration with state environmental agencies. Several green parties have been founded and some have enjoyed success locally – without ever breaking through at national level. The movement has found itself at loggerheads with the Yeltsin and Putin regimes on a number of issues. One of its biggest struggles was against a proposal by the Ministry of Atomic Energy in 2000 to begin importing nuclear waste from other countries for reprocessing. Ecological organizations collected 2.5 million signatures in favour of a national referendum on this issue, only for one quarter of them to be ruled out by the Central Electoral Commission, after which the government went ahead with the reprocessing programme.

During the author's visits to Russia in 2011/12, it was clear that environmental NGOs are still very active in both educational work and campaigning. Groups are fighting a number of issues connected with hydropower stations in Siberia, and the battle to keep Lake Baikal clear of the waste from a major cellulose plant was still in progress.

Environmental 'localism': an alternative tradition In an earlier chapter we referred to a leading environmental thinker, Oleg Yanitsky, and his work in bringing together ecological, social and cultural issues in a critique of growing individualism and consumerism in Russia. There are three areas where 'localism' is especially evident and important in this approach.

First, in its defence of local knowledge. This is not just the knowledge of local communities faced with globalization and wasteful development, but also that of the ecological advocates ('concerned professionals') who work with them. The problem, Yanitsky argues, is that the utilitarian approach to nature and extensive use of non-renewable resources typical of the Soviet period are simply being continued under new management. Referring to a number of environmental campaigns across Russia, he argues that neoliberals need to consider the slowness of real change. The current model of economic development in Russia is anti-ecology, hence the frequent 'mishaps' such as dams cracking up, oil pipeline emergencies and so on. His case study devoted to the Kamchatka peninsula in Russia's Far East (2007: 123–6) shows a vicious struggle going on between traditional communities (including small indigenous peoples) and new economic actors, in particular the poachers of the region's 'red gold' – salmon and the caviar taken from it (with ripped-apart dead fish often left in great mountains by the rivers).

Secondly, in its concern with the local built environment. Like the analysts of Russian civil society quoted in Part 1 of this book,

Yanitsky places the environmental movement within a longer historical perspective, quoting ideas about 'garden cities' dating from Tsarist times and an eminent thinker of the early twentieth century, Vernadsky, who included environmental alongside social and political thinking in his concept of a more balanced, peaceful life for future generations. Another example of the losses suffered by civil society in the 1920s was the break-up of local history associations seen by the Communist Party as a brake on headlong industrial development schemes (ibid.: 21–3). Yanitsky opposes outright several famous proponents of radical Soviet modernism, for example the Constructivists – architects from the Le Corbusier school – with their 'scientific', utilitarian box-houses for the new spartan, collectivist way of life. For Yanitsky, years of war (civil war, foreign intervention) inevitably meant de-ecologization, the loss of established ways of life, especially in the countryside, that had become more or less adapted to the natural environment. By contrast, the early Soviet years instituted a kind of 'barracks existence' (indeed, it was often called 'barracks socialism'; ibid.: 24–5).

Yanitsky takes this argument to the philosophical level, developing an opposition between the 'culture of location or places' and the 'culture of flows' (referencing Manuel Castells). To the latter belong the mobile, richer classes and their capital assets, moving between countries and around the world without impediment; to the former belong ordinary people, whose fate is much more closely tied up with where they were born, who have little money to send abroad and less chance of getting visas to travel.[1] This is a critique of modern nomadism and the mercenary way of life. Only freedom from the barracks, war or terror can provide the space in which to think about long-term issues like the natural environment.

Localism and the project Thirdly, in his account of the ideological development of Russian environmentalism, Yanitsky reaches a point in the mid-1990s where internationalist ecologists (increasingly influenced by their foreign partners) and local 'patriotic' ecologists found themselves in disagreement. At this moment, he says, the problem was solved in a pragmatic way – through a flood of foreign funding for small-scale projects. Thus, the big ideological issue (Russia's future ecological strategy) was broken up into a thousand small local problems to which different actors in the movement could address themselves.

All these comments are highly relevant for development pro-grammes in Russia and elsewhere. Civil society is full of 'localists' suspicious about government policies (and some of them no less suspicious of international agencies).[2] At the same time, no policy or programme means anything without implementers dedicated to a particular location and set of beneficiaries or local partners. Yanitsky discusses the 'projectization' of our working lives in the NGO sec-tor – cut into pieces of typically six months or a year according to the time-span of your current grant or service contract – and how this can hamper longer-term or strategic thinking. He also warns against the dangers of NGOs being incorporated in government. How to bridge the gap between grassroots initiatives and higher levels of decision-making, and stay independent, is indeed one of our major challenges.

Many donors now support advocacy by NGOs as a way in which the latter can influence government and improve the situation long-term rather than just provide day-to-day services. Russian NGOs are by now well acquainted with the development strategy 'teach people to use a fishing rod' rather than the charitable notion 'give them fish to eat'. Advocacy requires NGOs to encourage their target groups or clients to mobilize (as we saw in Chapter 7) so as to put their case to government as effectively as possible. It also requires a deeper, wider analysis than many local organizations are able to achieve in their daily work. Quite often, one of the problems is that govern-ment statistics and publicly available information are not adequately covering these issues.[3] In outlying regions of Russia like Urals and Siberia, there is a long way to go in research and development for alternative strategies. Indeed, the ecological movement is currently on the defensive, as the following quotes from friends in Russian NGOs make clear:

- 'Despite all our efforts in the 1990s, we have failed in many of our long-term goals – for example, in our attempts to get ecology into the mainstream school programme.' (Environmental activist, Perm)
- 'Management decisions are lobbied by business structures without

account of the interests of citizens and the natural environment.' (Quote from the resolution of the conference 'Actual ecological problems of Novosibirsk oblast', ISAR-Siberia and environmental network, 28 February 2012).[4]

- 'Many people think a victory was won at the Baikal Cellulose Plant with the move to closed cycle mode of water usage, but we are far from certain that pollution has been stopped there. The plant still operates all kinds of restrictions on independent monitoring activity.' (NGO Baikal Wave, Irkutsk)[5]

2 Challenges in developing a national anti-globalist movement in Russia

The environmental movement is undoubtedly one of the strongest civil society sectors in Russia today, uniting people under the classic slogan 'think global, act local'. But as we have seen, it comes up against mighty political and economic opponents. To overcome them it is necessary to win political and economic arguments at the national level. And from the early 2000s Russian civic and political activists began to put together an alliance against globalization – or, as many preferred to call it, an alternative or *alter*-globalization movement.[6]

This is a movement with deep roots in Slavophile nationalism and among conservative thinkers who right up to the Bolshevik revolution promoted Russia as a special civilizational centre, opposing Westernization and what they saw as its evils – immorality and the commercialization of life. In its 2000s interpretation, the main enemy for anti- or *alter*-globalists is neoliberalism and world domination by the USA.[7] The alternative is provided by grassroots social movements, including workers' organizations, the pensioners' and housing movements, environmentalists opposing nuclear plants or reprocessing facilities, anti-debt campaigners, and so on. Some of these social movements have a local focus and an everyday social or political character, as we saw in Chapter 7. Others focus on higher-level national or international policy issues and opportunities for action. This includes protests around the World Trade Organization (WTO) and participation in World Social Forum (WSF) events.

Anti-global mass actions in Russia began in November 2001 with the country's first street protest against the policies of the WTO. In the following year, similar demonstrations were held at the time of George Bush's visit to Russia and in 2006 during the G8 meeting in St Petersburg. These protests were not as large as demonstrations held in London, Paris, Genoa or Prague; nor did they escalate into Gandhi-type non-violent action (mass sit-downs, etc.). Nonetheless, they were very new for post-1991 Russia – anti-capitalist actions taking a lead from global civil society. Moreover, this was followed up by a series of Russia Social Forum meetings held during the mid-2000s (linked loosely to the World Social Forum). Five such forums were held in Siberia in 2003–08, in the cities of Barnaul, Novosibirsk, Tomsk and Irkutsk, as well as two national events in Moscow. A report of one of the meetings held in Novosibirsk says that 250 participants attended from thirteen regions. Izhevsk and Perm were described as examples of active social movement coordination; another important action discussed was a car workers' strike in the city of Togliatti; and an ecological section attracted fifty people.[8] In general, these meetings seem to have had the same character as the global meetings of WSF – that is, an inclusive and non-sectarian attempt to find ways of bringing about progressive social transformations (De Sousa Santos 2006: 182–7).

In an oblique, indirect relation with Russia's *alter*-global movement are a range of other national campaigns active in Russia today. One of these is the Global Campaign against Poverty (GCAP).[9] The focus of this coalition of about forty NGOs from different regions around Russia is social policy development. Its aim is to help organizations working with poor and marginalized groups to lobby for reforms at national level – quite an ambitious aim given the size of Russia. Building on almost ten years' work carried out at local level on issues like unemployment, sustainable livelihoods and small business development, GCAP now focuses on family and child poverty and the working poor (e.g. low-paid public sector workers, rural communities), many of whose incomes are below the official subsistence level. Its demands are similar to those made at Social Forum meetings. For example, given Russia's poor health ratings, one of the campaign's demands is to lift state spending on health from 4 to 6 per cent of GDP.

Russia joins WTO In December 2011, Russia was admitted to WTO (eighteen years after first applying) and in summer 2012, soon after Putin's resumption of the presidency, the Duma ratified the agreement. This decision carries many risks for Russia. The manufacturing sector faces big competition with the West and China, while it has hardly recovered from the 1990s recession; and Russian agriculture will always require special government support because of the country's harsh northern climate. Materials produced for an anti-WTO conference on the eve of the Duma debate claimed that membership will cost Russian 26 trillion roubles (just under US$1 trillion) by 2020, reducing economic activity by 5 per cent and manufacturing and agricultural outputs by 12.7 per cent each. The human damage was estimated as an extra 4.4 million unemployed. The main anti-WTO lobbyists represented at this meeting were trade unions and employers' associations in the sectors most at risk (agriculture, the food industry, machine building, leather and footwear, chemical, electronics, timber processing, white goods and auto parts).

Is there an alternative to WTO? In addition to support for the at-risk economic sectors listed above, a list of policies proposed at the same conference included the following: 1) reform the tax code (e.g. introduce a progressive income tax scale, a tax on property worth more than US$1 million, give tax inspectors the right to ask where your money came from); 2) nationalize mineral resources (concessions for oil and gas extraction can be issued to national or foreign companies, but the resources themselves should belong to the state); 3) prohibit government officials, managers of state enterprises and owners of businesses bought at bankruptcy auctions from opening offshore bank accounts; 4) reduce energy prices in the domestic market; 5) reform the legal system.[10] That this economic platform enjoys support from such a wide range of actors is a definite plus. But a hard defensive battle lies ahead now.

Challenges of coordinating action at national level The national scene is crucial for any campaigning with long-term objectives. This is the top level of representative democracy and decision-making – also the level in any state apparatus at which the main repressive policies and actions are adopted against the population. Reading journals like *Alternativa*, *Levaya Politika* and *Neprikosnovenny Zapas* opens the curtains on the daily problems of civic and political activists in reaching this level. Many had expected the economic crisis of 2007/08 to result in a wave of protest actions in Russia (using the example of western Europe), but this has not really happened. The trade unions are under more pressure from employers, and while a few protests have taken place, these mainly local and solidarity actions are weak. There are some more permanent coalitions – GCAP is one, the Union of Coordination Councils another – but the tendency is for each new struggle to bring forth a new coalition that supplants previous ones. Meanwhile police pressure on protesters is intensified and any demands are labelled 'political'. Community and trade union activists are fully extended in carrying out their own functions and responsibilities, and find it hard to support each other's meetings. Indeed, some activists remain determinedly 'localist' or resist any political affiliations, left or right.[11]

The political environment for civic activism is a complex one in Russia today. This book has focused on the liberal and progressive elements in the civil society space, but it should be noted for the sake of objectivity that nationalists (not to speak of the Orthodox Church) have large followings too. Indeed, CP leader Zyuganov has been active for fifteen years in various popular or patriotic fronts close to the nationalist wing, abandoning many traditional communist positions for a new eclectic ideology in which the key ideas are to shore up the state and restore people's power against the 1990s 'occupier regime' (Urban and Solovei 1997; Medvedev 2008a: 460–97). This readiness to 'think the unthinkable' and explore new alliances helps to explain his party's electoral success, but also repels many others from left and democratic positions. The dilemma about whether to share platforms with known nationalists or racists was mentioned in the previous chapter. This issue came up regularly in the pro-democracy movement during 2011/12 and it arises in the anti-globalist movement too.

As any study of political activism in Russia's regions will show, protesters against corruption, unemployment and poor housing come from all shades of political opinion. Even a slogan like 'social justice' can be used in a variety of different ways. And the main barrier to *alter*-globalism and progressive alternatives is currently at least not ultra-right groups or parties like Zhirinovsky's liberal democrats; it is the centre-right, corporatist 'party of power' led by Putin and

Medvedev. A worsening economic crisis in Russia will lead inevitably to social crisis – that is, reducing oil and gas revenues will force the government to try to cut social spending. Particularly under threat are education and the housing sector. It is precisely in the social sector that the government-aligned Federation of Independent Trade Unions is strongest, hanging on to what is left of the strong positions that unions occupied in the Soviet period. This means that teachers, doctors and nurses and other *budgetniki* are not able easily to speak out – indeed, in 2011/12 they voted for United Russia and Vladimir Putin in large numbers.[12]

And there is another challenge. According to analysts at the Institute of Globalization and Social Movements, the Russian *alter*-global movement lacks internationalism and has been unable to develop links with other campaigns (such as the Occupy! movement) around the world that would be able to help it expand its support base and, for example, appeal to youth.[13] Indeed, my own observation is that Russian NGOs and social movements working on poverty or globalization issues have very little visibility in countries much closer to home – such as their next-door neighbours in Caucasus and Central Asia. And the participation of FSU visitors and allies at major meetings in Russia is quite limited too – a serious challenge for the movement.

Here Kazakhstan is the exception, geographically and with its large ethnic Russian population much closer than the other countries of Central Asia to the Russian Federation. The trade union movement is stronger in Kazakhstan than in the rest of Central Asia, with active union sections in several foreign-owned mining and manufacturing companies.[14] In the civil sector, Kazakhstan's NGOs are working closely with local and national government on 'social order' contracts on the Russian model; they liaise closely with NGO counterparts in Urals and Siberia. The problems with democracy development in Kazakhstan are similar to Russia's.

Kazakhstan has been from the start one of the strongest proponents of CIS and Eurasian cultural and religious dialogue in general. President Nazarbayev has made many statements on these topics and they often have quite an official tone. But this is still positive. The ongoing development of a Customs Union between Russia, Belarus and Kazakhstan means that civic and political associations in these three countries will increasingly have to address their economic, political and social problems as part of a single space. If Kyrgyzstan and Tajikistan eventually join the Customs Union (which is their governments' declared policy), activists there will have to do the same.

3 NGOs campaigning for international accountability in Central Asia

Back in the USSR, there was a significant divide between donor (richer) and recipient (poorer) Soviet republics – though this was downplayed in the official propaganda. The divide now takes a new form between independent states – and is out in the open. If we look at the situation around accountability – that is, the responsibility that the state and business sectors (plus larger organizations and institutions of all kinds) have to citizens – perhaps the situation is something like this. On the one side, there is Russia, where one of civil society's main tasks in the past ten years has been to try to influence government and gain its support for a range of reforms and development initiatives; also richer ex-republics like Kazakhstan, where the same kind of NGO–government mechanisms have been put in place gradually since 2005. Historically and logically, social and economic demands were made on government first, on business a little later (since business was in such a primitive and disorganized condition).

On the other side are poorer countries like Kyrgyzstan and Tajikistan, where from the 1990s the international agencies and donors gained an increasingly powerful role, supporting and in some respects substituting themselves for weaker governments. In many of these countries transnational companies in sectors like mining and energy play a dominant role. And here too, some interesting examples of lobbying and monitoring by citizens at different levels can be found.

In Central Asia, a variety of studies on civil society development have charted the encounters between newly established NGOs and the donors. They show how by the early 2000s key NGO leaders and activists had got acquainted with the wider world of Western-funded development and human rights. At the same time, international donors tried in different ways to coordinate their actions in the region and share the feedback gained from local civil society. In many sectors the country UN office played a lead role in these efforts; and many development programmes included a networking component. For example, INTRAC's 2001–04 programme for civil society development in Central Asia included a component on improvement of communications and dialogue between donors and civil society. As part of this, its country offices ran quarterly round tables to bring together donor policy and practice in civil society development in Almaty, Bishkek and Tashkent. While these were primarily meetings for donors, local NGOs attended for particular discussions and made presentations. However, no formal mechanism has yet been created by which the NGO sector as a whole can select 'official' representatives to donor forums – an unsatisfactory situation that continues up to this day.

International NGOs like Greenpeace, Save the Children or Oxfam occupy a special position in the hierarchy of donor–NGO relations: an intermediary role in many respects. For most of them the region was quite new in 1990, and for some (as we have seen with VSO) the intervention was to be quite limited in time. Many seem to be comfortable with the current framework of donor policy and funding, but others have been on occasion openly critical of globalization, geopolitical competition and their effects in Central Asia.[15] In fact, sometimes INGOs were more critical than their local NGO partners, many of whom were *perestroika* liberals hoping and believing that the new aid system would work out well for the region.

Over the twenty-plus years since the Central Asian republics received their independence, the funding situation has changed several times, radically. Some donors left the region after achieving their 'transitional' aims; some countries (like Turkmenistan and Uzbekistan) moved largely outside the donor orbit, relying on other resources and alliances. Those agencies like USAID and the EU that stayed active in Central Asia began to transfer their funds through central government budgets or support to local self-government. The United Nations system had always viewed national government as its main partner, with NGOs as subsidiary, implementing partners.

Another of the major changes is the way in which international agencies have gradually redrawn the boundaries of aid programmes. The EU is a case in point. In the 1990s, it had two programmes (PHARE for eastern Europe and the Baltic States, TACIS for CIS). A key moment for FSU countries and civil societies came in the mid-2000s with the advent of the EU's Neighbourhood Policy. The Caucasus was included but Central Asia excluded from this advantageous status. In fact, the Central Asian countries more and more found themselves in 'catch-all' development programmes, in a variety of artificial regions linked to the Middle East, Afghanistan, South or even South-East Asia by policy-makers located in London, Geneva or Washington.

This is not to decry well-intentioned efforts by INGOs to make the new regions work, or to help local civil society influence the donors' choice of priorities and modes of activity. In the run-up to the launch of the EU's neighbourhood policy, for example, leading European NGOs adopted a proactive stance. The Aprodev group of aid agencies brought together their Central Asian partners to discuss the new EU strategy, took them to Brussels to study EU institutions and policies, and helped to set up a lobbying group called the 'Central Asia Platform'. The new lobby argued for programme priorities defined by Central Asian NGOs and platform members carried out baseline work analysing local NGO perceptions of the EU and its communication and funding mechanisms in the region. And as a result of these and many other efforts, the EU developed an ambitious funding programme for Central Asia for 2007–13.

The EU's Central Asia strategy has many strong points. However, since 9/11 civil society development has had to compete with the security agenda, economic development and EU access to the natural resources of the region for attention and funds. NGOs were included in EU poverty alleviation initiatives in Tajikistan and the Fergana Valley, in various partnership, democracy and human rights programmes – and many good projects have been implemented across the region. But the drawbacks are serious: 1) the volume of support to civil society is limited; 2) the programme is oriented on relatively big (bureaucratically cumbersome) grants, excluding smaller and less experienced NGOs; and 3) the EU deals with government, business and civil society in largely separate compartments (hence the human rights critique of EU policy in repressive states).[16]

Meanwhile, leading NGOs from Central Asia had begun their own critique of the work of international agencies. The overthrow of President Akayev in Kyrgyzstan in March 2005 was accompanied by a wide, civil-society-led, discussion about the results of development initiatives over the past fifteen years. One of the most dramatic results of this was the rejection by Kyrgyzstan of the World Bank's HIPC (highly indebted poor countries) programme. Using information and arguments from INGOs involved in debt relief and global accountability issues, plus a certain amount of local prejudice about poor countries in other continents, CSOs swung the Kyrgyz government against the HIPC scheme and it was abandoned in early 2007. In the other countries of the region, lobbying efforts were not as spectacular, but individuals and organizations were accumulating vital knowledge and experience of the complex issue of accountability – that is, the responsibility of organizations to the wider community (taxpayers, beneficiaries, local partners and the like). Indeed, from the mid-2000s the World Bank and other international financial institutions (IFIs) have responded to pressure from global civil society and included NGOs in discussions around donor policy as part of the 'Aid Effectiveness' debate.[17]

Case study: NGO Forum at the Asian Development Bank The Asian Development Bank (ADB) is a major player in the Caucasus and Central Asia, providing grants and credits to a wide range of development projects, both with individual countries and through the regional association CAREC. Like the World Bank, it has been for many years the object of attention from civil society groups concerned about issues such as value for money, corruption and the environmental impact of programmes. The NGO Forum on ADB (an independent body not funded by the bank) is a broad alliance initiated by groups in South and South-East Asia, which in the mid-2000s began to extend its monitoring and lobbying activities into the FSU region; their collective aim – to 'support each in order to amplify their positions on ADB's policies, programmes and projects affecting life forms, resources, constituents – the local communities'.[18]

The monitoring of ADB projects is an extremely difficult task, even for experienced NGOs and independent experts. These are typically enormous, multi-year projects supported by a large, closed bureaucracy: multinational companies, ADB programme management units and their government counterparts. A good example is road infrastructure projects such as the western Europe to western China road complex that passes through the steppes, deserts and mountain chains of Central Asia. This was one of the first projects that the fledgling Caucasus and Central Asia group within the NGO Forum set out to monitor. After a couple of years of uphill struggle, at a meeting held in October 2010, member groups from Kazakhstan reported on progress in community consultations on a US$17 million project for the part of the road that passes through their country. Activists had held workshops to inform the population (where there was nil previous knowledge of ADB), and one of the key emerging issues was its environmental impact. The result: over forty complaints forwarded to the Bank, the formation of a monitoring committee, and useful contacts established with local authorities and the relevant ministries in Kazakhstan.

At the same meeting, colleagues from Tajikistan reported on another ADB road project, this time linking Dushanbe to the Kyrgyzstan border via the Rasht Valley. They too had experienced problems with access to information: the ADB website is in English and many project details are considered confidential to the Bank and national government. The second problem they identified was lack of attention to the rights of those affected. The rules regarding compulsory resettlement for villagers whose houses were due for demolition (including provision of equivalent housing and/or monetary compensation) were not being observed. Disputes about the valuation of property and small businesses lost during the construction work remained unresolved.

NGO Forum meetings, like those of other monitoring groups, are a valuable way of sharing ideas on international development policy and practice. Thus, alongside the discussion on road projects, another NGO expert reported on Kyrgyzstan's energy policy (where international agencies and transnational companies play a key role), and a third topic for discussion was an ADB project to improve the investment climate in Kyrgyzstan. The paper demonstrated how national governments are able to release grants and credits from the IFIs by passing laws advocated by the banks. In this example, a public–private partnership law had been pushed through the Kyrgyzstan parliament in 2009 by the then prime minister and the Ministry of Economic Development. Its aim was to help attract new investment, support sustainable economic growth and job creation. However, it was adopted without public consultation, environmental or community safeguards, and in the opinion of civil society experts, failed to ensure the responsibility of private sector businesses to society as a whole. In some areas there were clear loopholes for corruption. The formal adoption of the law released over US$35 million in grants from ADB plus US$1 million in technical assistance.

All in all, Kyrgyzstan is viewed by ADB as a 'pro-reform' country (an image established by President Akayev in the 1990s by virtue of implementing economic shock therapy, joining the WTO and pursuing a 'multi-vector' foreign policy). According to the NGO Forum, since collaboration with ADB began in 1994, the country has received over seventy grants for technical assistance to the value of US$41.2 million. The report on the investment climate project says a lot about what is going on these days in the 'good governance' field. That is, it illustrates the serial adoption of government reforms as a way of keeping the foreign aid and credits coming in (and payments to government staff, consultants and expert groups). In the 1990s this work was mostly contracted out to international consultants, but now local experts have an increasing share of the pie. The trouble is that many of the reforms are not implemented, and many others don't work.

Case study: Extractive industries and oil revenues transparency The Extractive Industries Transparency Initiative (EITI) has its origins in the lobbying efforts of CSOs in different countries to gain an element of transparency in the mining (extractive) industries. Formally established with the support of Tony Blair in London in 2003, the initiative promotes a number of principles and mechanisms for monitoring the revenues that states around the world receive from transnational companies working on their territory. EITI has an international board, but countries agreeing to use its methodology operate independently, setting up their own multi-stakeholder groups and secretariat. Kyrgyzstan signed up in 2004, and its approach was validated formally in 2010. Just over twenty CSOs are part of the consortium monitoring the work of foreign-owned mining companies, 90 per cent of which is for gold extracted and processed by two companies, Kumtor and Makmal. Kumtor, much the larger of the two, is owned by Centerra, a Canada-based multinational in which the Kyrgyz government has a large share, while Makmal is operated by Kyrgyz Altyn, a wholly state-owned company.[19]

The members of the civil society consortium include environmental and anti-corruption NGOs operating at national level, and also a range of smaller groups based in the regions where mining activities are taking place. The consortium has opened five offices at community level and provides information to wider society through a website. However, it has major problems in gaining access to information. The first of these is that while private companies have signed up and provide reports, tax law in Kyrgyzstan prohibits the disclosure of certain kinds of commercial information and the data is not 'disaggregated' to show different kinds of revenue from different companies. And secondly, the accounts provided by the government itself do not fully meet EITI standards. This means that there are limitations in what civil society activists can tell concerned local citizens.

In some ways, EITI in Kyrgyzstan is a clear success. It has gained government and private sector recognition and implemented the global methodology – with twenty-six companies providing the required financial reports in 2011. It has lived through some very stormy times, in particular the years after the 2005 revolution when there was huge public pressure to revoke mining contracts, via land occupations and the blocking of roads around the country. Indeed, gold mining remains one of the hottest potatoes in national politics, with demands for nationalization continuing to be made up to this day.[20] Here, once again, we see the unclear boundary between civic and political action.

Quite similar to EITI are a variety of schemes to ensure that the vast incomes from oil and gas in countries like Azerbaijan and Kazakhstan are properly received and spent by the state. Several of these schemes were initiated by the Soros Foundation, one of the most influential and innovative donors in PSS, set up by the financier George Soros and therefore very much an IFI 'insider' organization. In the Caucasus and Central Asia region, several of the NGOs involved in oil revenue monitoring have become members of Revenue Watch, a non-profit policy institute based in Washington, DC. Its funders include not just the Open Society Institute (i.e. Soros) but also the Norwegian Oil for Development Fund.

Some members of Revenue Watch's Eurasia 'hub' have experience in monitoring state budgets, others in EITI. Because of the technical nature of the work, it is often led by higher education institutions or think tanks that provide training, information and expert advice to local activists. Work on state budget transparency has had significant results in several countries of the region. For example, civil society pressure in Azerbaijan led to the setting up of a National Budget Group that reviews state budgets and has persuaded the government to improve the posting of information on its official website. Civil society representatives on the budget group produce a 'citizens' budget' – a simplified version for distribution to the public. Azerbaijan set up a State Oil Fund in 2001 and over the next ten years accumulated US$70 billion in the fund – of which US$40 billion has been spent and US$30 billion saved (mainly in foreign bonds and assets).

In Kazakhstan, the letting of oil and gas prospecting and extraction contracts to foreign companies in the 1990s led to a major scandal ('Kazakhgate') involving pay-offs by companies to the president and senior government advisers. Fifteen years later, the Bota Foundation was set up with large amounts of money emanating from the country's oil revenues. This is now a major source of grant assistance to NGOs and as such can be counted as a success for the efforts to fight corruption and increase budget transparency. However, the main figures implicated in Kazakhgate were not brought to justice and the experts at Revenue Watch still see a problem in managing money coming into the Eurasia region from the mining, oil and gas sectors.[21]

This brings us to one of the most strategic questions for civil society activists working in the accountability field: how to relate to national government in the course of negotiations with international banks and transnational companies. Is government an ally or an adversary in the struggle? Should CSOs use information gained from close liaison with the IFIs to launch attacks on government policy – e.g. where they see faults or problems in education or health programmes?[22] Or should they try to work with their own governments, either to limit the damage from IFI policy, or reduce the credit burden falling on low-income countries as a result of these programmes? The experience of the NGO Forum is that in some cases – for example, the road schemes in Kazakhstan – campaigns relating to ADB have helped civil society develop accountability mechanisms within their own government. Activists now have better relations with local officials, can request information according to set procedures, and are even sometimes called in by government as experts (but within certain political limits).

Where corruption or major inefficiency by state officials is concerned, it is of course not so easy to make common cause with government. But some successes in tackling this problem have been recorded. Thus in Tajikistan and Kyrgyzstan, misuses of ADB funds in irrigation projects have led to court cases against contractors for misuse of funds, and the Bank effectively admitted responsibility and made financial amends.

A short summary. All these issues are extremely political. Any large civil society network will include 'reformists' and 'rejectionists' regarding the role of IFIs and the effects of globalization. The debates can be very heated. The difficulty of getting a response to formal complaints submitted to banks and governments, and the time involved in this, leads many to question the value of a reformist approach. It is hard to involve the general public in such complicated issues, and yet when they get involved they can have a very powerful impact – as the 2005/06 anti-HIPC campaign and continuing pressure for nationalization of mines in Kyrgyzstan show clearly.

Here the character of the NGO Forum at ADB and the Revenue Watch network as regional groupings stretching far beyond Caucasus and Central Asia is important. These networks have access to specialized resources and the ability to organize regional meetings and produce good-quality, well-researched publications, all of huge importance to local civil society. While is difficult to argue that forums and funds with head offices outside the FSU are locally owned, they are at the present time an important ally and resource, as local NGOs begin the slow and complex process of entering global civil society.

4 Conclusion: what about the major Russian companies?

Finally, we should briefly consider the question of how open or amenable Russian companies are to checks by civil society, or even to project-level collaboration with the civic sector. Some of these companies are among the largest in the world, with large empires outside Russia and FSU – that is, in Europe, the USA and other continents. Many of them are in the oil and gas industry and most have close links with officials in the Russian government.

The history here is that in the 1990s top enterprise managers and senior state officials were actively encouraged by Boris Yeltsin to join in the privatization process – in particular the infamous 'loans for shares' deal that helped Yeltsin win the 1996 presidential election. Prime Minister Viktor Chernomyrdin, who helped to steady the ship for Yeltsin in the middle of that decade, was an ex-head of Gasprom. Other well-known oil and gas companies that have had close links with government include Yukos – privatized then renationalized by Putin (with the imprisonment of its boss Khodorkovsky); Slavneft – privatized, then partially renationalized; and Rosneft – partially privatized.[23] Putin's position is for, not against, privatization. However, he has been concerned to draw back strategic resources into the state sector and to 'show who's boss'. During the 2000s, the links between government and business became ever closer. In this, government-aligned business associations like *Delovaya Rossiya* (Business Russia), *Opora* (Support) and the Russian Union of Industrialists and Entrepreneurs have played a big role. And they do their best to keep others out.[24]

Russian NGOs have been trying for more than ten years to influence business – that is, to help introduce corporate social responsibility (CSR) in the sector. A cross-sector group at the United Nations Development Programme's Russia office has played an important coordination role in this. And in a recent publication on programme evaluation by NGO experts from around Russia, alongside articles about the monitoring of state employment and municipal services, there are case studies assessing CSR projects launched by major companies like RusAlum and Sakhalin Energy. It is just a first step – there is a huge task ahead given the corrupt and chaotic way things have gone in the past two decades (see Kuzmin et al. 2009).

In Central Asia the situation is rather different. For historical reasons, Russian business has a significant presence in the post-Soviet space. In countries where Russians are in a minority, going into business has been a logical and widespread choice for ambitious young people seeing less chance of advancement in the state sector. There are many Russian-owned businesses with a high profile in the region: mobile telephone companies such as Megafon and MTS are one example, the dairy/foods business with an English-sounding name, Wimm Bill Dann, another. In some countries there have been serious clashes (shareholder and legal battles) around the ownership and control of these companies.

To this day the major Russian companies involved in oil and gas extraction, hydroelectric energy, the electricity and aluminium industries and so on stand rather to one side of the development sector. As a recent report by the Eurasia Heritage Foundation on the engagement of Russian companies in Kyrgyzstan and Tajikistan notes, despite the fact that FSU countries are often seen as a 'security belt' for Russia, 'there is no established practice of joint international development assistance projects by the Russian government and business, and no partnership concept has been formulated so far'. The report puts this down to the lack of a modern international development agency in Russia, plus mistrust between the government and business sectors and the absence of incentives for the latter to get involved in 'social and innovational strategies' (Eurasia Heritage Foundation and UNDP Russia 2010).

Thus, while corporate social responsibility is slowly establishing itself within the Russian Federation, in close liaison with Russian NGOs, it is still hardly on the agenda in what we have called the 'third' or 'outer' periphery. Russian-owned businesses lag significantly be-hind the practice of other transnational companies involved in the negotiations around accountability described in the previous sec-tion of this chapter. And the Russian government lacks a significant partner for its development strategy in the region – unlike agencies from other continents and countries that try to link development and private sector objectives closely. When this is added to the problems affecting all investors in fragile states, the Eurasia Heritage Founda-tion/UNDP report concludes that it is a difficult environment and a lot of work needs to be done. We can agree with that. Without a civil society input it will be hard to achieve significant results.

9 | RUSSIA AS A BRIC

1 Introduction: Russia – a middle-income country

If we look at Russia and its neighbours in PSS, we can see that a 'north–south' divide is beginning to emerge out of the ashes of Soviet levelling egalitarianism. As we have seen in earlier chapters, centre–periphery relations are being re-created in various kinds of ways – that is, via the exclusion, marginalization or relative power-lessness of different groups in the 'three peripheries'. The biggest internal economic boundary in the region is now the border between the three founders of the CIS Customs Union (Russia, Belarus and Kazakhstan) and the ex-republics to the south in the Caucasus and Central Asia.

At a conference held in Almaty in 2011 to discuss this new divide, Russian experts highlighted figures that show clearly the difference between the more prosperous/less prosperous countries in the post-Soviet space. Thus Russia, Belarus, Ukraine and Kazakhstan all have more developed economies, an income per head of the population of US\$6,500 or more, and a Human Development Index (HDI) over 0.7. All are in the top seventy countries globally and all except Russia improved their HDI positions in the last decade. By contrast, the countries of the ex-Soviet south have less than US\$5,000 income per head of the population (with the exception of Armenia) and an HDI of 0.6 or less. More practically, research papers produced at the meeting showed why Central Asia migrants continue to come in such large numbers to Moscow, Novosibirsk, Yekaterinburg and other northern cities right up to the Polar Circle. The wages are between five and ten times higher than at home.[1]

Speakers at the Almaty conference noted that the placing of Russia in the BRIC group of countries – Brazil, Russia, India and China – seems to locate it globally in a middle position somewhere between North and South (i.e. the world's richest and poorest countries). Just to take one example, one can see important similarities between Russia and India. In both countries economic growth over the last few years has been significantly higher than in the USA and Europe; in both we can see the emergence of a bigger middle class, huge internal migration and increasing inequality. Both Russia and India can now be described as 'post-foreign aid' countries, with Delhi as sensitive as Moscow about international agencies' interference in its affairs, and imposing the same kind of restrictions on external funding for local NGOs.

The four BRIC countries are all very large in size and with significant internal development challenges that include problems of access, poor infrastructure, and the special needs of smaller or indigenous peoples. As we have seen, there is a 'south' within the Russian Federation as well as within the wider post-Soviet space: the autonomous republics and districts (plus several 'Russian' provinces) that have unemployment and poverty levels two or three times higher than the country average and exist on subsidies from the centre.[2] All this makes it hard to imagine that Russia could match US or European indices for GDP per head in the near future. Indeed, locating Russia as a BRIC country is often more relevant and useful than comparing it with the USA or Europe.

2 Russia's development model today

With the help of the analysis made in the previous chapters, we can try to sum up key aspects of Russia's development model twenty years after the collapse of the USSR. The approach here is to look at things as they are 'in actual fact', not what we might wish them to be.

First, it is clear that Russia still maintains a 'strong state'. Some of the historical and cultural factors behind this have been alluded to in earlier chapters. Starting in 1999, after the discrediting of democratic forces arranged around Yeltsin, the Russian people have on three occasions elected as president a candidate with a KGB background, a strong commitment to the military, the arms trade, to standing up to US global hegemony and NATO's eastward expansion. The insurgency (struggle for independence) continues in the northern Caucasus and terrorist attacks and explosions have continued throughout the last decade, reaching to the heart of Moscow and strengthening the hand of the country's hawks. This is all abundantly clear.

Is a strong state necessarily authoritarian? Seemingly there is a tendency for this to be so. Indeed, populist leaders like Boris Yeltsin or Vladimir Putin achieved their popularity in part by showing that they were strong – and what easier way to do this than by being authoritarian? Often this is at the expense of civil society activists or groups. Looking at this question from the standpoint of social movements, Tilly and Tarrow (2007: 55–7) define four types of regime that opposition groups may have to contend with: 1) high-capacity democratic, 2) high-capacity undemocratic, 3) low-capacity demo-cratic, 4) low-capacity undemocratic. Here 'capacity' means the ability of a state to design and carry out the policies and programmes that it might wish to. On a grid of this kind, the analysis in my book places Putin's Russia towards the high-capacity and the low-democracy ends of the spectrum. It has greatly enhanced its capacity under the current leadership, and it has a lower democracy rating than at the height of *perestroika* in the late 1980s. But it is a mixed picture. Indeed, Russia has continued to be the 'composite' or 'hybrid' type of regime that several Western analysts called it over a decade ago.[3]

The question about whether Russia's strong state can become a developmental state, diversifying the economy beyond its raw materials extraction base and tackling the problems of human and social development referred to so often in this book, is a more open one. Russia is pursuing a 'catch-up' modernization strategy, oriented to Western indicators and performance. It belongs in the second or third wave of modernizing countries – the BRIC countries and others – that have the advantage of being able to learn from the West's mistakes, but also the problems of how to compete effectively with it. As in several other countries, accelerated modernization has been pursued via the 'seen hand' of a dominant government apparatus (civil service, government institutions). Those in power enjoy patron–client relations with agencies lower down the admin-istration hierarchy, with the business sector and citizens. Corruption is endemic. Reform is difficult.

How could the regime address these problems? The collection edited by Arinin (2010) quoted in Chapter 7 has some useful propos-als. One addresses the failure of the current model to think or act strategically, suggesting that the government should invite inde-pendent experts to bring new ideas to bear on social and economic issues, moving to a knowledge-based economy, more meritocracy and fewer clan- and special-interest-based appointments. Another proposes that regional leaders should be given more space in which to operate. A third recommends steps towards 'direct democracy' – that is, people's power. A fourth recommends the three-sector approach to development and in particular economic modernization. Today real influence on economic development is exercised by government and business alone, while civil society is a 'bystander'. Citizens' groups need to take on check-and-control functions and become themselves a generator of social innovations, taking an active part in formulating the guiding principles and value (ideology) of society.[4]

Putting the model on the map: the Yaroslavl World Political Forum An attempt to raise strategic issues facing Russia before an international audience took place during the writing of this book. This was the second 'World Political Forum' hosted by the Russian government in Yaroslavl in September 2010. The title suggests that this is an attempt to match the Davos World Economic Forum or indeed the civil-society-led World Social Forum. The meeting featured a keynote address by then president Dmitri Medvedev and was described by one of Russia's leading journals, *Expert*, as an attempt to show that Russia is determined to help shape the world political agenda, responding to economic crisis and trying to find solutions to the problems it has thrown up.

The main topics of the Forum were technological and economic modernization, the future of democracy, issues of security and international law. Domestic stars abounded, even some old enemies like the communist Zyuganov and arch-privatizer Chubais (who agreed on the need for the state to support national technological innovation and development – e.g. in the energy sector). Carlotta Peres (UK) argued that after the excesses of liberalism, state interventions will spark a new period of development of productivity and an increase in mass demand. She argued that there are no old productive sectors, only outdated means of production. The Forum took place in the lead-up to Russia's accession to the WTO and, interestingly, a contribution by Eric Rainert (Norway) argued that the country's position outside WTO gave it many advantages. He compared Russia's industrial strategy unfavourably with the approach adopted by both China and India.[5]

Immanuel Wallerstein led the section on democracy, arguing that this is a fluid concept, that there is no perfect democracy anywhere. It consists of two sides – government and people. It can be extended. Russian speakers argued that forced democracy does not work (viz. Iraq and Afghanistan). Lord Skidelsky (UK) defended Western 'pro-democracy' military interventions, claiming the reverse – that is, that democracy is an absolute and that adjectives like 'managed' or 'sovereign' democracy used frequently by the current Russian regime mean that it does not actually exist.

A local critic summed up President Medvedev's speech at Yaroslavl: all the talk about democracy and modernization hides a basically conservative agenda whereby the government will take responsibility for technological development as a precondition for economic prosperity and therefore democracy. The regime's true focus is on economic liberalization. It is a paternalistic approach because the regime claims to have sorted out the main issues arising from the chaos of the 1990s, so now all it needs to do is maintain the course it has set for society. It is a conservative approach because while Medvedev is ready to hand over elements of regulation and responsibility to society/civil society, he immediately makes a distinction between 'good' and 'bad' guys and argues that government should support only the former (Morozov 2010).

Sovereign democracy, neoliberal modernization There are several key political concepts on which the Medvedev/Putin government based itself at the start of the 2010s. Indeed, 'sovereign democracy' was one of these, developed in the middle part of the previous decade by Putin's aide Surkov. Why did the regime promote this idea? Perhaps there were two main reasons: 1) to assert the particularity of the Russian experience (problems) in developing democracy after the fall of the USSR; 2) to say to other countries 'hands off our political system' or 'stop interfering in our internal affairs'. Indeed, is there any country in the world that would not prefer to be sovereign and not pushed around by others? It is more a question of whether they have the strength to achieve this.

Beyond that, Russian political scientists have some arguments of their own. For example, Kuznetsova (2010) writes that in recent years academic arguments on democratization often come up against two problems. First, the erosion of democratic legitimacy in the advanced countries because of low voter turnout, mass media influence on political culture, and the lack of significant differences between the main parties. Secondly, the enforcement of democracy on countries like Haiti and Afghanistan and the limited success of these military operations. Once again, it is hard to disagree with the Russian position. Is there anyone in the West who thinks that the democracy under which they live is not 'managed'? How many people think that the actions in Haiti or Afghanistan were successful? Opinion surveys show not many.

At the same time, Kuznetsova notes another key argument repeatedly put forward by Medvedev and Putin, around the linkage between liberal democracy and a country's economic well-being. Russian government spokesmen argue that the economic crisis of 2008–10 has undermined the argument that democracy is good for economic development and prosperity. 'Undemocratic' states like China or the Persian Gulf regimes have done better than democratic ones. In 2008, the gross domestic product of the USA fell by 2.8 per cent, of Europe's twenty-seven countries by 4.2 per cent – while China's rose by 8.7 per cent (ibid.: 282), exposing to doubt the West's claim to be in the van of economic development. These arguments enjoy widespread credence in Russia, where many experts continue to hold the line that economic issues are more important for society than liberal democracy.[6]

A third key issue is around corruption and what lies behind corruption – political and economic morality or culture. It is increasingly admitted by political scientists and economists in Russia that not only did free market shock therapy fail in the 1990s, 'culture shock therapy' failed too. That is to say, many Russians have remained very traditional in their views and way of life (including adherence to many values promoted in the Soviet period). It was hoped that economic freedom would create a middle class and via this new class some new 'European' values would be born and transmitted to society at large. But many of these hopes have been disappointed.

No doubt about it, Russia gained a significant degree of freedom in the *perestroika* period and after. In fact, it can be argued that what was most important at that time was not democracy but freedom: both for Russia and the soon-to-be free countries of FSU and eastern Europe. In the words of one analyst, Russia can be described as 'a free country with an authoritarian regime' (Inozemtsev 2010). It seems a paradox but, he points out, Russian citizens enjoy a multiparty political system, free speech, the right to openly criticize Russia's rulers, a variety of national media outlets, access to Western newspapers, free access to the internet, a market economy, freedom to travel abroad ... And at the same time there is systemic corruption in Russia. Freedom has led to a situation where 'there are no citizens left'. Everyone is out to make money. This is a 'destructured society' unable to organize itself and pursue common aims. 'By the end of the 2010s, the basic principle of Russian reality had taken shape: free conversion of power into money and property and back again.' Power is now a 'kind of business', and the global market economy is one of the main supports for this, because: 1) Europe is ready to buy as much oil and gas as Russia can sell, 2) there are a multitude of offshore tax havens where entrepreneurs and government officials alike can hide their money.

All these 'paradoxes' (as we charitably called them in Chapter 1) have led to what another liberally inclined analyst admits is 'resentment' among the people. The fact is that for many in the post-Soviet elite, the economic side came first (i.e. making money), European culture and values somewhat later. A significant section of the population that voted for Putin and Medvedev are reacting against this; they support the government's populist stance against both the liberal elite and the oligarchs. In a recent article called 'How to depose the authoritarian majority: not an easy task', Urnov argues that the pro-democratic camp needs to think how to reduce resentment and how to turn Russian culture from authoritarian to democratic – via a kind of 'cultural reprogramming'. This would include 1) undermining old myths and stereotypes, 2) providing mass training in democratic management at all levels, 3) assuring government support for civil society, educators and cultural workers (Urnov 2010: 78–88).

In his own contribution to the collection on Russia's modernization, Arinin agrees. While statistics produced by the Russian Academy of Sciences show that 40 per cent of Russians live in poverty, and data from the Institute of Sociology show that the incomes of the richest exceed the incomes of the poorest by a factor of thirty to thirty-five, we are witness to the 'incompetence and irresponsibility' of the elite and government officials, the greed, egoism, and corrupt machinations of Russian business. Which in turn leads to a lack of work motivation of much of the general population' (Arinin 2010: 46–52). And the children of the elite are no better ...[7]

Another reason for the problems of the right: the strength of the left in Russia By summer 2011, the papers were regularly asking questions and speculating about the future of the Medvedev–Putin tandem, in particular would both stand for president in 2012? And if only one of them, which one would stand? Indeed, quite apart from the media hype, it was an interesting question. Putin was clearly the senior and the more powerful of the two, but as noted in an earlier chapter Medvedev had demonstrated liberal colours attractive to many inside and outside Russia. Typical of these were his comments at a major annual event, the St Petersburg Business Forum, quoted in the daily *Kommersant*, to the effect that 'Our previous model of power no longer works for me', 'We have to move from the manual system of economic management to market controls', and 'We are not creating state capitalism'. Another article in the same paper describes Medvedev's plan for more sell-offs of state-owned companies. Other observers expressed fears that the election of Putin would lead to economic and political 'stagnation' in Russia.[8]

An analysis of the political parties for the 2011 Duma elections shows that almost all the main parties wooed voters with left-sounding programmes. The communists offered nationalization of the raw materials extraction, electricity, machine-building and aviation industries; increased spending on rural development, transport, science, education and health. On the centre left, Just Russia promised to stop privatization and impose taxes on luxury goods and money transfers abroad, raise social sector salaries and return to the 'solidarity' pension system. The 'party of power', United Russia, sounded quite left too, with its programme to create 25 million 'modern' jobs over twenty years, to raise average wages by 50 per cent in two years, and impose a property tax on the wealthy. This left only Zhirinovsky's Liberal Democrats and Prokhorov's *Pravoe Delo* (Right Thing) clearly on the right.[9]

According to polls quoted at a round table entitled 'Who is Left in Russia and the world?', held in April 2012, the majority of voters in Russia consider themselves 'left' – 40 per cent as socialist, 20 per cent as communist. This is despite the history of Bolshevik repression of other strands in the socialist movement – the Mensheviks, Social Revolutionaries and others – and the gradual drift into dictatorship and a one-party hierarchy. As often during discussions of this kind, there was not a huge amount of agreement at the round table. For some, the communists clearly espouse right-wing positions, while other dismiss Just Russia as a creation of the Kremlin, and for others ultra-left groups have little influence with the wider public.

The 2011/12 elections were a major success for the left and there would seem to be many points around which to build unity. As one participant at the round table put it, it should be easy to be socialist now when capitalism is so clearly defined in Russia; as another remarked, the most important positions for socialists are clear – a socially oriented government, democratization, tolerance of minorities, confidence that 'another world is possible' ... But according to a third, the mass protests of December 2011–March 2012 haven't yet produced a clear political platform (let alone a socialist one). This means, according to a fourth, that there is a long road ahead for the left to gain cultural-values hegemony. Despite its left majority, today Russia is one of the most right-wing countries in the world.[10]

The postscript to this is that Putin and United Russia indeed made a great many promises to the Russian people as part of the 2011/12 election campaign. Some of these were quoted above. Others included building 1,000 new schools in five years and doubling the house building programme by 2016 while reducing mortgage lending rates, doubling road building in ten years ...[11] Only time will tell how much of this will be delivered in the third decade after Russia's capitalist revolution.

3 Russia, the BRICs and G20

The term BRICs was coined by Western bankers who at the turn of the twenty-first century were beginning to place their bets on the high growth rates of emerging-market economies in different continents (despite the earlier stock market crashes in Russia and East Asia). These sources are still bullish, and one can regularly read optimistic forecasts in English-language newspapers such as *Moscow News* or *Moscow Times*. 'Ready for a BRIC century', proclaims a typical article in the latter, noting that the BRICs are already among the ten biggest economies in the world and they may represent four out of the top five by 2050. 'How long will it take the investors to accept that growth markers are actually fiscally more prudent and financially in better shape than in the Western world?' asks the head of Goldman Sachs Asset Management.[12]

Indeed, the BRICs are a significant group of countries, especially if you add South Korea, South Africa and Mexico, as some do, to the original foursome. They are huge recipients of foreign investment. If you look more widely at 'emerging countries' or 'emerging markets', these now make up 82 out of 191 countries, some 46 per cent of the land territory of the globe and 68 per cent of its population. The BRICs have many things in common – not just the recent high growth rates but also a tendency to corporatism and state-led development. In this sense, the Russian development model is one of the main options in the early twenty-first century.

One of the big questions is: what can Russia or the BRICs do with the global recognition they have achieved? What new ideas or policies of interest to the world audience can they suggest? The experience of NATO countries' interventions in Asia, the Arab world and Africa in recent years seems to indicate it will be hard to reduce Western political-military hegemony. Despite the BRICs' opposition, there was little change from the Iraq and Afghan scenarios – even UN acquiescence to the Libya bombardment. Experts commented on the Libya situation on Russian TV to the effect that the BRICs have not yet developed a shared platform. To date, they are more of an economic than a political counterweight to the West. Their actions are mainly bilateral – e.g. Russia and China resisting the US military bridgehead and listening-post in Central Asia – rather than multilateral.[13]

So will the advent of the 'BRIC century' mean any change in global politics or the policies of the international financial institutions? Will it help the smaller, poorer countries in any way?[14] The BRICs have made big play of their willingness to put major new funds into international development programmes, but will this come to fruition?[15] Perhaps the comments of veteran Marxist Samir Amin, quoted in *Left Politics*, are relevant here. According to Amin, we are in a 'grey period' when lots of 'monsters' may appear. The USA has not given up its stake in military domination of the globe. The main conflicts are North–South, capitalism–socialism, centre–periphery. Some in the new ruling class in Russia may have the 'illusion' that they will be able to find a place at the global top table, but they are unlikely to be successful. In reality, we must aim for social progress (not necessarily socialism) and try to create social blocs in a multi-polar world.[16]

The position of Russia and the BRICs is sometimes described as 'realist' in international and development matters. This undoubtedly reflects the disillusioned, hard-headed view of many Russian analysts and President Putin himself on foreign policy issues – where they see Western pressure and hypocrisy on all sides. The international development policies of Russia and China are described as realist because their aid to foreign countries follows their own national interests and is given 'without strings attached' (Bebbington 2008; Cheru and Obi 2010). For example, in recent years China has invested huge resources in infrastructure building projects in Africa, gaining access to raw materials for its own economy without making demands for political reforms in the recipient countries. Perhaps this is a practical or realistic approach. On the other hand, one could argue that the commitment to 'sovereign democracy' is a principle being applied here, or that the economic exchanges are fair to both sides. And many people question whether Western aid is really so altruistic.

Civil society at the crossroads In autumn 2011, INTRAC and civil society partners in Europe, Asia, Africa and Latin America launched a project comparing the recent experience and future challenges of civil society globally. On the one hand, economic growth has elevated many previously 'developing' countries to middle-income status and several have joined the G20 as major world economic powers. On the other, developed countries face massive public debt and significant constraints on government budgets. Over the past thirty years, Northern and Southern NGOs alike have taken on major tasks in international development. In doing so, their functions have expanded from a relatively narrow but respected repertoire (e.g. in poverty reduction) to encompass a wide range of more contested activities (e.g. defending a range of rights and political positions). The bipolar world of the time of the Cold War was succeeded in the

1990s by a 'new world order' where the USA had supreme dominance, but now a new period is beginning. Global governance has become more complex as new problems of reordering power (e.g. with the BRICs and G20 countries demanding more influence) are layered on top of the old issues of poverty and exclusion.[17]

The 'Civil society at the crossroads' project produced over twenty case studies of civil society development and social movement struggle – in the UK, the Netherlands, Greece, Chile, Argentina, Greece, South Africa, India, Indonesia and Russia to name a few. The case studies considered the character and activities of registered NGOs and informal networks and campaigns; the main problems facing citizens in organizing themselves; the role of traditional and new media; and some of the main demands being made on governments across the world. Perhaps it is not so surprising that civil society in the BRIC countries faces similar challenges.[18]

To continue an international comparison made at the start of this chapter, colleagues from INTRAC's partner organization PRIA noted that as India's buoyant economic growth in 2000–10 brought in more resources for government, social sector spending had begun to increase – often with the participation of CSOs. In India, this is not only in service delivery; there are some new rights-based programmes (e.g. in the health and employment sectors) and experiments with progressive governance – giving CSOs more access to government information, allowing them to undertake a monitoring role. Civil society has shown itself willing to take on the challenge of creating social accountability (e.g. the mass anti-corruption movement led by young urban activists). And the government is trying to tie civil society into the system of service contracts, meanwhile tightening up the regulatory framework for civil activism. All this echoes trends in Russia that were described in Chapters 5 and 7 of this book.

In South Africa, by contrast, civil society colleagues noted a worrying sense of disillusion. Many political activists from the liberation struggle had moved from the mass democratic movement into government after the fall of the apartheid regime. The new government is keen to press them into service delivery in an attempt to meet the basic needs of the population.[19] But spaces for freedom of expression and association are reducing, at the same time as South Africa remains one of the most unequal societies in the world, with its model of capitalism having many of the same glaring faults as in Russia today.

Indeed, the BRIC countries can hardly promote social progress abroad if they do not practise it at home. A recent report produced by Oxfam and disseminated by its Moscow office is quite relevant in this respect. Entitled 'Left behind by the G20?', the report calls on members of this group not to forget issues around inequality or to delude themselves that economic growth by itself will bring about a reduction in poverty in their countries. The G20 countries now include in their ranks more than half of the world's poor (remember India, China ...). And in all G20 countries except four, income inequality has continued to grow since 1990.[20]

At a round table organized in Moscow to discuss the report, Russian experts discussed how their government might best set about reducing poverty and inequality. Some emphasized economic measures to encourage job creation and small business growth, others more effective social transfers (i.e. redistribution of resources to depressed regions of the country) and targeted social assistance programmes, others again a rise in the minimum wage, more generous child benefits for poor families, a progressive income tax, and measures to tackle gender inequality. All agreed on the need for a more strategic vision of sustainable development.

The comparisons of Russian performance with that of its BRIC partners seemed to be quite helpful in the analysis of policy options. Thus one speaker noted that inequality in Brazil has come down slightly, reflecting successful social and economic policies in that country. In India it is rising but only slowly, thanks to efforts to reduce poverty and unemployment. In China inequality is growing faster, owing no doubt to the speed and breadth of market reforms. In Russia, the Gini rating has stabilized but at far too high a level. Steps to boost wages and the more than doubling of state pensions in 2006 were key steps in the last decade, it was noted, but much more needs to be done.[21]

A presentation of the 'Civil society at the crossroads' global report and Russia civil society case study in Moscow and Novosibirsk in early 2013 elicited significant interest and agreement. In Moscow, participants discussed why the anti-global movement has been less vocal than in other countries, the role of individual citizens alongside

TABLE 9.1 Gini inequality coefficient in Russia and other countries

Country	Russian Federation	Brazil	China	India	Poland	South Africa	USA
Gini coefficient (2000–10)	40.1	54.7	42.5	33.4	34.1	63.1	40.8

Notes: 1. The Gini coefficient measures inequality by comparing the distribution of income and consumer spending by individuals and households. A score of 100 reflects 'absolute inequality' while 0 reflects 'absolute equality'. The figures are taken from the latest year between 2000 and 2010 for which figures are available in each country; 2. In Russia and China the main damage to the egalitarian system inherited from communism was done in the 1990s. Thus the Gini coefficient in Russia grew by 77 per cent in the 1990s and only 3 per cent in the 2000s; in China by 20 per cent in the 1990s and 3 per cent in the 2000s.

Source: UNDP *Human Development Report* 2013

organizations in social action, and the increasing role of business and private philanthropy in charitable projects. In Novosibirsk, participants focused on the latest government clamp-down on democracy NGOs, the huge socio-economic challenges still facing the Siberian and eastern regions, and the prospects for the new Putin regime in tackling them before popular anger erupts again.

Russia, Central Asia and China It seems impossible from a Central Asia vantage point to avoid a comment on the relations between Russia and China as BRIC partners. In Central Asia, the question of competition or potential stress between these two big neighbours is frequently mentioned by analysts, though in the official media their collaboration in the Shanghai Security Organization is emphasized. As noted in Chapter 6, the contributions of China and Russia to international development in the region are significant, but for some reason treated in a separate compartment from Western aid.[22] China's economic influence is huge, via the ancient trading routes through the Tien Shan and Pamir mountains into the markets of Central Asia, whereas the Russian influence is overtly political and military as well as economic. However, development experts in Russia have for several years now been looking at different approaches.

Russia has now taken the first steps, as Petrovsky recommended (2007: 162–73) in creating a kind of RUSAID similar to USAID, not just coordinating humanitarian and technical aid to developing countries but also adding a new 'human dimension' to its foreign policy. According to Oxfam Russia, as part of the preparations for Russia's presidency of the G20 in 2013 and the BRICs in 2014, national experts had begun work on an 'innovational' development model and a new 'cooperation paradigm'. This would maintain the country's aid priorities in the health, education and food security sectors but add, for example, private sector contributions (which, as we saw in Chapter 8, have been relatively meagre to date). In Central Asia, we can see the beginnings of Russian support to independent NGOs, whether through the Russian diaspora or other routes, as part of this new development initiative.

One of the problems that development projects face in Central Asia is the lack of political unity and strong intergovernmental institutions in the region. While Kyrgyzstan and Tajikistan pursue a 'multi-vector' strategy in which it is difficult sometimes to see where the priority lies, Uzbekistan switches direction completely from time to time, entering and exiting CIS bodies in a confusing way. China's raw materials and infrastructure building focus can be clearly seen in Kyrgyzstan – major road-building projects and the plan for a railway over the Tien Shan mountains and down into the Fergana Valley. But the political risks in this seem enormous, since nationalist elements are strongly against the giving up of natural resources or territorial integrity. The advent of the CIS Customs Union is a major factor here, and China has already begun to adjust its marketing strategy in Central Asia with the downgrading of bazaars in Kyrgyzstan in favour of new entry points directly into Kazakhstan.

In Russia itself, the influence of and 'danger' from China are big issues especially beloved of nationalists. Unfortunately, there is a history of conflict between the two countries from the communist period. The orientation of most of the Russian elite to European culture and Western economic contacts means that Russia has yet to develop a real Asia strategy in which the key partner would naturally be China.[23] Thus, while Russia is stagnating and ambitious young people are frustrated by the lack of new opportunities, many Russians see China as more of a threat than an opportunity, worried by any strategy that might seem a detour from the European path of development. Closer trading ties seem to them to bring the risk of greater immigration from China, indeed of being swallowed up by it (while in reality more people from Russia are currently going to live in China than the reverse).

All this is bad news for the regions that border China – Siberia and the Russian Far East. Indeed, Russia can hardly hope to compete with China as a producer of manufactured goods – its labour costs are too high. However, it can supply oil and gas (the subject of protracted negotiations between the two countries[24]) and, as another expert writes, we should not forget the products of Siberian agriculture – forestry and water management – using the advantages of Russia's huge reserves and the possible benefits of future climate warming. Both food and paper are required in growing volumes in China, new labour power could be brought in from Central Asia, and investment both from East Asia and the West. A focus on agricultural development in Siberia might offend some (as not befitting a great power like Russia), but the trouble with high-technology industries such as rockets, nuclear power or aircraft manufacture, the same expert writes, is that alone they can't solve all the problems we have beyond the Urals.[25]

So here we come back to the vision of Siberia as a bridge between West and East, North and South, as promoted by experts like Boiko and Alexeyev (see Chapter 3). At the same time, the government needs to think about how the current population of Siberia could adapt to a strategy like this (including the need for further scientific and technical development and labour competition from China). By contrast, in the absence of an Asian or Eastern strategy, whenever there is trouble in Russia, the threat of the country falling apart is raised – for example, so-called Siberian 'separatism'.[26]

4 Development in the three peripheries: conclusions and prospects

In the complex, competitive and often violent global context, with a government determined to maintain control over both the business and civil sector, what can we conclude about the possibilities for development in the three peripheries we have identified?

First periphery: excluded and marginalized groups in Russia's cities and towns Robbed of their work and savings in the 1990s, disoriented by the paradoxes of undemocratic democracy and impoverished prosperity, excluded groups – with the exception of some exceptionally well-organized and self-aware associations (such as the miners and railway workers) – were slow to react. However, this book has followed Russian experts in charting the movement back to civic engagement and protest (even if some of the most vulnerable and marginalized do not generally take part in it). Russia's electorate has rejected purist neoliberalism and we have seen how hard the Putin and Medvedev regimes have had to try to head off popular discontent. The government has invited civil society to contribute to social services development and has begun to submit its services to regular monitoring by civic groups. Indeed, much of this is top-down or formal, but there is positive, innovative, independently organized experience from around the country that activists can learn from or make common cause with.

Structurally, however, it will not be easy to get back what was stolen from the people in the 1990s. Indeed, staunching the flow of capital being exported year by year by the richer classes seems to be beyond the power of the current government. Entry to WTO threatens to create another structural obstacle to poverty reduction, especially in the old industrial regions of Russia and the wide belt where climatic conditions make agriculture more expensive and less competitive.[27] Therefore deep social and economic divisions will remain.

The days of Western aid to solve these problems are in the past now. As noted by VSO's country director when the volunteer programme closed some ten years ago, Russians do not need 'aid', they need cooperation and opportunities to exchange ideas and experience with other countries. As we have noted on several occasions, networking, organizational and citizens' links will be very important here, especially if the international political situation deteriorates. Indeed, we cannot rule out the possibility that CSOs will have to work in conflict situations or via citizens' diplomacy in the absence of good intergovernmental relations.

Second periphery: nations and regions in the Russian Federation's outer fringes The unravelling of privileges enjoyed by smaller nations in the Soviet Union continues. However, a lot depends on whether they are large or small, titular or non-titular nations – and as we saw in an earlier chapter, whether they are sitting on large oil and gas or other mineral reserves. In most autonomous republics and districts of the Russian Federation, Russians make up the majority and this limits centrifugal tendencies; in almost all cases, these areas have been part of Russia for 200–300 years. Our short analysis of the Urals and Siberia regions points to the huge challenge in maintaining many of the urban settlements and industrial towns established in the Soviet period. The traditional Western-facing focus of Russian government policy has hampered the development of the east. Writers like Schedrovitsky have stressed the need to create coordinated development programmes in these regions, and in late 2012 President Putin announced a big new plan for the Russian Far East. The Federation Council in Moscow surely has a big role to play – but is not often in the news with eye-catching initiatives or decisions. Therefore it seems likely that regional development will continue to be a challenge.

On the other hand, a well-prepared and inclusive south- and east-facing development 'vision' for the Russian Federation could be a very attractive document. The geography from the polar region through tundra and taiga belts to the coniferous and deciduous forest and steppes to the south is a unique, grand and still largely untouched environment. The multinational indigenous peoples and their historic links living side by side with the Russian population; the Trans-Siberian railway as a transport route between Europe and Asia, the Volga and Siberian rivers playing a similar north–south communications role; the minerals extraction and industrial traditions of the Urals; new high-tech centres building on the region's higher education base; the cultural and architectural wealth of the Orthodox and Islamic religions – these are significant assets for any development strategy. Eurasian thinkers have much to contribute. But the on-off war in the Caucasus must somehow be brought to an end in a way satisfactory to all sides. Compulsory participation in a development strategy, however attractive the strategy, is not good in the long term.

Third periphery: Russia's cousins in the ex-Soviet republics The problems and possibilities outlined above mean serious limitations in what kind of assistance the ex-Soviet republics can expect from

Russia. On the one hand, the majority of Russian bilateral aid is likely to go to its FSU neighbourhood. This has been the case with major donors like Britain or France (which devote half or more of their development aid to their ex-colonies).[28] The setting up of a unified RUSAID will replace the current unsatisfactory situation where fifteen or so government ministries and departments take decisions coming under this general heading. But will Russia actually take on a bigger international development role? And will it focus on close-to-home regions like Caucasus or Central Asia? The Russian population's gradual exit from the region and the steady fall in the status of the Russian language in some of these countries both pose problems. As noted in Chapter 6, Tajikistan has not up till now received the attention or assistance it needs – including from Russia. In Kyrgyzstan, Russia made a highly publicized US$2 billion grant and credit package in 2009 – only for then president Bakiev to seriously let his partners down.[29]

These problems are raised from time to time in the Central Asia press by a range of experts from strategic and analytical institutes in Russia. Often, their articles are strongly anti-American. Sometimes they are extremely frank in their criticism of the political elite in Central Asia. For a serious tranche of criticism, here are some notes from a 2011 interview with a senior expert from the Russian Institute of Strategic Studies. The main points in this article: Kyrgyz politicians are still offering pipe-dreams to their electorate. The political system has not matured and there are still too many parties. Kyrgyzstan's habit of trying to rewrite agreements signed with foreign governments does not inspire confidence. The two revolutions in Kyrgyzstan show how property is being redistributed without attention to the concerns of companies that previously invested in the country. The idea of outing corrupt officials seems like a return to Bolshevik repression. Kyrgyzstan's multi-vector foreign policy means the country going cap in hand to one foreign capital after another ...[30]

On the other hand, without a coherent development policy and long-term practical programmes, initiatives like Putin's promise of a Eurasian alliance made before the 2012 presidential elections do not inspire great confidence in the region. Comments in the Dushanbe papers were along the lines of 'we'll wait and see what it really means' or 'he can't just call and expect us to come running' ...[31]

Priorities for civil activists Arising from the above, there seem to me four areas where NGO and social movement activists are already playing or could in the future play a vital role in promoting development in Russia. This is not intended as a complete list, simply one that addresses important issues that have been brought up in this book and can be taken up in grassroots campaigns and projects, or at provincial and national level.

1 Represent local communities

- Standing up for local people, particularly the more disadvantaged. Nobody can do this better. In Yanitsky's vocabulary, 'defending places in a world of flows'.
- Promoting cultural and regional diversity. For example, the Urals and Siberian cities visited in the writing of this book all have different images and feeling. Yekaterinburg and Novosibirsk – Soviet industry and modernism; Irkutsk – Russia's nineteenth-century grandeur. Ulan Ude – a Buddhist and Mongolian component. Maintaining historic place-to-place and community-to-community links (across geographical, cultural and other boundaries).
- Using bottom-up, interactive and participatory approaches. Foreign donors and NGOs like VSO and INTRAC have played a big part in the renewal of development methodology, and now Russian NGOs are taking this on in their own way.
- Continuing the difficult search for agreement between different groups (NGOs, trade unions, political parties, large and small organizations) for negotiated common goals. The *alter*-global and pro-democracy movements both show the challenges here – but also the importance of finding unity.

2 Advise and assist government

- In domestic policy, continuing the joint search with local and national government for quality services. At present, only 4 per cent of the population rate NGO services as 'good'. Trying to bring good practice in social policy at local level to the national level.[32]
- Taking the initiative in lobbying and monitoring government, rather than waiting for invitations to participate in formal, ineffective bodies.
- Promoting development of Russia's distant, more backward regions – including depressed towns and villages, Siberia and the

Far East, the autonomous areas … Lobbying for more government funds for NGO programmes in the regions.

- Helping advise the new RUSAID as it takes shape – arguing for a progressive, non-imperialist approach in the Russian government's education, culture and economic development programmes. Here Russians who have returned from the Caucasus and Central Asia can play a special role, using their better understanding of these regions.

3 Tackle racism and xenophobia

- Human rights groups already pay constant attention to the risk and actuality of national and ethnic conflict within Russia – in particular Chechnya and the northern Caucasus; it is vital to continue this work.
- Helping ensure that 'patriotic' discourse does not exclude non-Russians and that Russian 'civilization' is not taken to mean simply its European aspects, but includes Asian, eastern and southern elements with a multi-ethnic commitment.
- Increasing work with work migrants and the issues around identity and integration that migration is bringing up. Some examples from visits to Urals and Siberia: grant competitions promoting tolerance in schools and the community; the tradition of celebrating different national festivals; carefully targeted housing and employment programmes; local research into sensitive or controversial issues taking account of minority views. Trade unions have started paying serious attention to migrants but they could do more.

4 Develop regional and global links

- Humanitarian efforts are already commonplace in PSS. An example, activists from the NGO Urals House (*Uralsky Dom*) came down to Osh with 40 tons of humanitarian aid immediately after the 2010 riots in southern Kyrgyzstan.[33] The CIS Intergovernmental Committee for Humanitarian Initiatives brings together people in the educational and cultural spheres from Azerbaijan and Armenia (still bitterly suspicious of each other twenty years after military hostilities ended). Each year the committee organizes an orchestra with musicians from different CIS countries; recently they organized the first direct flight from Baku to Erevan to take the orchestra on its tour …

- Working actively in global alliances (e.g. the environmental movement or the World Social Forum) to strengthen the Russian presence in these forums. Though many Russians concluded in the 1990s that the Soviet Union had 'given too much aid' to poorer countries, there are many around the world who still remember and respect that assistance.

- Some of the best examples of NGO networking are among disadvantaged groups. One example from earlier in this book was the importance of networking for minority peoples from the far north. The disability movement is another good example: organizations set up in Russia and the Baltic countries with the help of VSO in the late 1990s are now promoting modern approaches across the FSU region. Examples that this author has seen in Bishkek include work with special needs education, Down's syndrome and other specialist areas.

It would be good if civil society activists and progressive-minded people in other countries could support this important work, in whatever way they can.

POSTSCRIPT

A right-wing country with a left-leaning population. A population enjoying many freedoms despite an authoritarian regime. A regime in the Thermidor (consolidation) mode after a pro-capitalist revolution. A civil society disillusioned by the events of the 1990s but re-engaging in the second half of the 2000s, whether through official channels, local initiatives or if need be on the streets. These are some of the viewpoints and contradictions emerging from this book's analysis of present-day Russia.

I hope that the book reflects the positive spirit of many NGO and development workers working alongside people, movements and communities in struggle. It has 'discovered' – that is, traced back – a tradition of citizens' involvement in democratic and development processes in Russia from Tsarist through Soviet times to the present. Impressionistically but reasonably convincingly, I hope, the examples provided in its early chapters have shown that the country possessed a multifaceted progressive movement in the late nineteenth and early twentieth century and many activist and policy choices were available in 1917; indeed, many were taken up by the revolution.

The book has pointed to the Westward- and Eastward-facing aspects of the Bolshevik regime and other streams within the movement – other socialist paths – that students of Russian history and political thinking might wish to investigate further. From a development point of view, I was particularly interested in grassroots initiatives, the role of volunteers and community workers, and policies that can be seen as forerunners of local government decentralization and regional policy within the Russian Federation. Another key issue for me was how civil society can help preserve some kind of autonomy or identity for smaller national groups. In all these areas there is a rich history but no easy path forward given Russia's centralized state system, determined to hold its own against the forces of Western political hegemony and economic globalization.

For Marxists, the transition of communist countries back to

capitalism in the 1990s has posed many difficult questions. In reality some lessons can be seen increasingly clearly. First, the Soviet Union's attempt to leap over the capitalist stage of development was ultimately unsuccessful (indeed, there were elements of state capitalism in the Soviet system, as left critics noted at the time). Secondly, the shock therapy practised in the Soviet bloc in the 1990s to bring these countries back to the global capitalist orthodoxy entailed serious losses for the broad masses of citizens. However, later chapters in this book showed how Russia is slowly recovering, with people and organizations re-entering the struggle at various levels for the public good, a bigger say in government and control over their own lives. And this can hardly be achieved without an ideological commitment to some form of progressive social change.

Many Russians admire what they see in the West; indeed, many have settled in Europe and the USA since 1991. As a traveller and resident in FSU for many years I too can look with new eyes on positive things I see in western Europe: the many institutions in public ownership, examples of tolerance and good citizenship, improvements in technology, communications and the general standard of living that the founders of Marxism saw as essential to socialism. But there are aspects where the Marxist critique of capitalism remains as strong as ever: as regards the individualism and marketization reaching into people's heads and their daily relationships; and above all the unequal power relations that this book tried to focus attention on when considering questions around development.

This brings us to a third lesson from the recent changes in the region. If Russia has gone back to capitalism – the capitalism that many socialists forecast for it at the end of the nineteenth century – then the struggle for a better or more advanced system is still ahead. If we reread the classics on the transition to socialism, we will see that they made the point forcefully: transitions are never simple or brief processes – they include periods of advance and retreat (periods sometimes lasting centuries).

A fourth idea springs out of Alexander Zinoviev's view, developed during the 1970s and 1980s in the period of 'real socialism', that communism is not a system that 'comes after' capitalism. Rather it is a system adapted to war and emergency conditions and one which objectively and for a time can meet many of the priorities of the majority of the population (e.g. full employment and provision of basic services). However, 'communal relations' between people (by which Zinoviev means something rather specific – that is, the mode of life of people occupying a 'communal apartment'[1]) are far from ideal and have to be enhanced by more modern systems, institutions, laws and customs. Unfortunately for the Soviet Union, these reforms had not been implemented before the regime destroyed itself. What are we trying to say here, via this play on words? That communism tried to lead people to the famous 'bright future' but in actual fact the collectivism that people lived was very much determined by violence and privation. And the system proved incapable of meeting their gradually increasing expectations.

In a recent book on Stalin's victims, the biographer of Bukharin, Stephen Cohen, notes how hard the anti-Stalinist movement in Russia was hit by the 1990s. As economic and social collapse proceeded, people had little time for critiques of a past that was beginning to look better than the present. However, I would agree with Cohen that this state of public opinion will gradually change. Too many families lost parents and grandparents – imprisoned, executed or simply disappeared – for this issue to die. This is the kind of long view we need to take in looking at development in Russia (see Cohen 2011).

On the other hand, in the 1930s and today, the class war in Russia was/is far from over. History shows that the richer peasants hung on to their resources, nationalist groups fought back when they could (even in collaboration with the Nazi occupiers), and that a new bourgeoisie was there in the making under developed socialism, including in the upper reaches of the Communist Party. What is the answer? How should socialists proceed? This question has been asked many times since Khrushchev's secret speech in 1954. The answer has to lie in a more democratic socialism and greater respect for human life. But how many generations will the poor and powerless have to wait for their political and economic rights? When will the gap between rich and poor, powerful and powerless, begin to be reduced? Here we are back with the questions raised about international development in the early chapters of this book. And the answers are not so encouraging.

In their book on Russia 'in search of utopia', Martyanov and Fishman pose different strategies which it is worth returning to for a moment. Could Russia opt out of the corrupt capitalist system again? It seems unlikely at the moment. Could it re-create a new 'empire of the periphery'? Russia's newly independent neighbours in the region would have objections to that. Arguing for an all-encompassing moral revolution, the authors state that localist, multicultural and post-modern solutions will not adequately address global problems but will just maintain hierarchies. This is not my position, nor is it that of many others quoted in the book. But many of us would concur with the authors that Russia should not accept its current position in the world system, because: 1) it is consigned to the sidelines, 2) slavery and injustice are perpetuated (Martyanov and Fishman 2010: 247–55).

What of the role of civil society? This book has argued throughout that citizens and free associations can contribute a lot to development – indeed, they have played a key role at several stages of Russian history. But we have also seen the complex relation between civil society and political society (see the chequered history of *narodov-lastiye* or people's power). As Kruzhkov concludes, in the USSR civic questions were progressively politicized, a process that seems to distort them gradually (as the struggle for power pushes values and traditions to one side). Revolution, war communism and the one-party state gradually destroyed the environment in which the Russian intelligentsia could thrive, posing the harsh question 'are you for or against us?' and decimating its opponents. War, terrorism and the war between the state and terrorists are all bad for civil society today. The Russian model shows that super-politicized society can erode or destroy civil society.

Many of these dangers exist within coloured revolution too, if it turns violent, as we saw in a short description of recent events in Kyrgyzstan. In the FSU, coloured revolution can be defined as the continuation of *perestroika* in a situation of continuing political conflict and imperfect or inoperative multiparty election systems. External players like the USA and Russia are involved in a big way. The question of government legitimacy is fundamental to the outcome of these upheavals, as is the level of self-organization or determination of the opposition forces. If there is major violence, there will be little celebration and a much longer time for the wounds to heal, or indeed for the new forces to consolidate their power.

A final word on the 'three peripheries': the excluded classes in the cities, the depressed regions of Russia, and the poor neighbours. My analysis certainly does not want to pose these groups against one another – which is the path often taken by racists and nationalists. All this book could really do was to point to some very complex problems and show how NGOs and social movements are engaging with them. A comparison of levels and types of disadvantage and the social and economic policy options in Russia needs a more thorough, expert analysis. But on one aspect the conclusion is pretty clear: the newly independent countries and Russia need one another. There is a potential shared gain from migration to Russia's cities and depressed regions resulting in creation of jobs, increased skills and incomes, more chances of local development, more remittances to the countries of the ex-Soviet south. Secondly, there are aspects of shared language, history and culture, mostly good things, decent values that are worth keeping.

But the top-down model of development will struggle to understand or open up the space for civic dialogue, more complex and negotiated development options in Russia and in wider PSS. The crude, egoistic forms of private sector development are a considerable worry, as is the failure of Westward-facing elites to give time and resources to the south and east. Modernizing catch-up strategies are not going to achieve major redistribution of resources back to the people. The Russian left needs to abandon resentment and rediscover internationalism and the many potential allies that exist around the region for progressive social change. Despite what has been said above about the difficult balance and unclear boundaries between political and social/civic action, these problems require a political solution. My book is intended as a contribution to that, an outsider view maybe, but certainly that of an engaged observer.

NOTES

1 Capitalism, civil society and development

1 One of the first comparisons between the claims of civil society and the reality of transition was Hann and Dunn (1996).

2 See Aleksandrova and Grishina (2004).

3 See Toschenko (2001). The author defines 'paradoxical man' as 'not just the contradictions within society, its social groups, layers and institutions – it is a real life situation for people, when a person pursues mutually exclusive strategies at one and the same time, often not noticing the paradoxical nature of his own consciousness and behaviour'.

4 See Salmenniemi (2009) and Howell and Pearce (2002: 39–62) for a full discussion of these issues.

5 This phrase is from Yakovenko's analysis of culture, politics and propaganda in a chapter on the Russian character as 'anti-Greek' (2009: 37–63).

6 The Decembrist revolt took place in St Petersburg on 14 December 1825 when approximately three thousand army officers, disillusioned with the Tsarist regime after their experiences in the Napoleonic wars, refused to swear allegiance to the new Tsar, Nicholas I. The four main leaders were executed and a large number of other officers were exiled to Siberia and the Far East.

7 For example, the Centre for the Study of Civil Society at the Higher School of Economics in Moscow, and the Centre for Social Policy and Gender Studies at Saratov University.

8 See the case study on the Anti-Slavery Society in Tilley and Tarrow (2007: 1–26).

9 Examples taken from Yakobson et al. (2011).

10 'The second edition of capitalism in Russia', articles by Boris Kagarlitsky and Alexander Tarasov, *Levaya Politika* [Left politics], 7/8, 2008.

2 The Soviet period

1 See, for example, the discussion around 'revisionism' in Soviet studies with Sheila Fitzpatrick and others in 'Revisionism in retrospect', *Slavic Review*, Vol. 67, No. 3, 2008, pp. 682–704.

2 See Kordonsky (2010). In Russian, the contrast is between реальный, 'real', and на самом деле, 'in actual fact'.

3 This section adopts the grouping of development schools from Rist (2008).

4 Rist (2008: xi–xii). Not a phrase that applies well to eastern Europe or FSU given the region's economic and social crisis.

5 Accessed from ruxpert.ru/download/GDP_per_capita_PPP_2013_(cur_int_usd).xls.

6 The name given to supporters of the party *Narodnaya Volya* (People's Will) in late nineteenth-century and early twentieth-century Russia.

7 See Shanin (1985) and Alec Nove, 'Russia as an emergent country' (in Nove 1979), for two classic accounts of underdevelopment in Tsarist and Soviet Russia. Shanin pays particular attention to the peasant class in Russian society, showing the structural problems that

the Soviet regime had to contend with in trying to implement socialism, catch up and surpass the advanced capitalist countries.

8 See, for example, Szymanski (1979) for an analysis against these big political claims at this time.

9 The post-1945 'invention of development' started with President Truman's four-point plan in 1949. The language of developed/developing replaced the language of colonizer/colonized in official media, building on analyses of 'stages of development', e.g. by Schumpeter. Lenin had also written on imperialism as the highest stage of capitalism. Development skirted uncomfortable issues like exploitation and the role of the state and gave primacy to GDP (Rist 2008: 76, 93–104).

10 Kagarlitsky (1999: 121–44) and regular articles in *Levaya Politika*.

11 For a description of Soviet aid to one of its main beneficiaries, newly independent India, see Clarkson (1978).

12 This section is based on Kruzhkov (2005), telling a story known to Western students of Soviet history from the works of E. H. Carr, Victor Serge and Isaac Deutscher, to name just a few. Kruzhkov quotes a very broad definition of 'people's power' by another contemporary political scientist, Korolev: 'The totality of actions of the majority of the population, indirectly carrying out a political role through the dissemination and assertion of objectively coercive social standards. This means standards that any professional politician or administrator has to take into account if he wants to attain and keep power' (ibid.: 17–20).

13 Lenin had polemicized with proponents of the Russian village commune for decades, arguing that the latter could never form the basis for socialism and that large-scale industrialization was essential for the modernization

of Russia and the creation of a mass working class. See Bideleux (1985) for an account of arguments on both sides. A bitter struggle ensued with the Socialist Revolutionaries, one of whose supporters fatally injured Lenin in an assassination attempt in 1921.

14 Several early Soviet decrees are quoted by Kruzhkov (2005).

15 For example, during the early 1920s almost every settlement and district unit had its own Peasant Mutual Society and the Central Bureau of Proletstud catered to the welfare needs of students much as voluntary associations had done before the revolution. These voluntary associations offered alternative ways of solving social problems, but the authorities doubted their long-term utility and the political reliability of their participants. New mass movements such as the Soviet Committee for Peace, the Union of Atheists or the Union of Women had an explicitly communist ideology.

16 The darker side of state-led development included the use of forced labour in mines, construction sites and new industrial projects. Solzhenitsyn, Roy and Zhores Medvedev and others began to expose this in the 1960s and 1970s. Since *perestroika*, the analysis of forced labour has delved deeper, including regional studies in the Urals. See several volumes in the series История Сталинизма [History of Stalinism], ROSSNEP, Moscow.

17 I recorded it in an unpublished book entitled *In the Red Corner*. (The 'red corner' in Russian traditional culture is a corner of the room where an icon hangs on the wall and candles are traditionally lit. In Soviet times this name was given to a display area for political information and notices in public buildings.)

18 For useful accounts of the impact of Soviet development in Central Asia, see Wheeler (1964), Shaw (1995), Akiner

et al. (1998), Roy (2000) and Jones-Luong (2004).

19 See, for example, Sullivan (2002) for arguments against wholesale mar-ketization and commercialism; mass cul-ture and its tedious and boorish aspects; and an examination of the manipulation of democracy and the failure to create a more participatory political society in the West. Or Dosuzinas and Zizek (2010) for a discussion about how to rebuild the political and philosophical base for communism.

20 INTRAC – International NGO Training & Research Centre, a UK-based organization working to support develop-ment and civil society around the world – www.intrac.org. From 2001 to 2004, our programme for civil society in the five ex-Soviet countries of Central Asia was supported by the UK government's De-partment for International Development.

21 In Ulan Ude, one complainant had previously had her electricity cut off for non-payment of bills, another complained that the temperature from the central heating was too low to be tolerable. They both won, but the court did not award monetary compensation or relieve them of the obligation to pay their bills (Humphrey 2010: 247). And in Tajikistan, influential international agen-cies like the World Bank have not made household central heating a priority.

22 For fuller answers to these dif-ficult questions, see Zharkevich (2010b).

23 In August 1991, Yeltsin banned the Communist Party of the Soviet Union and confiscated its huge property assets. However, in November 1992, after an appeal to the Constitutional Court, the party and several other politi-cal groups won a reversal of some of these decisions.

3 Moving east and south

1 See V. V. Alekseyev's chapter on regional issues in Russia in S. Chatterjee

et al. (eds) *Asiatic Russia*, Delhi: Shipra, 2009.

2 See the chapter by S. V. Makarchuk on Russian social democrats' attitude to local self-government between the two revolutions 1905–17 in Lamin (2004). Lenin criticized the Menshevik policy of so-called 'revolutionary' self-government as opposed to open rebellion, accusing them of 'tailing the monarchist bourgeoisie instead of heading the forces of the revolutionary proletariat and peasantry'.

3 These quotes are taken from the socialist press Голос социал-демократа [Voice of the Social Democrat], 22, 1910, p. 3, and Луч [Ray of Light], 26 April 1913, respectively.

4 GOELRO: the reconstruction and electrification plan put forward by Lenin in 1920.

5 In fact, from as far back as the 1960s and 1970s there had been a significant out-movement from Siberia to other regions of the USSR.

6 Boiko (1998: 8–10). Similar demands were made in the Urals region at this time – for example, by Eduard Rossel, governor of Sverdlovsk Oblast, whose eagerness to open up the region to new influences and investments provided an opportunity for VSO, the British Council and others to establish programmes in Yekaterinburg.

7 Waldron (2010) notes that Count Uvarov – coiner of the famous Tsarist slogan 'autocracy, orthodoxy and nationality' – paid considerable atten-tion to the Asian lands bordering Russia during his presidency of the Academy of Sciences, viewing the pioneering spirit as central to the formation of a healthy Russian nation. The harsh conditions of Central Asia were a good test of character and travels in these sparsely inhabited areas did not risk significant armed resistance from indigenous peoples, unlike in the Caucasus.

8 The Siberia volume in the *Historia Rossica* (Russian History) series, Dameshek and Remnev (2007), is a similarly valuable new approach, focusing among other issues on centre–periphery relations in the Tsarist period.

9 Interestingly, historians of Russian culture note that nomads were often seen in a positive light as open to new influences; whereas the more settled peoples were portrayed as oppressed, unreliable religious fanatics. The ancient cities of Bukhara and Khiva took on a romantic glow only after they became Russian protectorates (Abashin et al. 2008: 324).

10 Whole new concepts came into being as people moved from nomadism to a settled way of life. For example, the idea of 'boundaries' and 'another person's land' appeared for the first time in the 1870s. New practices were enforced through a mixture of carrot and stick. For example, in the effort to establish money relations as the primary form of economic exchange, the head of staff of the Siberian administration is quoted as advising Russian traders to force Kazakhs to pay in cash and, if they took animals as payment, at very low rates (Abashin et al. 2008: 196–7).

11 Pan-Turkism began in the Ottoman Empire at the beginning of the twentieth century as a movement to bring all Turkic-speaking countries and communities together under the Turkish state. Pan-Islamism appealed to Muslims rather than Turks and opposed itself to colonialism. See also Khalid (1998).

12 Water shortage was a major issue forcing collective decision-making in pre-Tsarist Central Asia and determining the annual routes of nomadic tribes so as to maximize shared use of oases, rivers and ponds; or for agriculture. The arbiters in water matters were called *mirabs* and the creation and upkeep of canals and lock systems demanded a large amount of communal labour or *khashar*. Russian administrators called them 'water communities' (Abashin et al. 2008: 203–5).

13 Some of the fiercest fighting took place near the town of Przhevalsk (named after the explorer) at the eastern end of Lake Issyk-Kul close to the border with China. By contrast, a report from a police chief in one area read as follows: 'the Kyrgyz see the police and government officials as their enemies, they aren't attacking the Russian population at all' (Abashin et al. 2008: 290). In the mid-2000s a small monument commemorating the uprising was built on the road from Bishkek to Issyk-Kul.

14 Several early decrees are quoted in Kruzhkov (2005), also materials from the 1920 Baku Congress of Peoples of the East, and the Congresses of Oppressed Peoples in Paris, 1920, and London, 1923.

15 In 1989, there were still fifty-three different national units (autonomous regions, territories, etc.) within the USSR.

16 From the 12th Congress of the Bolshevik Party, quoted in Kruzhkov (2005).

17 See T. D. Mamsurov, *Регионы – Центр: проблемы согласования интересов* [Regions and centre: problems in coordinating different interests], Moscow, 2000, pp. 58–9, quoted in Kruzhkov (2005).

18 For example, Kamalov (2011). The CERCEC conference at which Kamalov's paper was presented posed the interesting question of where the FSU region fits in the usual North–South development paradigm twenty years after independence for the countries of Caucasus and Central Asia.

4 Political mobilization

1 The term frequently given to a set of events in the former Soviet Union whereby the opposition challenged

and then overthrew the current regime (as happened in Georgia, Ukraine and Kyrgyzstan in the 2000s).

2 For an insightful view of Putin's political origins in St Petersburg, read the chapter on his boss, liberal mayor Anatoly Sobchak, in Medvedev (2008a: 321–72); and the same author for Putin's first terms in office (2008b).

3 In China a stratum of civil servants had formed from 2000 BC wielding great influence, whereas the development of a merchant or burgher class was much slower. Historians debated over whether culture and geography could significantly alter the main stages of development. Thus in Central Asia and other regions affected by water shortage or desertification communities were forced to set up and administer water committees, and here too the role of the state tended to grow and the role of private sector entrepreneurs was less.

4 Thus, in *The New Central Asia*, a chapter on the Sovietization of Central Asia is followed by one on the 'recomposition of solidarity groups' in the Soviet period and another on political factionalism based on clan and geographical roots (Roy 2000).

5 Kirgizia was the name used in Soviet times to refer to what is now the Kyrgyz Republic or Kyrgyzstan.

6 See his poems 'Арзымату' (1892) and 'Пять кабанов' (1897) in the collection *Poets of Kirgizia* in the Biblioteka Poeta series, 1980, pp. 67, 82.

7 Mikhail Frunze, the Red Army commander who led the Bolsheviks' military victories in Turkestan in 1919/20 and who gave his name to the capital of the Kyrgyz Republic (now renamed Bishkek).

8 See Hopkirk (1984) for a derring-do story of British intelligence agents.

9 See Sheila Rowbotham, *Women, Resistance and Revolution*, New York: Pantheon, 1972; William Mandel, *Soviet Women*, New York: Anchor Books, 1975.

10 Bischel (2011). This study is part anthropological, focusing on metaphors like 'virgin' land (new, untouched) or 'generous steppe' (because if you give the 'hungry' steppe water, she will become fertile and produce food for all). The Yagnob people trace their history back to soldiers fighting in Alexander the Great's army. An article in *Steppe Magazine* (8: 36–55) claims that many of them died from chemical poisoning in Zafarabad in the early years.

11 Or see www.sakharov-center. ru and its sections on 'Mythology and ideology in the USSR'.

12 The events of 2005–07 are analysed in more detail in Buxton (2011: ch. 4).

5 Local government decentralization

1 In the projects described above, VSO benefited from partnerships with UK NGOs such as the National Society for the Protection of Children, Health-prom and Mencap, as well as specialist units set up by local authorities such as Kent Social Services, working with social policy experts at Kent University.

2 See also Nadezhda Borisova's article on Perm, 'Город: режимы жизни' [City: real life regimes], *Neprikosnovenny Zapas*, 2, 2010, pp. 92–102.

3 See the booklet by V. Vyuzhanin (2010).

4 For example, a flat rate income tax of 13 per cent and a cut in corporation tax from 35 to 24 per cent.

5 Regional elites hung on to their privileges and secret income sources. 'According to the principle of bureaucratic hierarchy on which elites have been formed since Soviet times, offering obedience to any new master means the possibility of keeping your own political autonomy and sphere of influence. This includes shadowy spheres that usually exist and are protected most of all'

(*Nezavisimaya Gazeta*, 29 March 2007, quoted in Van Zon 2010).

6 For an early portrait of *Nashi*, see Ishkanian (2008: 58–85). According to the author, *Nashi* grew rapidly to over 200,000 members in its first three years. It can be seen as a pre-emptive move against the youth movements of the type that spurred coloured revolutions in a series of FSU countries. Activities include volunteering in social projects, organizing political demonstrations and rallies. The movement's manifesto stresses 'sovereign democracy' and 'civil society' and calls for the liquidation of oligarchic capitalism and a struggle against fascism and intolerance of ethnic minorities.

7 Russian Federation Law no. 18-FZ on registration of NGOs (2006) was heralded as an 'unprecedented assault on the work of human rights groups' (Human Rights Watch Europe and CA Division). Freedom House noted, 'the government intensified crackdown on NGOs, particularly those receiving foreign funding' (quoted in Javeline and Lindemann-Komarova (2010: 171–3). The authors argue for a less biased view of Russia in the West.)

8 The same article notes that to register an NGO in Russia costs 2,000 roubles ($66) plus the cost of legal advice – although the latter is available free from NGO resource centres and a number of websites.

9 Russian Federation Law no. 131-FZ, 'On General Organizational Principles of Local Self-Government in the RF'.

10 Babenko (2009). See Table 2.1 for some comparisons between Russia and other countries.

11 BAM was a flagship project during my stay in Moscow in the late 1970s, the subject of many an article by journalist colleagues at Novosti. It proposed a new railway running north of Lake Baikal to open up new regions for development

and relieve rail freight pressure on the Trans-Siberian Line.

12 There are new kinds of 'regions' that the government should develop too – not just geographical areas but innovatory economies, the biosphere or 'virtual post-economy' that may help Russia to compete globally (Schedrovitsky et al. 2005: 94–7, and subsequent articles).

13 Perm's 2010 Human Development Report shows male life expectancy in Kudymkar, the centre of the ex-autonomous area, as less than fifty years and male and female life expectancy taken together as only fifty-five years.

14 The criteria for making these comparisons included: 1) individual attitudes identified in a sociological survey (trust, solidarity, social responsibility, etc.); 2) an analysis of social practice (involvement in voluntary groups, habits of mutual assistance, level of information on social or political issues, etc.).

15 A similar report produced by the head of Perm's NGO resource centre for the Volga *okrug* focuses on human and organizational capacity issues familiar to INTRAC. He notes issues such as a cut in number of NGOs, traceable to tougher reporting requirements; solid but ageing leaders of NGOs; increasing financial dependence on government grants and contracts; difficulties in working in a more long-term way or in finding properly qualified staff; hence the public's low opinion of NGO services (V. Vyuzhanin, *Volga region NGO report*, 2008).

16 Quoted from a presentation on NGO development by ASI's president Elena Topoleva at the Bearr Trust conference in London in November 2011.

17 As one volunteer put it, 'There are those who say that VSO volunteers cannot change the attitudes of the countries of the FSU (and a few who say we should not even try because that means imposing our western values).

We agree: VSO will not change anything in the FSU. We cannot impose anything either. What volunteers can do is to show colleagues that there are alternative ways of doing things, which could have advantages if they choose to adopt them. And we can strengthen the arm of those who already think the same way.' Dr Richard Waldram, 'Dear health volunteer', Volunteer orientation paper, Yekaterinburg, 2000.

18 See Marquand (2009). This describes major donor ecological and sustainable development projects in Siberia; also the issues relating to what level of aid interventions worked best in Russia, how to disseminate results and influence policy.

6 Development challenges

1 Enclaves, areas belonging to one republic but fully surrounded by the territory of another republic, were one of the Soviet time-bombs that independence set off.

2 As Lena Jonson puts it in her book on Russian foreign policy under Putin, the Islamic question has become 'securitized' in Russia – that is, it is presented to the public as a 'life or death' matter and moved up the political agenda accordingly. This means that things that are quite unalike are frequently 'put in the same boat' (Jonson 2004: 10–15).

3 For some first-hand stories about religious leaders in Soviet-era Uzbekistan, Tajikistan and Afghanistan, see the early chapters of Whitlock (2002).

4 Бизнес и Политика [Business and politics], Dushanbe, 13 November 2011, p. 4.

5 In Kyrgyzstan, CSO groups made a serious attempt to challenge the strategy of development 'subordination' to rich countries after the 2005 revolution, even rejecting a World Bank debt relief programme because it seemed to condemn the country to an indefinite aid treadmill.

6 See 'Rogun dam as a guarantee', Азия Плюс [Asia plus], 12 October 2011, p. A13; 'Tajikistan and Uzbekistan – who will make the first move to make up?', 'Uzbekistan's complaints about the Rogun dam', Business and Politics, 13 November 2011, p. 4.

7 The president has now removed the Russian ending 'ov' from his surname but we retain it to avoid confusion.

8 The government's argument was that families are bankrupting themselves in an attempt to keep up with the neighbours, by organizing more and more extravagant family ceremonies.

9 Or the investments were rendered ineffective by the war in neighbouring Afghanistan.

10 See Babadjanov (2011). Babadjanov's article on social alienation was based on materials from the Complex Sociological Study, UNDP Regional Centre, Bratislava.

11 Russia has been the main destination for migrants from Kyrgyzstan and Uzbekistan, too. A smaller number of migrants from all three countries head for Kazakhstan.

12 From the International Organization for Migration (IOM) Tajikistan website, press item dated 23 April 2012.

13 Estimates from the director of the World Bank in Russia, Mikhail Rutkovsky, IOM Tajikistan website, press item dated 8 February 2012.

14 Вести трудовой миграции [Migrant labour news], 5(29), May 2011.

15 Asia Plus, 16 March 2012.

16 From the IOM Tajikistan website, press item dated 28 May 2012. Here the technicalities are crucial. There are three ways to work legally as a migrant in Russia: 1) via the quota, if your employer is official and registered; 2) as a qualified specialist; 3) fill out a 'patent'. This

costs 1,000 roubles per month (US$35), extendable for up to one year. It was designed for self-employed occupations but is actually used much more widely.

17 'Who killed Khursheda?' (St Petersburg), *Asia Plus*, 7, 30 March 2006; 'Tajik killed in Volgograd', *Asia Plus*, 22 June 2006, p. A9; 'Nazis kill Tajiks in Russia', *FC*, 1, 16 July 2007; 'Public execution on internet', *Asia Plus*, 16 August 2007; 'Tajikistan ambassador on threat to migrants in Russia', *Asia Plus*, 22 April 2009, p. A5; 'A Kyrgyz woman migrant: "Russians are so nice. But why are they killing us?"', *Komsomolskaya Pravda*, 28 April 2012.

18 Data from Статистика.ru.

19 This is quite different from other post-colonial situations – the absence of an influential foreign landowner or plantation class in the post-independence period.

20 While some fathers continue to send remittances, others do not. It has proved very difficult for wives to get alimony payments, and when their marriage was either unregistered or registered during a religious ceremony in the mosque, they have no legal redress at all. Among the latest effects of new technology are the so-called text-message divorces. On the other hand, having a migrant in the family increases its income-earning potential. Many migrants earn enough to be able to buy a car or build a new house in their ancestral village. A gap is opening up between these families and poorer families where nobody is working abroad. See Ulmasov (2011: 26–40).

7 Beyond alienation

1 See Tony Wood, 'There is no alternative: Russia on the eve of the presidential election', *London Review of Books*, 34(4), 23 February 2012. And in the same edition of *LRB*, the views of left activist Kirill Medvedev, 'They

treat us like shit', on youth and student actions at the time of the elections.

2 *Russia Today TV*, 17 October 2011.

3 In a collection of essays entitled *Socialism-21*, Putin's tightening up of the new market economy regime is compared to Napoleon re-establishing of order during the Thermidor period after the French (bourgeois) revolution (Smolin 2009).

4 Anna Ochkina's analysis of employment policy in Russia was placed on the IGSO website in April 2009.

5 See too Anton Oleinik, *Власть и рынок* [Power and the market], ROSSPEN, 2011, for a more technical analysis focusing on the tensions between government versus capitalist or oligarchic power during the 2000–10 decade in Russia.

6 *Аргументы и факты* [Arguments and facts], 7 June 2006.

7 Saturday (*subbota*) voluntary work sessions to clean up the courtyard, school grounds or town park.

8 See too Rose (2009). After an analysis of popular scepticism, cynicism and 'patience' around the region resulting from the lack of any visible gains from transition, Rose concludes that 'autocratic regimes are good at teaching people to wait' (p. 36) but distinguishes patience from loyalty. Later chapters show the evolution of popular response, e.g. the 'steady but positive trend since 2001 towards normalization of Russian society' (p. 175).

9 A shorter version of these case studies focusing on 'social capital' can be found in Petrenko (2008: chs 7, 8 and 10).

10 See too Shomina (2008) for an analysis of community development around housing issues.

11 For example, many old or infirm people living in prime locations were swindled out of their flats or simply murdered for them.

12 Advising work migrants is another important line of work. There are

significant numbers of migrants from the Caucasus and Central Asia in all the main Siberian cities. Local NGO activists consider that the attitudes to them are not so hostile as in Moscow and St Petersburg. However, they are far from fully integrated into society, and some tension is felt.

13 With fines up to US$30,000, according to *Moscow Times*, 24 May 2012.

14 *International Herald Tribune*, 15 July 2011, pp. 1, 4.

15 From the IGSO website, 19 June 2011.

16 They note as an exception the work by Elena Zdravomyslova on social/public movements, published in 1998. Also a number of Russian social scientists responding to the new wave of activism, among them Irina Khaliy, Sergey Patrushev, Oleg Yanitsky and Yevgeny Gontmakher. They express particular thanks to the latter, now head of the Social Policy Centre in the Institute of Economy at the Russian Academy of Sciences, for giving prominence to these issues. And they approve of his distinction between social and political movements – and in particular the definition of three types of activism: 1) 'everyday activism' around a single problem; 2) 'human rights activism' around not just our problems but those of other people; 3) 'political activism', demanding citizens' control over government.

8 NGOs challenging power

1 A counter-case is the fact of migration of poorer people from PSS to Russia itself. In fact, his localist argument leads Yanitsky into a rather negative view of migration, fitting into a gloomy view of the decline of human resources in Russia today (2007: ch. 6).

2 See Kordonsky (2010: 132–40) on what he calls NIMBY ('not in my backyard') local campaigns in Russia, e.g. against closure of village schools, build-

ing of new roads or cutting down of trees by new owners. His argument is that in many cases people are taking a limited or selfish view. However, this is in the nature of civil society protest worldwide – and very often local people *know better*.

3 The author has personal experience of working with colleagues in Central Asia to strengthen research skills for NGOs. The experience shows that studies by civic activists can influence government practice and decisions at local level and help build alliances for change at higher levels (where of course international NGOs are already active). See the INTRAC website, www.intrac. org, for a variety of publications on action research in Central Asia.

4 The resolution gives as examples the illegal cutting down of trees (a major struggle was going on in Akademgorodok around the threat to local forests), the damage caused by oil pipeline breakdowns, and plans to open mining activities in national park areas in the mountainous Altai region. See the site ecodelo.org/info.

5 In early 2013 Putin finally agreed to close the plant. Now the urgent task is to find cleaner and more sustainable occupations for the inhabitants of Baikalsk town.

6 For an optimistic survey of left prospects at this time see Kagarlitsky (2007), in particular chs 10–12.

7 Buzgalin (www.alternativy.ru, 3 March 2006). For extended analyses of radical trends in global civil society, see works by Kaldor, Tarrow and Batliwala and Brown.

8 See Библиотека журнала Альтернативы [Library of the Journal Alternativa], *Кто сегодня творит историю: альтерглобализм и Россия* [Who is making history today: alterglobalism in Russia], Moscow, 2010 for detailed accounts of Social Forum events by Russian participants.

9 This coalition is currently coordinated by Oxfam Russia (an organization that with other leading international NGOs has actively supported the World Social Forum).

10 See 2012 campaign booklets by N. N. Aleksandrov (ed.), *ВТО: Что ждёт Россию? Мировой опыт* [WTO: What can Russia expect? World experience], and K. A. Babkin et al., *Последствия присоединения России к ВТО* [The consequences of Russia joining WTO]. Some of these demands (e.g. anti-corruption measures) were incorporated, albeit in an incomplete form, in Putin's new programme after the 2012 presidential elections. Thanks to Yevgenia Konovalova at the HSE Civil Society Unit for her assistance in this case study.

11 These comments are taken from the report of a conference organized for social movement and trade union activists in May 2010, sponsored by the Institute for Globalization and Social Movements and the Rosa Luxemburg Foundation, with the aim of examining the effect of the world economic crisis on solidarity efforts in Russia. *Left Politics*, 3/4, 2010, pp. 43–61.

12 From the same May 2010 conference.

13 Boris Kagarlitsky's article on the 2006 G8 protests in St Petersburg, *Взгляд* [Viewpoint], 17 June 2006. For more commentary on these themes, see the websites www.ikd.ru and www.igso.ru.

14 In autumn 2011 a major oil workers' dispute in western Kazakhstan led to civil disturbance and the shooting dead of several activists in the small town of Zhanozen. Left political parties, unions and human rights activists lined up a strong campaign to defend the workers, but at the cost of the imprisonment of leaders of the campaign.

15 For example, the critique of post-9/11 aid policy in the region by Christian

Aid in publications like *The New Cold War*, or Oxfam GB's work challenging global poverty and trade relations.

16 See the paper by the International Crisis Group (2006).

17 See a variety of publications on the websites of leading INGOs, including INTRAC, www.intrac.org.

18 See www.forum-adb.org.

19 Gold production at Kumtor accounts for around 10 per cent of Kyrgyzstan's GDP. This case study is based on a report by Chiara Fabrizio for INTRAC in July 2012.

20 At the time of writing a parliamentary commission was deliberating how to get a better deal from Kumtor and local campaigners were pressing for nationalization.

21 Revenue Watch press release, 27 April 2011.

22 In both education and health the threat of privatization is a major issue across the FSU region. Readers will not be surprised to learn that the major donors actively support privatization.

23 See Sim (2008), where the three above companies are case studies.

24 According to Boris Nemtsov, a long-time liberal opposition leader with good relations with international business, the pro-government associations are 'blood brothers' with government, 'the gang that rules over business'. *Moscow Times*, 17–19 June 2011.

9 Russia as a BRIC

1 In April 2011, average wages in Tajikistan were only 9 per cent of those in Russia; in Kyrgyzstan and Moldova they were 30 per cent of the Russian level; in Ukraine a surprisingly low 39 per cent; and in Kazakhstan an impressive 70 per cent. Figures quoted by Vladimlr Mukomel, Institute of Sociology, Russian Academy of Sciences, at CERCEC conference, Almaty, August 2011.

2 See Zubarevich (2010). On the one hand the growth rates of the backward areas are higher than the average for Russia; on the other hand the labour market is significantly more restricted. The Putin–Medvedev government has invested heavily in politically strategic republics like Chechnya and Tatarstan but smaller, southern or mountainous areas like Kalmykia, Tuva or Altai still have official poverty rates around 35–45 per cent.

3 See, for example, the articles by Archie Brown, Lilia Shevtsova and Michael McFaul in Diamond and Platter (2002). And more recently the debate in *Slavic Review* (2011, Vol. 68, No. 3) about how authoritarian Russia is today, where a review of Luke March's book *Managing Opposition in a Hybrid Regime: Just Russia and Parastatal Opposition* led to the commentary 'From overlooking to overestimating Russia's authoritarianism' by Stephen Kotkins. The latter argues that the West overlooked the authoritarian nature of the pro-Western Yeltsin regime and runs the risk of overstating Putin's authoritarian approach.

4 See contributions in Arinin (2010) by Gaman-Golutvina (p. 18), Chirikova (pp. 25–6), Komarova (pp. 46–8) and Pavlenko (pp. 171–2).

5 Rainert argued that WTO entry tends to enrich previously modern productive sectors, while monocultures and raw-material-resource-based economies suffer. India and China used 'imitation strategies' so as to replace foreign imports with home-produced goods. Russia, by contrast, took up the idea of 'comparative advantage', according to which the structure of production in a given country is not important. Pavel Bykov and Olga Vlasova, 'Modernizers of all countries', Эксперт [Expert], 36, 13–19 September 2010, pp. 17–24.

6 Kuznetsova herself calls for a 'decoupling' of the notions of sovereignty and democracy, arguing that the European Union shows positive efforts by countries to give up sovereign freedoms for wider social gains. But these arguments are less widely accepted than they were a decade ago when the euro was quite new and European enlargement still held out many hopes in the East.

7 Children of the current political elite are close to power and money but they don't have the 'legitimacy' of their parents of the 1990s. 'All in the family', *Moscow Times*, 2 August 2011, p. 8.

8 See respectively *Kommersant*, 1, 18 June 2011, and *Nezavisimaya gazeta*, 28 July 2011.

9 These points are taken from a short analysis of electoral platforms in *Arguments and Facts*, 2011, No. 39, p. 7.

10 Round table 'Who is "left" in Russia and the world: boundaries and additions to the term "left" yesterday and today? Who can or can't we call "left" in modern Russia?', International Memorial, Moscow, 27 April 2012, www.hro.org/print/13959 info@hro.org.

11 See 'What Putin said in his inauguration speech', *Russky Reporter*, 10–17 May 2012, pp. 26–7. A year later the promises were beginning to cause a strain. See *Kommersant*, 19 November 2012, p. 3, as the Medvedev government began to lose popularity, struggling to fulfil the extravagant promises made by Putin in his presidential campaign. And despite extensive TV coverage designed to show the prime minister as a dynamic, charismatic leader.

12 *Moscow Times*, 2 August 2011, p. 9. Or 'BRIC countries strong as world enters new economic crisis', *Moscow News*, 22–25 June 2012, p. 5, with comment during the G20 summit in Mexico.

13 Comment on Russia Today TV, 16 October 2011.

14 Colonel Gaddafi asked this question at the UN General Assembly a year

before his demise, using his chairman-
ship of the African Union to warn that
discussions about middle-level countries
like India and Brazil taking a place at
the Security Council appeared to ignore
the interests of poor countries in Africa
and Asia.

15 'Brazil, Russia, India, China offer
IMF financial aid for wider policy role',
The Australian, 27 April 2009. At a
meeting of the four countries it was
announced that they would be willing to
contribute to a quadrupling of the IMF's
resources by purchasing bonds. But they
expected to get their shares in decision-
making bodies at the IMF increased
accordingly – to help the IMF tackle
its 'democratic deficit' Brazil's finance
minister said. In the same year a World
Bank–Department for International
Development (UK) project began to
provide technical assistance to Russian
ministries and agencies, including the
development of new university courses
on international aid, and work with journalists and officials on the management
of aid programmes.

16 *Left Politics*, 3/4, 2008, pp. 102–5.
See the efforts of left activists to forge
links between Russian NGOs, social
movements and trade unions described
in the previous chapter. In Central Asian
countries, the formation of a social bloc
capable of pressing for social progress is
lagging seriously behind.

17 Information on 'Civil society at
the crossroads' is available at www.
intrac.org or via INTRAC's partners
Community Development Resource
Association (South Africa), Society of
Participatory Research in India (PRIA),
ICD (Chile), PSO (Netherlands), EASUN
(Tanzania).

18 Several of the case studies were
brought together in a special edition of
the journal *Development in Practice* (vol.
23, August 2013) edited by Brian Pratt,
Rajesh Tandon and David L. Brown.

This includes a Russia case study by the
author bringing together some of the
information on civil society history and
current practice used in this book.

19 The dangers of civil society
incorporation in the state agenda were
mentioned in earlier chapters. For an
interesting analysis of the experience of
consultative committees across Russia,
see Tarasenko (2010). The author's finding was that committees set up to local
'recipes' without waiting for orders from
the Public Council at federal level work
more effectively.

20 'Left behind by the G20? How inequality and environmental degradation
threaten to exclude poor people from
the benefits of economic growth', Oxfam
Briefing Paper 157, 19 January 2012, www.
oxfam.org.

21 See papers by Yevgeny Gontmakher from the Institute of Contemporary Development, Lilia Ovcharova from
the Independent Institute of Social Policy
and others on the Oxfam Russia website.

22 Lewis (2008) comments on
mistakes made by the USA in Central
Asia, including the 'geopoliticization of
values', the turning of democracy into a
'foreign policy tool', and the 'nationalist
discourse' of US foreign policy. The
Americans tried to make separation
from Russia a precondition for friendship with USA – but failed. The Central
Asia states deserved a more unified
development effort.

23 For a Westernizing view, see
Travin (2010). This review of Russian foreign policy since the late 1990s takes as
its starting point Samuel Huntington's
prediction that the third world war will
erupt in a conflict between Russia and
China, focusing on the latter's alleged
global ambitions.

24 See *Moscow News*, 15–18 June
2012, pp. 8–9, for comment on the
Russia–China gas deal; *Moscow Times*,
20 June 2012, p. 5, for difficulties in

Russia–China relations and Far East issues during the economic boom.

25 Sergei Karaganov (dean of the faculty of world economy and world politics at the Moscow Higher School of Economics), 'Asian strategy', *Rossiskaya gazeta*, 17 June 2011, p. 20.

26 'Disunited Russia: once a colony, always a colony', *Vlast*, 16 April 2012, on sources and actors in Siberian separatism, pp. 14–23.

27 *Vedomosti*, 18 June 2012, p. 3, on the likely effects on agriculture of WTO entry.

28 Similarly, newer donors among the BRICs countries mainly focus attention on their 'own' regions or countries that are historically friendly: for example, Brazil prioritizes Mozambique; China aids African countries where it has long had important political allies like Angola and Zimbabwe, and so on.

29 The Russian money fell prey at least in part to the financial machinations of Bakiev's son Maxim. For local comment on this, see *Delo*, 8 April 2009. For details of the Russian grant to Kyrgyzstan, *Obschestvenny Rating*, 25 February 2010; for the founding of the Development Institute and results of the Development Fund for 2009, *Arguments and Facts*, 10, 2010.

30 Interview with the editor of the journal of the Russian Institute of Strategic Studies, Adzhar Krutov, *Obschestvenny Rating*, 10 February 2011, pp. 6–7.

31 *Asia Plus*, 77, 12 October 2011. A representative of the People's Democratic Party of Tajikistan (the ruling party) commented: while many in Russia feel nostalgia for the USSR, it will be impossible to revive it, though we welcome elements of economic integration. A Tajikistan Community Party representative said: if Putin thinks that he just has to mention this idea and people will come running, he is sorely mistaken. Nobody in the FSU will want to unite on a predatory programme promoted by oligarchs like Chubais or Deripaska.

32 The chapter 'Current practices of Russian NGOs' in Yakobson (2011: 35–43) has useful latest information on NGO–government relations in Russia and the level of efficiency of NGO operations in the social sector; also new methodologies used by NGOs in various spheres – with children, the homeless, etc.

33 Leonid Grishin, NGO *Uralsky Dom*: 'It's a long way to the restoration of peace in Osh', *Fergana.ru*, 8 August 2010.

Postscript

1 A communal apartment is a flat divided into small sections, typically each occupied by a (poor) family, after it has been confiscated from the rich.

REFERENCES

Abashin, S. (2011) 'Mustakillik and Uzbek memory policy', CERCEC (Centre d'études des mondes russe, caucasien et centre-européen) conference paper, Almaty, August.

Abashin, S. and V. Bushkov (2004) *Ферганская долина: этничность, этнические процессы, этнические конфликты* [Fergana Valley: ethnicity, ethnic processes, ethnic conflicts], Moscow: Nauka.

Abashin, S. et al. (2008) *Historia Rossica – Центральная Азия в составе Российской Империи* [Historia Rossica – Central Asia in the Russian Empire], Moscow: Novoye Literaturnoe Obozrenie.

Ablazhei, N. and E. Vodichev (2009) 'Siberia: scenarios of colonisation and the demographic landscape', in S. Chatterjee et al. (eds), *Asiatic Russia: Partnerships and communities in Eurasia*, Delhi: Shipra.

Abuseitova, M. K. (2011) 'Myths and reality in Central Asian history', CERCEC conference paper, Almaty, August.

Akiner, S. (1997) 'Between tradition and modernity: the dilemma facing Central Asia women', in M. Buckley (ed.), *Post-Soviet Women: From the Baltic to Central Asia*, Cambridge: Cambridge University Press.

— (2002) 'Prospects for civil society in Tajikistan', in A. Sanjoo (ed.), *Civil Society in Comparative Muslim Contexts*, London: I.B. Tauris.

Akiner, S. et al. (eds) (1998) *Sustainable Development in Central Asia*, London: Routledge.

Aleksandrova, A. and E. Grishina (2004) *Городская бедность в России и социальная помощь городским бедным: аналитический доклад* [Urban poverty in Russia and social assistance to the urban poor: analytical report], Moscow: Institute of Urban Economy Foundation.

Alexeyev, V. V. (2009) 'The integration of Russia: the historical experience and today's problems', in S. Chatterjee et al. (eds), *Asiatic Russia: Partnerships and communities in Eurasia*, Delhi: Shipra.

Arinin, A. I. (ed.) (2010) *Модернизация России как условие её успешного развития в XXIом веке* [The modernization of Russia as a precondition of its successful development in the 21st century], Moscow: ROSSNEP.

Babadjanov, R. M. (2011) 'Социальная отчуждённость и её роль на формирование уровня жизни и рынка труда' [Social alienation and its role in the formation of living standards and the labour market], in *Трансформация экономики Таджикистана: состояние, проблемы и перспективы* [Transformation of the economy of Tajikistan: state of play, problems and perspectives], Dushanbe: Russian-Tajik (Slavic) University and Friedrich Ebert Foundation.

Babenko, M. (2009) 'Understanding Russia's demographic challenge', *UNDP Journal*, 14.

Bank Watch (2009) Special Caucasus and Central Asia issue, March.

Batyrbaeva, S. (2010) *Эпоха Сталинизма в Кыргызстане в человеческом измерении* [The Stalinist epoch in Kyrgyzstan: the human dimension], Moscow: Russian Political Encyclopaedia.

Bebbington, A. et al. (2008) *Can NGOs Make a Difference? The Challenge of Development Alternatives*, London: Zed Books.

Bideleux, R. (1985) *Communism and Development*, London: Methuen.

Bischel, C. (2011) 'In the name of victory – turning the "hungry steppe" into new land', Lecture at the University of Central Asia, Summer.

Boersner, D. (1957) *The Bolsheviks and the National and Colonial Question*, New York: Hyperion.

Boiko, V. (ed.) (1998) *Сибирь в геополитическом пространстве 21ого века* [Siberia in the geopolitical space of the 21st century], Novosibirsk: Siberian Branch of the Russian Academy of Sciences.

Bradley, J. (2011) *Voluntary Associations in Tsarist Russia*, Cambridge, MA: Harvard University Press.

Bridger, S. and F. Pine (1998) *Surviving Post-Socialism: Local Strategies and Regional Responses in Eastern Europe and Former Soviet Union*, London: Routledge.

Busygina, I. and A. Khainemann-Gruder (2010) *Федерализм и этническое разнообразие в России* [Federalism and ethnic diversity in Russia], Moscow: Russian Political Encyclopaedia.

Buxton, C. (2011) *The Struggle for Civil Society in Central Asia: Crisis and Transformation*, Bloomfield, CT: Kumarian.

Bykov, A. N. (2009) *Постсоветское пространство: стратегии интеграции и новые вызовы глобализации* [Post-Soviet space: strategies of integration and new challenges of globalization], St Petersburg: Aleteia.

Bykov, P. and O. Vlasova (2010) 'Модернизаторам всех стран' [To modernizers of all countries],

Ekspert, 36, 13–19 September, pp. 17–24.

Cheru, F. and C. Obi (2010) *The Rise of China and India in Africa: Challenges, opportunities and critical interventions*, London: Zed Books.

Cheryomukhin, A. (2007) 'Community, identity and social capital', Azerbaijan Psychological Association, for INTRAC Conference on Community Development, Amman, Jordan.

Chokushev, V. (1968) *Классовая борьба и упрочнение советской власти в киргизских аулах 1918–24* [Class struggle and the consolidation of Soviet power in Kirgiz villages 1918–24), Frunze.

Chotonov, U. et al. (eds) (1998) *История Кыргызстана: XX век* [The history of Kyrgyzstan in the 20th century], Bishkek.

Clarkson, S. (1978) *The Soviet Theory of Development: India and the 3rd World in Marxist-Leninist Scholarship*, Toronto: University of Toronto Press.

Clement, C., O. Mirasova and A. Demidov (2010) *От обывателя к активистам* [From bystander to activist], Moscow: Tri Kvadrata.

Cohen, S. (2011) Жизнь после ГУЛАГА: возвращение Сталинских жертв [Life after the GULAG: the return of Stalin's victims], Moscow: Novaya Gazeta Publishers.

Cox, R. with M. G. Schechter (2002) *Political Economy of a Plural World: Critical reflections on power, morals and civilization*, London: Routledge.

Dameshek, L. M. and A. V. Remnev (eds) (2007) *Сибирь в составе российской империи* [Siberia within the Russian Empire], Moscow: Novoye Literaturnoye Obozrenie.

De Rivero, O. (2001) *The Myth of Development*, London: Zed Books.

De Sousa Santos, B. (2006) *The Rise of the Global Left: The World Social Forum and beyond*, London: Zed Books.

Deacon, B. (1992) *Social Policy, Social Justice and Citizenship in Eastern Europe*, Farnham: Ashgate.

Diamond, L. and M. F. Platter (eds) (2002) *Democracy after Communism*, Baltimore, MD: Johns Hopkins University Press.

Dobronravin, N. (2010) 'Глобально лишние: негосударственные народы и сырьевое государство' [Globally superfluous: non-government peoples and the resource state], in V. Gelman and O. Marganiya, *Пути модернизции* [Paths to modernization], St Petersburg: European University.

Dosuzinas, C. and S. Zizek (eds) (2010) *The Idea of Communism*, London: Verso.

Earle, L. et al. (2004) *Community Development in Central Asia*, INTRAC.

Easley, R. (2009) *Emancipation of Serfs in Russia: Peace arbitrators and the development of civil society*, London: Routledge.

Eurasia Heritage Foundation and UNDP Russia (2010) *Engagement of Russian Business in International Development Assistance in CIS Countries (Kyrgyzstan and Tajikistan)*, Moscow.

Evans, A. (2006) 'Vladimir Putin's design for civil society', in A. Evans et al. (eds), *Russian Civil Society: A Critical Assessment*, Armonk, NY: M. E. Sharpe, pp. 147–57.

Gelman, V. and O. Marganiya (2010) *Пути модернизции* [Paths to modernization], St Petersburg: European University.

Gelman, V. et al. (2002) *Автономия или контроль: реформа местной власти в Российских городах 1991–2001* [Autonomy or control: local government reform in Russian cities 1991–2001], Moscow: Letny Sad.

Giffen, J. et al. (2005) *The Development of Civil Society in Central Asia*, INTRAC.

Gontmakher, Y. (2000) *Social Policy: Lessons of the 1990s* [Социальная политика: уроки 90-х], Gelios ARB.

Gray, J. (2002) *False Dawn – the Delusions of Global Capitalism*, London: Granta.

Hann, C. and E. Dunn (eds) (1996) *Civil Society: Challenging Western Models*, London: Routledge.

Harris, J. R. (1999) *The Great Urals: Regionalism and the evolution of the Soviet system*, Ithaca, NY: Cornell Unversity Press.

Harwin, J. (1996) *Children of the Russian State 1917–95*, Aldershot: Avebury.

Heathershaw, J. (2005) 'Discourses of danger', *Central Asian Survey*, 24(1): 196ff.

Hemmett, J. (2007) *Empowering Women in Russia: Activism, aid and NGOs*, Bloomington: Indiana University Press.

Henry, L. (2010) 'Russian environmentalists and civil society', in A. Evans, L. Henry and L. Sundstrom (eds), *Russian Civil Society: A Critical Assessment*, New York: M. E. Sharpe, pp. 211–27.

Hopkirk, P. (1984) *Setting the East Ablaze: Lenin's Dream of an Empire in Central Asia*, London: John Murray.

Howell, J. and J. Pearce (2002) *Civil Society and Development: A Critical Interrogation*, London: Lynne Rienner.

Humphrey, C. (2002) *The Unmaking of Soviet Life: Everyday economies after socialism*, Ithaca, NY: Cornell University Press.

— (2010) *Постсоветские трансформации в азиатской части России* [Post-Soviet transformations in the Asiatic part of Russia], Moscow: Natalis.

Imanaliev, K. (2004) *Kyrgyzstan, a Word about Homeland*, Bishkek: Uchkun Press.

Inozemtsev, V. (2010) 'Что случилось с Россией?' [What happened to Russia?], *Neprikosnovenny Zapas*, 6.

International Crisis Group (2006) *What*

Role for the European Union?, CG Asia Report no. 113, Brussels: ICG.

— (2011) *Central Asia: Decay and Decline*, CG Asia Report no. 201, 3 February.

Ishkanian, A. (2008) 'Democracy promotion and civil society', in M. Kaldor et al. (eds), *Global Civil Society 2007/8*, London: Sage, pp. 70–1.

Javeline, D. and S. Lindemann-Komarova (2010) 'A balanced assessment of Russian civil society', *Journal of International Affairs*, 63(2).

Jones-Luong, P. (ed.) (2004) *The Transformation of Central Asia: States and Societies from Soviet Rule to Independence*. Ithaca, NY: Cornell University Press.

Jonson, L. (2004) *Vladimir Putin and Central Asia: The shaping of Russian foreign policy*, London: I. B. Tauris.

Kagarlitsky, B. (1999) *New Realism, New Barbarism: Socialist theory in the era of globalization*, London: Pluto.

— (2000) *The Return of Radicalism: Reshaping the left institutions*, London: Pluto.

— (2007) *Политология революции* [The political science of revolution], Moscow: Algoritm.

— (2008) *Empire of the Periphery: Russia and the world system*, London: Pluto.

Kamalov, A. (2011) 'Post-colonialism in Central Asia', CERCEC conference paper, Almaty, August.

Kara-Murza, S. (2002) *Истмат и проблема Восток-Запад* [Historical materialism and the East–West problem], Moscow: Eksmo.

— (2005) *Потерянный Разум* [Lost reason], Moscow: Eksmo.

— (2011) *Проект 'Путин'. Кремль. Отчет перед народом* [The 'Putin' project. Kremlin. Report to the people], Moscow: Algoritm.

Kassymbekova, B. (2011) 'Helpless imperialists', *Central Asian Survey*, 30(1): 21–38.

Khalid, A. (1998) *The Politics of Muslim Cultural Reform*, Berkeley: University of California Press.

Kolmogorova, D. (2010) 'Укрупнение российских регионов' [The enlargement of Russian regions], in I. Busygina and A. Khainemann-Gruder, *Федерализм и этническое разнообразие в России* [Federalism and ethnic diversity in Russia], Moscow: Russian Political Encyclopaedia.

Kordonsky, S. (2010) *Россия – Поместная федерация* [Russia – a federation of estates], Moscow: Evropa.

Kotz, D. M. and F. Weir (2007) *Russia's Path from Gorbachev to Putin*, London: Routledge.

Kozyrev, M. (2010) 'Глобализация, опыт СССР и сценарии развития экономики Рассии' [Globalization, the experience of the USSR and scenarios of development of the Russian economy], *Levaya Politika*, 13/14: 119–38.

Krasilschikov, V. (2010) 'От авторитаризма к демократии на путях модернизации' [From authoritarianism to democracy on the path to modernization], in V. Inozemtsev (ed.), *Демократизация и Модернизация: к дискуссии о вызовах XXI века* [Democracy and modernization: contributions to the discussion about challenges in the 21st century], Moscow: Yevropa.

Kruzhkov, A. (2005) *Проблемы народовластия в России* [Problems of people's power in Russia], Moscow: Institute of Modern Economy and Law, Russian Academy of Sciences.

Kuleshov, V. V. and A. V. Yevseyenko (1998) 'Базовые социально-экономические процессы в Сибири: тенденции и прогнозные сценарии' (Basic socio-economic processes in Siberia: tendencies and prognoses), in V. Boiko (ed.), *Сибирь в геополитическом пространстве 21ого века* [Siberia in the geopolitical space of the 21st century], Novosibirsk: Siberian Branch of the Russian Academy of Sciences.

Kuzmin, A. et al. (eds) (2009) *Оценка программ: методологии и практика* [Programme evaluation: methodology and practice], Moscow: Presto Publishers.

Kuznetsova, E. (2010) 'Демократия в эру ограниченного суверенитета' [Democracy in an era of limited sovereignty], in V. Inozemtsev (ed.), *Демократизация и Модернизация: к дискуссии о вызовах XXI века* [Democracy and modernization: contributions to the discussion about challenges in the 21st century], Moscow: Centre for Study of Post-Industrial Society and Evropa Press.

Lacquer, W. (1994) *The Dream that Failed*, Oxford: Oxford University Press.

Lamin, V. A. (ed.) (2004) *Местное самоуправление в истории Сибири XIX–XX веков* [Local self-government in Siberian history of the 19th–20th centuries], Novosibirsk.

Lane, D. (ed.) (1995) *Russia in Transition*, Longman.

Laxter, G. and S. Halperin (eds) (2003) *Global Civil Society and Its Limits*, London: Palgrave.

Lewin, M. (2005) *The Soviet Century*, London: Verso.

Lewis, D. (2008) *The Temptations of Tyranny*, London: Hurst & Co.

Lovell, S. (2006) *Destination in Doubt: Russia since 1991*, London: Zed Books.

Makarchuk, S. V. 'Городское самоуправление в теории и практики российских социал-демократов. 1905–17 гг' [Urban self-government in the theory and practice of Russian social-democrats. 1905–17], in V. A. Lamin (ed.) *Местное самоуправление в истории Сибири XIX-XX веков* [Local self-government in Siberian history in the 19th–20th centuries], Novosibirsk.

Manning, N. and N. Tikhonova (eds) (2004) *Poverty and Social Exclusion in New Russia*, Farnham: Ashgate.

Marquand, J. (2009) *Development and Aid in Russia: Lessons from Siberia*, St Antony's series, London: Palgrave Macmillan.

Martin, T. (2001) *The Affirmative Action Empire: Nations and nationalism in the Soviet Union 1923–39*, Ithaca, NY: Cornell University Press.

Martyanov, V. S. and L. G. Fishman (2010) *Россия в поисках утопий: от морального коллапса к моральной революции* [Russia in search of utopias: from moral collapse to moral revolution], Moscow: Ves Mir.

Massell, G. (1974) *The Surrogate Proletariat: Moslem women and revolutionary strategies in Soviet Central Asia 1919–29*, Princeton, NJ: Princeton University Press.

Matveeva, A. (2008) *Perils of Emerging Statehood: Civil War and State Reconstruction in Tajikistan*, London: LSE.

Medvedev, R. (2008a) *Политические портреты* [Political portraits], Moscow: AST.

— (2008b) *ВВ Путин: продолжение следует* (VV Putin: to be continued).

Mersianova, I. V. (2008) 'Роль индивидуального субъекта и его персональных практик в формировании ГО в России' [The role of the individual subject and personal practice in the formation of civil society in Russia], in L. I. Yakobson (ed.), *Факторы развития гражданского общества и механизмы его взаймодействия с государством* [Factors of development of civil society and mechanisms of interaction with government], Moscow: Higher School of Economics.

Morozov, V. (2010) 'Охранительная модернизация Дмитрия Медведева' [The defensive modernization of Dmitry Medvedev], *Neprikosnovenny Zapas*, 6.

Nazpary, J. (2002) *Post-Soviet Chaos: Violence and Dispossession in Kazakhstan*, London: Pluto.

Nove, A. (1979) *Political Economy and Soviet Socialism*, London: George Allen & Unwin.

Olimova, S. (2000) 'Islam and the Tajik conflict', in R. Sagdeev and S. Eisenhower (eds), *Islam and Central Asia: An Enduring Legacy or Evolving Threat?*, Washington, DC: Center for Political & Strategic Studies.

— (2011) *Человеческий капитал и неравенство в независимом Таджекистане: взаимосвязь и взаимохзависимость* [Human capital and inequality in independent Tajikistan: interconnections and interdependence], CERCEC Conference paper, Almaty.

Olimova, S. and M. Olimov (2014), 'Human capital and inequality in Tajikistan: intercommunication and interdependence', in S. Hohman et al., *Development in Central Asia and the Caucasus: Migration, democratisation and inequality in the post-Soviet era*, London: I. B. Tauris.

Petrenko, E. S. (ed.) (2008) *Гражданское общество современной России: социологические зарисовки с натуры* [Civil society in Russia today: sociological studies from the field], Moscow: Institute of the Public Opinion Fund.

Petrovsky, V. (2007) *От империи к открытому миру* [From empire to an open world], Moscow: Russian Political Encyclopaedia.

Pickup, F. (2002) 'Local level responses to rapid social change in a city in the Russian industrial Urals', PhD thesis.

Piirainen, T. (1997) *Towards a New Social Order in Russia: Transforming structures and everyday life*, Dartmouth.

Politkovskaya, A. (2004) *Putin's Russia*, London: Harvill.

Pratt, B. (ed.) (2003) *Changing Expectations: The concept and practice of civil society in international development*, Oxford: INTRAC.

Rahnema, M. and V. Bawtree (eds) (1997) *The Post-Development Reader*, London: Zed Books.

Rashid, A. (1994) *The Resurgence of Central Asia: Islam or nationalism?*, London: Zed Books.

— (2002) *Jihad: The rise of militant Islam in Central Asia*, New Haven, CT: Yale University Press.

Razzakov, A. and E. Gulmetov (1968) 'Роль городских партийных организаций в подъёме хозяйственно-культурной жизни кишлака в период создания фундамента социализма' [The role of urban party organizations in improving economic and cultural life in villages during the period of the creation of the foundations of socialism], in *Компартия Узбекистана: в борьбе за победу советской власти и построения социализма* [The Communist Party of Uzbekistan: the struggle to establish Soviet power and build socialism], Tashkent.

Rist, G. (2008) *A History of Development*, London: Zed Books.

Romanov, P. and E. Yarksaya-Smirnova (2009) *Общественное движение в России* [Social movements in Russia], Moscow: Library of the Journal of Social Policy.

Rose, R. (2009) *Understanding Post-Communist Transformation: A Bottom Up Approach*, London: Routledge

Roy, O. (2000) *The New Central Asia – the Creation of Nations*, London: I. B. Tauris.

Sagdeev, R. (2000) 'Central Asia and Islam: an overview', in R. Sagdeev and S. Eisenhower (eds), *Islam and Central Asia: An Enduring Legacy or Evolving Threat?*, Washington, DC: Center for Political & Strategic Studies.

Salmenniemi, S. (2009) 'Теория гражданского общества и постсоциализм' [The theory of civil society and post-socialism], in P. Romanov and E. Yarksaya-Smirnova, *Общественное движение в России* [Social movements in Russia], Moscow: Library of the Journal of Social Policy, pp. 96–119.

Schedrovitsky, P. et al. (2005) *Формула Развития: сборник статей 1987–2005* [Formula of development: collection of articles 1987–2005], Moscow: School of Cultural Policy.

Sedaitis, J. and J. Butterfield (eds) (1991) *Perestroika from Below*, Boulder, CO: Westview Press.

Sergeyev, V. M. (1998) *The Wild East: Crime and lawlessness in post-communist Russia*, Armonk, NY: M. E. Sharpe.

Shanin, T. (1985) *Russia as a 'Developing Society'*, London: Macmillan.

Shaw, D. (ed.) (1995) *The Post-Soviet Republics: A Systematic Geography*, Harlow: Longman.

Shomina, E. S. (2008) 'Само-организация жителей на локальном уровне' (Residents' self-organization at the local level], in L. I. Yakobson (ed.), *Факторы развития гражданского общества и механизмы его взаймодействия с государством* [Factors of development of civil society and mechanisms of interaction with government], Moscow: Higher School of Economics, pp. 263–90.

Sim, L.-C. (2008) *The Rise and Fall of Privatisation in the Russian Oil Industry*, London: Palgrave.

Smolin, O. N. (2009) 'Новейшая революция в России и перспективы социализма XXI века' [The new revolution in Russia and perspectives for socialism in the 21st century], in *Социализм-21: 14 текстов постсоветской школы критического марксзма* [Socialism-21: 14 texts from the post-socialist school of critical Marxism], Moscow: Cultural Revolution.

Sullivan, S. (2002) *Marx for a Post-Communist Era*, London: Routledge.

Sundstrom, L. (2003) 'Women's NGOs in Russia', in G. Laxter and S. Halperin (eds), *Global Civil Society and Its Limits*, London: Palgrave, pp. 146–63.

Sundstrom, L. and L. Henry (2006) 'Tensions and trajectories', in A. Evans et al. (eds), *Russian Civil Society: A Critical Assessment*, Armonk, NY: M. E. Sharpe, pp. 305–25.

Sviagelskaia, I. (1995) *The Russian Policy Debate on Central Asia*, Former Soviet South Project, Royal Institute of International Affairs.

— (1997) *The Tajik Conflict*, Russian Centre for Strategic and International Studies, Moscow.

Szymanski, A. (1979) *Is the Red Flag Flying? The political economy of the Soviet Union*, London: Zed Books.

Tarasenko, A. (2010) 'Инкорпорирование некоммерческих организаций в процесс государственного управления в России' [The incorporation of non-commercial organizations in the process of government rule in Russia], in V. Gelman and O. Marganiya, *Пути модернизации* [Paths to modernization], St Petersburg: European University.

Tilly, C. and S. Tarrow (2007) *Contentious Politics*, Colorado: Paradigm.

Tomasova, A. K. (1998) *Социальный заказ в регионах России: проблемы и перспективы* [Social order in Russia's regions: problems and perspectives], Moscow: Charities Aid Foundation.

Toschenko, Zh. T. (2001) *Парадоксальный человек* [Paradoxical man], Moscow: Gardariki.

Travin, D. (2010) 'Угроза с востока' [The threat from the East], in V. Gelman and O. Marganiya, *Пути модернизции* [Paths to modernisation], St Petersburg: European University, pp. 225–60.

Ulmasov, P. U. (2011) 'Мигрант' [The migrant], in *Функции семьи в переходный период к рыночной экономике* [Functions of the family in the transition period to a market economy], Institute of Economy and Demography & Friedrich Ebert Foundation, Academy of Sciences of the Republic of Tajikistan, pp. 26–40.

Umarov, Kh. (2010) *Кризис в Таджикистане: глубина действия, формы проявления, пути преодоления* [The crisis in Tajikistan: its depth and consequences, and possible strategies to overcome it], Dushanbe: Centre for Economic Studies, Tajik Institute for Innovation and Communication Technologies and Friedrich Ebert Foundation.

Urban, J. and V. Solovei (1997) *Russia's Communists at the Crossroads*, Boulder, CO: Westview Press.

Urnov, M. (2010) 'Ниспровергнуть авторитарное большинство: непростая задача' [How to defeat the authoritarian majority: no easy task], in V. Inozemtsev (ed.), *Демократизация и Модернизация: к дискуссии о вызовах XXI века* [Democracy and modernization: contributions to the discussion about challenges in the 21st century], Moscow: Centre for Study of Post-Industrial Society and Evropa Press.

Van Zon, H. (2010) *Russia's Development Problem: The cult of power*, London: Palgrave.

Vyuzhanin, V. (2010) *Энергия социального партнёрства: городскому конкурсу социально значимых проектов в Перми 10 лет* [The energy of social partnership: the town competition for socially useful projects is ten years old], Perm community affairs department and Urals NGO support centre.

Waldron, P. (2010) 'Przheval'skii, Asia and Empire', *SEER*, 88(1/2), January/April.

Wheeler, G. (1964) *The Modern History of Soviet Central Asia*, London: Weidenfeld & Nicolson.

White, A. (2004) *Small Town Russia*, London: Routledge.

Whitlock, M. (2002) *Beyond the Oxus: The Central Asians*, London: John Murray.

Yakobson, L. I. (ed.) (2008) *Факторы развития гражданского общества и механизмы его взаимодействия с государством* [Factors of development of civil society and mechanisms of interaction with government], Moscow: Higher School of Economics.

— (ed.) (2011) *Справится ли государство в одиночку? О роли НКО в решении социальных проблем. Российские общественные организации и решение социальных проблем: ретроспектива* [Can government cope on its own? On the role of non-commercial organizations in tackling social problems. Russian public organizations tackling social problems: a retrospective view], Moscow: Higher School of Economics.

Yakobson, L., I. Mersianova, O. Kononykhina et al. (2011) *Civil Society in Modernizing Russia*, Civicus World Alliance for Citizen Participation & HSE, Moscow.

Yakovenko, I. G. (2009) *Политическая субъективность масс* [The political subjectivity of the masses], Moscow: Novy Khronograf.

Yanitsky, O. (2007) *Экологическая*

культура [Ecological culture], Moscow: Nauka.

Zaionchovskaya, Zh. et al. (2009) *Иммигранты в Москве* [Immigrants in Moscow], Moscow: Tri Kvadrata.

Zharkevich, I. (2010a) *Civil Society and Political Accountability in Tajikistan*, INTRAC.

— (2010b) *Examples of Good Practice in Bridging Social Capital*, INTRAC.

Zinoviev, A. (1994) *Коммунизм как реальность: кризис коммунизма* [Communism as reality: the crisis of communism], Moscow: Tsentropolitgraf.

Zubarevich, N. (2010) 'Социо-экономические различия между этническими регионами и политика перераспределения' [Socio-economic variations between ethnic regions and the politics of redistribution], in *Федерализм и этническое разнообразие в России* [Federalism and ethnic diversity], Moscow: Russian Political Encyclopaedia.

INDEX